TRACED WITH FIRE
WRITTEN IN BLOOD

A JOURNAL OF
GEORGIA CIVIL WAR HISTORY

Co-edited by R. Olin Jackson and Daniel M. Roper

Published by Legacy Communications, Inc.
P.O. Box 585
Armuchee, GA 30105-0585
1-800-547-1625
www.georgiabackroads.com

International Standard Book Number (ISBN):
ISBN-10: 1-880816-22-9
ISBN-13: 978-1-880816-22-6

Library of Congress Control Number:
2009932607

For Additional Copies:
Legacy Communications, Inc.
Post Office Box 585
Armuchee, Georgia 30105-0585
1-800-547-1625
www.georgiabackroads.com

Dedication

Dedicated to the memory of the soldiers of Georgia,
who served their state in the hour of her greatest need.

Acknowledgements

None of the authors who contributed to this book did so for fame or fortune. No writer, they'll tell you, could survive on the pay earned by those who write for a regional history magazine like *Georgia Backroads*, from whose pages each chapter of this book was taken. Nor is there much fame or notoriety involved in magazine writing.

Instead, these writers toiled entirely for the satisfaction that comes from identifying, researching, and writing about matters that interest them. While earning a living as a realtor, teacher, lawyer, private investigator, photographer, or in some other vocation, these "amateurs" devoted the time necessary to pursue their avocation, their passion – history.

May there always be laborers who toil purely for the love of it – Georgians so enthralled by our state's rich heritage that each is willing to devote the time and effort needed to add each additional chapter to our history books.

We are indebted to each of the "citizen historians" who contributed to this book:

Marion Blackwell, Jr.
Brian Brown
Anne Buckner Burgamy
Ray Chandler
Emma Cottrell
Gary Elam
Alexandra Filipowski
Hugh T. Harrington
Mary Frazier Long
Deborah Malone
Jim Miles
Daniel M. Roper
Zack C. Waters
Michael Williams

TABLE OF CONTENTS

NIGHTS OF THE ROUND TABLE

With war between North and the South imminent, a social club comprised of a Georgia town's most eligible bachelors and maidens met for the last time. That night, none could foretell what fates awaited these knights who would serve their country.

DANIEL M. ROPER

The Round Table met for the final time one late March evening in 1861 while the rain fell in torrents. Eleven members gathered at Belvidere, an imposing hillside mansion overlooking Rome, Georgia. Theirs was an exclusive society of lawyers, publishers, merchants, and ladies. Ostensibly, it was a reading club. Indeed, during its short life the Round Table discussed literature ranging from Shakespeare and Washington Irving to Poe's "The Raven" and "The Pit and the Pendulum." But there was more to it than that.

While the organization did promote reading, its real purpose was to facilitate the mingling of the town's most eligible young bachelors and suitable young women. Their good-natured banter, teasing, and flirting, all dutifully noted in the minutes, makes that clear. On one occasion, Miss Eddie Magruder read a passage from *Field's Scrap Book* titled

George T. Stovall was a lawyer, newspaper publisher, and the "best loved young man in Rome" on the eve of the Civil War.

"Woman": "This being a subject of unusual interest especially to the gentlemen," the club secretary recorded, "it was listened to with much pleasure and interest."

Each member of the Round Table was the target of playful darts thrown by others. Henry Gartrell was given the nickname Alligator, and his closest friend, George Stovall, was noted for his "ferocious mustache" and the tendency of his hair to stand on end "in fierce array giving him quite the appearance...of a fretful porcupine." The group also facetiously accused Henry Smith of "having taken on a melancholy and serious turn of late [so that] his numerous admirers and friends and fellow citizens and countrymen, Romans and lovers also, began to fear lest his constitution, like that of the late United States, was on the decline."

Frequent references to each other's appearance and relations with the opposite sex confirm that these knights were more interested in love than in literature. "The first reader for the evening was a Mr. Skidmore – whose face his most intimate

COURTESY DWINELL FAMILY

Melvin Dwinell was one of Stovall's closest friends and a fellow Round Table member. A native of New Hampshire, Dwinell moved to Rome before the war and became the editor of the Rome's *Weekly Courier* newspaper. Despite his northern background, he ardently supported the South, joined the Rome Light Guards, and was wounded in the arm while carrying the flag of the 8th Georgia Regiment at Gettysburg. He survived the war and spent the remainder of his life in Rome.

friends have never seen, being partly obscured by a luxuriant beard," the minutes for the January 25, 1861 meeting disclose. "This gentleman has an upward tendency of about six feet. He can tell at any time 'weather' it is going to rain or not. He never speaks without saying something and that always in an audible tone. His subject was 'Woman's Influence' – which no one, perhaps, felt more than himself."

Despite their protestations to the contrary, marriage was a matter of keen interest to the members of this select society. The Round Table's first meeting began "after a few preliminary remarks upon the state of the weather, the State of South Carolina, and, it may be proper to state, also a few side-bar statements upon the Holy Estate of Matrimony," the secretary recorded. Melvin Dwinell, editor of Rome's *Weekly Courier* newspaper, followed by reciting "Tis the Heart that Makes the Home," a poem "so beautifully and feelingly set forth that several heartless bachelors present resolved that henceforth they would be homeless no longer than would be necessary."

Isham Branham's February 1861 announcement that he was engaged to be married prompted much discussion and lamentation about his "fallen state." "Mr. Branham informed the Club that he had 'found a Pearl richer than all her tribe'…[We desire] to return acknowledgements to assure him our appreciation of his worth, our regret at losing him, and to hope that he may be half as happy as he deserves to be. We feel it our duty though to warn our friend that traveling in 'that land of promise,' that foreign country of which he speaks is attended with many difficulties.'"

In a parable equating wedlock with travel in a distant land, the Round Table cautioned Branham that a husband must abide by many rules: "You will find many articles which you now consider indispensable are contraband – positively forbidden – or subject to heavy tariff. Your old habits must be given up and a strict conformity of the rules and customs of their country observed. It's no use trying to smuggle in even one good coon dog and, as to pipes, anything which smells of tobacco is seized by their custom house officers. Feet on the mantle, whist parties, egg nogs, bird and oyster suppers, and forbidden books, papers, boots, etc are not allowed to lay round loose and handy and a speck of dirt throws 'em into a spasm. All this we speak from hearsay, never dangers be they real or imaginary, 'tis with some misgivings that we say good bye."

In his last official act before departing, Branham assured the group that he entertained "for each member a cordial esteem and undying friendship." He then alluded to the crisis engulfing the nation in extending his wish that "The R.T. circle remain unbroken – except by Secession to form a closer and more indissoluble Union."

The Round Table bid Branham an affectionate farewell at its February 22, 1861, meeting. Secretary George Stovall then inquired of his friends, "Who will be next to leave a vacant chair around our Table?" Just a month later, he stunned the others by announcing that he would "get married very soon himself." Indeed, his chair would become the next vacancy, but for reasons that neither he nor the club could envision.

By all accounts Stovall – who was a lawyer, newspaper publisher, and president of the Methodist Sunday school – had a kind heart. Years later, a Roman remembered him fondly, saying that "he stood for all that was noble and good in his young manhood. I think I may say that George Stovall was the best loved young man in Rome, at that time."

He had once been chided for failing to transcribe the minutes of an earlier Round Table meeting, but the members eventually concluded that his excuse was perfectly satisfactory. "It being Christmas week," the minutes detail, "he was solicited by the little boys and negroes to participate in the dignified business of popping fire poppers and climbing a greasy pole in front of Martin's Confectionary for prizes."

Round Table meetings were light-hearted affairs, yet the festivities were sprinkled with references – some subtle, others unabashed – to the growing divide between North and South. At one meeting, the secretary jokingly chastised two members who had seceded – "not to form that closer and more indissoluble union, alluded to by Secretary Branham, but only into an adjoining room." In similar fashion, the group toasted Georgia, "the great empire state of the South," and referred to Fort Sumter two months before the strategic federal outpost in

The Round Table met for the final time on March 29, 1861 at Hollis Cooley's house, Belvidere.

Charleston Harbor became a household name.

Sometimes, as at a January 1861 meeting, their patriotism burst forth exuberantly. "We all sang 'Dixie,'" William Skidmore wrote. "Feeling satisfied with our performance and highly pleased with the song, we concluded to sing, 'Dixie's Land.' By special request we then sang 'Dixie,' after which each member of the club was furnished with 'a copy,' and we finished the program by all singing 'Dixie's Land.'" Then the males gallantly vowed, "When the country calls for soldiers, the Gentlemen of the Round Table will be as prompt as minute men to respond, and second to none in pledging, in her defense, 'their lives, their fortunes, and their sacred honor.'"

And so the Round Table assembled for what proved to be the final time at Belvidere on a rainy March evening. The hostess for the occasion, Miss Martha Cooley, "introduced a resolution to suspend the society until Fall, and – strange to say – most of the ladies were in favor of it." George Stovall countered with a motion that "the Round Table would never adjourn finally until all the members thereof were married – and the one who remained single the longest would be entitled to the minutes, scrap box, book, etc." The group agreed to table Miss Martha's motion until the next meeting, to be held two weeks later, and adjourned.

Due to the inclement weather, the ladies remained at Belvidere the evening of the last meeting. As for the men, "Miss Martha said she could not bear to see the gentlemen go off in the rain. She kindly furnished them with umbrellas; then came the shaking of hands." Nevertheless, buffeted by rain and wind, they received a thorough soaking on their way home and the secretary noted it was "not until the bell at the depot had informed us that it was 'the wee sma' hours'" that they made it home.

True to their word, the men of the Round Table were ready for action when the simmering tension between North and South boiled over in April 1861. Of the seven who resided in Rome, six were members of the Rome Light Guards (the seventh, newly married Isham Branham, had moved to his wife's hometown and enlisted in the Fort Valley Infantry). Thirty-year-old Henry Gartrell, the only one to delay military service, volunteered later and led a cavalry company that served as Nathan Bedford Forrest's escort.

There was much business to attend to before the Light Guards volunteers departed. Melvin Dwinell appealed to his newspaper subscribers to pay up: "The editor and proprietor of this paper has devoted himself to the defense of the country, and expects in a few days to be ordered to the field of conflict. This is done at great, and almost ruinous, sacrifice of his business." Edward J. Magruder, Miss Eddie's brother, was married in a ceremony attended by his fellow Guards. George Stovall made his last will and testament on May 27, the very day the unit left for Richmond, Virginia. Within, he acknowledged "that the life of a soldier is exceedingly precarious, I deem it right and proper...that I should make a disposition of my property."

In May 1861, the Rome Light Guards went to Virginia under the command of Edward Magruder, a Rome teacher. Magruder married Miss Florence Fouche just days before the Guards left Rome.

Upon reaching the front lines, the Round Table men hung together. When Reuben Norton and Charles Smith, fathers of three Guards, traveled to Virginia in July, they found Charles and George Norton, Henry Smith, William Skidmore, and George Stovall faring rather sumptuously in Mess 10, Company A, 8th Georgia Regiment. In his diary, Reuben recorded, "I found Mess No. 10 lived finely, as they had plenty of means to buy anything they wanted...they had two negroes for cooks; butter and honey of the very best was plenty with them."

The two fathers joined the mess for dinner at noon on July 2 and enjoyed "fine beef, and the boys had procured some cherry pies and a pail of milk. I thought not a bad dinner for soldiers!" They had just finished when an alarm was sounded and the division assembled and formed in line of battle. It proved to be nothing, but it was apparent that the army would soon engage the enemy. A few days later, Reuben Norton left for Rome, parting with his son Charles in front of a hotel in Winchester, Virginia. "This was," he sighed, "the last time I ever saw him."

On July 23, Henry Gartrell received a telegram in Rome that George Stovall had been killed in action at the Battle of Manassas two days before. The next day, Reuben Norton learned that his son Charles had suffered the same fate along with "many others killed and wounded from Rome." He found out later that his son and George Stovall had been killed "side by side at the same instant, in front of their Company."

Seven months after the battle, the still-grieving father returned to Manassas. From there Norton went to the battlefield with "8 detailed men from the Light

Guards, to disinter the bodies of C.B. Norton and Geo. T. Stovall. We found them in a very wet place, the water standing over the boxes in which they were buried; after much difficulty, we succeeded in getting them in coffins and placing them on the platform at the railroad in Manassas." On March 6, 1862, Reuben Norton returned to Rome and, the next day, reburied his son's remains.

Stovall and Norton were the only Round Table members to die during the long war, but they were not the only casualties. William Skidmore was discharged due to disability in 1862; Melvin Dwinell was shot in the arm while carrying the regimental flag at Gettysburg in 1863; Henry Gartrell was captured in 1864 and spent a year in prison; and a few days before the surrender at Appomattox in 1865, Henry Smith suffered a wound to the arm "necessitating amputation above the elbow."

Following the Round Table's last meeting at Belvidere that stormy evening in March 1861, George Stovall and Henry Smith had "favored the party with a duet" as the gentlemen made their way home through the wind and the rain. They sang, "Thou Reign'st in this Breast," the depot bell sounded in the "wee sma' hours," and the knights of the Round Table carried on, blissfully unaware that loss of life and limb would commence before their hopes and dreams could be realized.

Today, George Stovall's knapsack is in the Museum of the Confederacy's collection in Richmond, Virginia. It was likely recovered by his comrades after he fell at Manassas and may have been given to Reuben Norton, who traveled to Manassas after the battle to recover the bodies of both his son and George Stovall, to pass along to the Stovall family.

FOR THE SIN OF THE FATHERS

The recent discovery of a 145-year-old store ledger sheds new light on Rome, Georgia's antebellum past, and the lives of those caught in the firestorm that ultimately led to the secession of Georgia from the Union, and the terrible war that followed.

DANIEL M. ROPER

Had he known the scrutiny that his purchases in the little store in Ridge Valley would receive 145 years later, the Reverend Richard Leigh might have declined to make them at all. Not that there was anything necessarily scandalous about buying gum camphor, whiskey, wine, gunpowder, two pounds of shot, and – perhaps in keeping with his preaching style – brimstone. But the thought of prying eyes probing his dealings undoubtedly would have been distasteful to him, and the knowledge of the pain and suffering that would follow in the next few years would have stopped him cold in his tracks.

The Rev. Leigh's purchases, and those of more than 150 others, are detailed on the brittle, yellowed pages of an old store ledger recently discovered in the attic of a long-neglected house near Rome, Georgia. The store patrons were widows, farmers, mechanics, blacksmiths, laborers, teachers, and "ministers of the gospel."

There was Sarah Boswell, who paid $2.00 for an ounce of asafetida, gunpowder, and two hoes; Thomas Miller who bought two Jews harps for 5 cents; George Crossly who spent $3.18 ½ for a wooden bucket, a tin bucket, six gun flints, quinine, Bateman's drops, salts, linen, flax thread, trace chains, fish hooks, shirting, and calico; and Jasper Martin, who forked over $2.55 for a pair of shoes and two wool hats and still had 20 cents left over to splurge on ½-pound of candy.

Just as did many of that day, the store honored the barter system, taking from its customers beeswax, chickens, eggs, and molasses in exchange for "store-bought" products. For the most part, the store did not sell items that could be made, grown, caught, killed, or obtained locally like milk, fruit, vegetables, and meat. The merchandise most commonly sold included schoolbooks, sugar, coffee, tobacco, whiskey, gunpowder, agricultural implements, household utensils, and footwear. Most of the transactions involved a few cents to a few dollars, but occasionally a shopper paid a princely sum for finery like a $5.25 coat or $20.00 Lever watch.

Early Store Records

Today, grocery and hardware stores still stock some of the same things listed in the ledger, but other items had unfamiliar names or uses. For instance, the brimstone purchased by Rev. Leigh was actually sulfur, and Mrs. Boswell's asafetida was a foul-smelling resin thought to fend off sickness. Other unfamiliar items included osnaburg (a coarse, heavy linen used for work clothes, sacks, and later in Confederate uniforms), copperas (used in making ink or dye), laudanum (a pow-

Grave of Reverend Richard Leigh

erful opium-based anesthetic), and various name-brand potions like Moffatts Pills, Opodeldoc, Eps Peppermint, and Harts Horn.

Though it is long-gone today, it was relatively easy in the year 2004 to identify the little store that once sold these items, even though the ledger itself does not specify the store's name or location. Nineteenth century maps of Floyd County clearly show a store called McGuire's – later Pinson's – in Ridge Valley, a farming community a few miles northeast of Rome. The ledger includes many sales to those who resided in the area around the location of this store including the Thomas McGuire family and several Pinson families.

The evidence suggests that the transactions recorded in the ledger took place near the beginning of the Civil War. The only date in the ledger, however, is an entry referring to a payment by B.W. Bell for "1 shirt got in Aug. 1859," as though that event had occurred a year or two earlier than the date the notation was made in the ledger.

Several entries in the ledger appear to refer to purchases made by slaves for owners, such as "Thomas Zuber per boy Turner" and "Joseph Googe per girl."[1] Zuber did not have a child named Turner, but both he and Googe did own slaves. This would lend credence to the presumption that the ledger transactions were recorded no later than the war years when slavery was still in effect.

To narrow things a bit, it seems that the ledger could not date much later than the start of the Civil War since commodities like laudanum, gunpowder, sugar and coffee were difficult or impossible to obtain during the war years, and if one was lucky enough to find them, they were usually sold at vastly inflated prices by mid-war. Moreover, Federal troops overran Ridge Valley in May 1864, shutting down schools and stifling commerce almost completely.

At the very least, it is certain that the ledger pre-dates early 1866 since the Rev. Leigh died in March of that year.

Beginnings in the Valley

By the 1860s, Ridge Valley's most prominent citizen was Joseph Watters. He, his

Joseph Watters

wife, and nine children had settled in Floyd County in 1835, the year of the Treaty of New Echota.[2] This pact, signed by several prominent Cherokee Indian leaders including Major Ridge, ceded all Cherokee land east of the Mississippi River to the United States. (Ridge Valley earned its name from Major Ridge, who at one time had lived there.)

Under the leadership of Chief John Ross, much of the Cherokee nation remaining in the Southeast (a substantial number emigrated without the use of force to the western United States) attempted to repudiate the treaty. President Andrew Jackson and Georgia governor George Gilmer, however, refused to yield. The infamous Trail of Tears followed in 1838, and Joseph Watters served in a Floyd County militia unit that assisted in rounding up the remaining Cherokees in preparation for their removal to the West. Watters, an admirer of Jackson, named his Ridge Valley residence Hermitage in honor of the president's Nashville plantation, and the little community was known by that name for many years.

After the departure of the Cherokees, Rome and Floyd County developed a slave-oriented agricultural economy similar to most of Georgia's largest cities and counties. By 1860, Floyd had a population of 15,195, of which 5,913 (39%) were slaves. This was comparable to Augusta/Richmond County (39%), Macon/Bibb County (42%), Columbus/Muscogee County (45%), and even Savannah/Chatham County (48%). In contrast, the other mountain counties had an overall slave population of just 14%.[3]

Unlike most Georgia mountain counties, Floyd had vast expanses of river bot-

Grave of Joseph Watters

COURTESY GEORGIA ARCHIVES

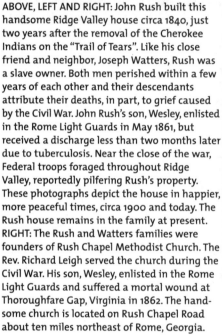

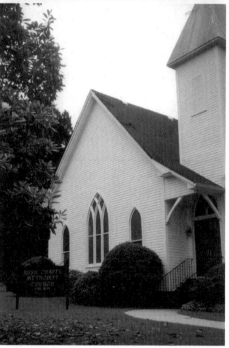

ABOVE, LEFT AND RIGHT: John Rush built this handsome Ridge Valley house circa 1840, just two years after the removal of the Cherokee Indians on the "Trail of Tears". Like his close friend and neighbor, Joseph Watters, Rush was a slave owner. Both men perished within a few years of each other and their descendants attribute their deaths, in part, to grief caused by the Civil War. John Rush's son, Wesley, enlisted in the Rome Light Guards in May 1861, but received a discharge less than two months later due to tuberculosis. Near the close of the war, Federal troops foraged throughout Ridge Valley, reportedly pilfering Rush's property. These photographs depict the house in happier, more peaceful times, circa 1900 and today. The Rush house remains in the family at present. RIGHT: The Rush and Watters families were founders of Rush Chapel Methodist Church. The Rev. Richard Leigh served the church during the Civil War. His son, Wesley, enlisted in the Rome Light Guards and suffered a mortal wound at Thoroughfare Gap, Virginia in 1862. The handsome church is located on Rush Chapel Road about ten miles northeast of Rome, Georgia.

tomland ideal for growing cotton. Consequently, wealthy planters with large farms needed slaves to work their crops. That certainly held true in Ridge Valley, where Joseph Watters owned 46 slaves, two plantations, and thousands of acres.[4] Other owners of large numbers of slaves in the area included John Rush (31), Thomas B. Pinson (39), Joseph Pinson (11), Susan McGuire (27), Erasmus Bearden (17), and Tillmon Dozier (17).[5]

Dealing with the Issue

Over the ensuing years, increasing abolitionist fervor and political power in the Northern states provoked the South's "fire-eaters" – the most fanatical defenders of slavery and the State's Rights issue who regarded secession as the optimal solution. Opposition to secession came from the Constitutional Union party, made up of moderates like Joseph Watters who considered the real danger to be the turmoil created by both the fire-eaters and abolitionists.[6]

Constitutional Unionists in the Southern states urged restraint despite their dependence upon slavery. "We claim for ourselves a fixed and unaltered opinion in favor of the institution of slavery," they declared in a resolution published in the *Rome Weekly Courier*.[7] "[We] are therefore, opposed to the continued agitation of this question, believing as we do, that it injures the institution, and in no way promotes the public good; but on the contrary disturbs the peace of the country."

With this principle in mind, Watters served several terms in the Georgia State Senate and as a delegate to the 1850 Georgia Convention that met to consider – and ultimately rejected – secession. Despite Unionist efforts to "pour oil on troubled water," the political climate staggered under a series of legislative and judicial blows. Enactment of the Fugitive Slave Act of 1850 and the Supreme Court's Dred Scott Decision (holding that slaves were property rather than citizens) infuriated abolitionists. Slave owners became equally irate when abolitionists hindered federal officials from taking runaway slaves into custody and returning them to their masters.

Unrest in the Church

Planters and politicians were not the only ones dealing with the divisive slavery issue. The discord ultimately reached the religious pulpits, where the Methodist Episcopal Church suspended a Georgia bishop because of his ownership of slaves. This led to a denominational split in 1844 and the creation of the Methodist Episcopal Church South, a schism felt even in little Ridge Valley. The McGuire's Store ledger includes three Methodist ministers: Richard Leigh, Whitfield Anthony and William H. Hickey. Each was a slave owner and became a member of the M.E. Church South.

Preachers sympathetic to slavery claimed that it had been ordained by God. "Southern masters," explained the Rev. Fred Ross of Huntsville, Alabama, "hold from God...the highest and noblest responsibility ever given by Him to individual private men on all the face of the earth."[8]

In keeping with this responsibility, some slave owners avoided selling a husband and wife, or parent and child, separately. An 1860 newspaper advertisement illustrates this practice: "Negro woman and her child [to be sold] together with a great many articles," the *Rome Tri-Weekly Courier* detailed. "The above pieces of property are offered at a bargain. Persons are requested to examine for themselves."[9]

Similarly, the *Rome Weekly Courier* advertised an estate sale to take place "before the Courthouse door, in the city of Rome, Floyd county, on the first Tuesday in January next, the following negroes, viz: Silas, a blacksmith, 38 years old; Amos, 30; Sam 21; Jourdan 25; Frank 20; Jeff 70; Mira 17, and her two children; Claressa 34; Julia 20, and her two children; Ruth 60...All the above negroes sold as the property of Jonas King, deceased, and sold for the benefit of the heirs and creditors of said deceased."[10]

The slave owners' ideas of humanitarian measures did nothing to placate abolitionists like the Rev. George Cheever, who believed that slavery violated the laws of God. "There is wanting the element of conscientious, stubborn, heart-felt, eternal hostility against slavery as sin, as reprobated and forbidden of God in the same catalogue with lying, perjury, murder, whoremongering, piracy, man-stealing, and guilt, that, by the law not of God only, but man, is worthy of death," he roared in an 1858 speech to the American Abolition Society."[11]

Inflammatory rhetoric like this helped convince the fire-eaters and even many moderate Southerners that the looming 1860 presidential election posed a real threat to the institution of slavery, the balance of political power, and Southern rights and economic well-being in general. "Next fall," the *Tri-Weekly Courier* warned early that year, "[abolitionists] will elect their candidate for the Presidency – as soon as the terms of the Northern Senators of other parties expire, their places will be supplied by Black Republicans – the Supreme Court will be remodeled, and the South reduced to a state of most degrading vassalage."[12]

Richard Watters died at the Confederate hospital in Shepardstown, Virginia (now West Virginia) and was buried in the local cemetery. A few years ago, the government replaced his tombstone and the original was sent to Georgia where it was placed in the Watters family cemetery at Hermitage

No Choice but War?

Thoroughly aroused by this prospect, Southerners drew a line in the sand. "Let the State of Georgia arm her military forces, encourage volunteer companies, provide arms and ammunition, and 'in time of peace provide for war,'" suggested the *Tri-Weekly Courier* on February 19, 1860. "This is what prudence demands. We are for peace as long as we can preserve our rights by adherence to it; but when 'forbearance ceases to be a virtue,' then we say, let the fight come. We have no fears of the final result of such a conflict. 'It may cost blood – it may cost treasure;' but we say, let us be prepared for the conflict when it may come."

Just as in many other communities, the young men of Ridge Valley answered this call for volunteers. Andy Bearden, John Bearden, Wilbur Leigh, Wesley Rush, and Richard Watters were among the first to join the Rome Light Guards, an infantry unit organized more than six months before the outbreak of hostilities. Six others from the valley later joined them (G.L. Aycock, Joel Aycock, W.H. Bearden, George McGuire, Lucius Beall, and John Pinson). These eleven had at least three things in common: youthfulness (their average age was 22), and the interesting fact that they themselves did not own slaves but their fathers did.

The Rome Light Guards is an interesting case study of slave ownership in a Confederate infantry company. The 1860 census for Floyd and neighboring Cass counties and other records on file in Rome's Sara Hightower Regional Library provide relevant information for 64 of the 76 Guardsmen listed in a roster published in the May 28, 1861 *Tri-Weekly Courier*. Of the 64, only six (9%) owned slaves.[13] At first blush, this appears to be a minimal amount consistent with the viewpoint holding that the typical Southern soldier was not a slave owner. However, the parents of another 27 (42%) of these Guardsmen did own slaves. Therefore, more than half of the 64 Guards identified on this roster had close ties to slavery and a more or less direct financial stake in its continued existence.[14]

Undeniably, Floyd County was a vibrant, agriculturally-rich area in which slaves were much more common, and therefore more likely to be owned by the soldiers' families from that vicinity than would those from most of Georgia's mountain counties.

Slave ownership for the Floyd Springs Guards, another infantry company from Floyd County, may have been more typical of units from the mountain counties. Relevant information was found for 68 of 93 men listed on a roster for that unit

published in the *Tri-Weekly Courier*. Of these, 4 (6%) owned slaves, 12 (18%) had close family ties to slavery, and 52 (76%) had no discernible ties to slavery. Most of the Floyd Springs Guards lived in a relatively remote valley between Johns Mountain and Horn Mountain.

Taken as a whole, most Southern soldiers in fact did not

Joseph Watters named his Ridge Valley home "Hermitage" after President Andrew Jackson's Tennessee plantation. Watters and his wife, Polly, had ten sons and three daughters. All of their sons served in the Confederate army and two were killed in action – Richard at Sharpsburg in 1862 and Francis at the Battle of Atlanta in 1864.

own slaves, but instead hailed from a region in which the enslavement of blacks had become a way of life, causing the entire Southern economy to hinge upon the institution. The number of Southerners was few indeed, who would not in some way be dramatically affected by the elimination of slavery.

Slave Owners in Floyd

Those Southerners with a direct financial stake in slavery were going to determine Floyd County's course in the 1860 elections and the subsequent secession proceedings, because slave owners controlled the political system in the county. The leading men in Floyd at the time – all slave owners – included Augustus Wright (attorney/preacher/former U.S. Representative), J.W.H. Underwood (attorney/U.S. Representative), Daniel Mitchell (attorney/planter), Thomas Watters (sheriff), John Lumpkin (judge/former U.S. Representative), Dr. H.V.M. Miller (physician), Alfred Shorter (planter), Simpson Fouche (planter/teacher), Wade Cothran (planter/trader) and Frank Shropshire (attorney). Even a few politically active individuals who did not own slaves (mostly younger, professional men like Melvin Dwinell, a newspaper editor, and E.J. Magruder, a teacher) openly supported the institution.

As these men grew increasingly anxious about the country's direction and argued among themselves about which of the three presidential candidates opposing Lincoln to support, their sons met for drill and military instruction. More than 1,000 enlisted in Floyd County companies in 1860 and 1861, ultimately destined for obscure places like Manassas, Seven Pines, Chancellorsville, and Vicksburg. Rome's slave owners would have scoffed at, dismissed, and fumed over the notion that slavery was sinful, but one thing was certain: if it was, the sons would be the ones to pay for the sin of their fathers.

The last opportunity for a peaceful resolution ended as the dogwood, redbud, and old-man's-beard trees burst into bloom in the valleys of Floyd in the spring of 1861. "The glorious news was received at Rome at 11:30 o'clock yesterday that Virginia has seceded from the Union...and there is fighting at Harper's Ferry and Norfolk!" the *Weekly Courier* trumpeted on April 26 of that year. Three months earlier, Georgia had withdrawn from the Union despite spirited resistance from the Constitutional Union party that had carried Ridge Valley, Floyd County, and the state in the November 1860 presidential election, but failed to check escalating secessionist sentiment following Lincoln's victory. Now Virginia needed the sons of Floyd.

The Rome Light Guards was one of the first units to leave Rome and its departure made quite an impression on the city. "Our heart fails us as we attempt to write upon the subject," the *Tri-Weekly Courier* sighed on May 28, 1861. "The company is made up almost entirely of young men...Most of the members have lived in the city or in the immediate vicinity; they are connected with the best families and of course are greatly beloved." The editor closed by imploring, "That they may all safely return is the fervent and earnest prayer of the entire community."

The Wages of Sin

Of the eleven Light Guards from Ridge Valley, Wilbur F. Leigh, son of Rev. Richard Leigh, was the first to fall. While serving as a litter bearer at Thoroughfare Gap, Virginia, he suffered a mortal wound on August 28, 1862. Three of his friends also succumbed to wounds received in combat: Richard Watters (Sharpsburg), G.L. Aycock (Fredricksburg), and Joel Aycock (Gettysburg). Of the remaining seven, six sustained wounds or received discharges due to disability. Only one – John Pinson was present when the Rome Light Guards, Army of Northern Virginia, surrendered at Appomattox Court House at war's end.

Pinson came home to a valley that had been devastated by the war. In 1864, the Union army had liberally foraged the countryside during its six–month occupation of Rome, and then burned much of the town on the night of November 10. After the Federals departed for Savannah, Floyd County was at the mercy of guerrilla fighters and outlaws for months. Joseph Watters and other Ridge Valley families suffered many depredations during this period.

"Because he was a prominent citizen and had given aid to the Confederate cause," a descendant recorded, "he was robbed by Federal troops who destroyed much of his property and took most of what remained. A broken man, he lived only a few years and died at his home in March 1866."[15] This scenario was repeated over and over again, as Southerners paid the ultimate price for the horror of war.

All of the above – the joyous departure for war; the sacrifices during the war years; the casualties suffered in battle; the family losses to disease, disability and death; the depredations and horrors following the war – were all yet to come, however, when Rev. Richard Leigh paid ten cents for an ounce of gum camphor and left McGuire's Store sometime around 1861. Perhaps he had picked up and thumbed through the pages of the *Tri-Weekly Courier* and read with approval the editor's brassy proclamation: "We say, let the fight come." Had Rev. Leigh known then what the future held for the people of his lovely little valley, and that the same newspaper would soon print his own son's name with the notation, "wounded mortally, and since died," he might have completely changed his way of thinking, and instead prayed: "Lord, if it be possible, let this cup pass from me."

Endnotes

1. Purchases by family members or friends are noted more formally in the ledger than are purchases by slaves. For instance, an entry for John Rush "per Hosea" refers to his son. Similarly, there are entries "per daughter," "per wife," "per Miss Edwards," etc. In contrast, entries "per boy" and "per girl" appear to refer to slaves.
2. Four more children were born thereafter.
3. In 1860, the total population of Georgia's twenty-three northern-most counties (excluding Floyd) was 153,555 of which 22,704 were slaves.
4. The 1860 census lists Joseph Watters as the owner of 46 slaves. During his

lifetime, Watters bought and sold more than 7,000 acres in Floyd County, although he never owned that much at one time.

5. All enumerated in the 1860 census in Floyd County's Watters District (except Rush, listed in the Etowah District).

6. The Constitutional Unionists referred to themselves as "conservatives," but the term "moderates" is used here for comparison to the more extreme positions of the fire-eaters and the abolitionists.

7. Issue of June 15, 1859.

8. Ross, Rev. Fred A., *Slavery Ordained By God*, 1857, J.B. Lippincott & Co., Philadelphia, p. 67.

9. Issue of January 12, 1860. Rome had several newspapers at the time including the *Rome Courier* and *Rome Tri-Weekly Courier*.

10. Issue of November 30, 1859.

11. Cheever, George Barrell, *The Fire And Hammer Of God's Word Against The Sin Of Slavery*, 1858, American Abolition Society, New York, p. 3.

12. Issue of February 4, 1860.

13. George Merck, Warren Barrett, Dr. J.M. Gregory, M.L. Sanders, and George Sandford are enumerated slave owners in the 1860 census. In addition, George Lumpkin almost certainly inherited the slaves of his father, John Lumpkin, who died in 1860, since George was the oldest son.

14. The actual percentage is probably higher. While 27 of the Guards were identified as having fathers (and sometimes mothers, in the case of widows) that owned slaves, no information was found for the other 31. Several of these men lived alone or in boarding houses and the identity of their parents – and whether their parents were slave owners – was not determined. Given the percentage of ownership among those identified, it is highly likely that some of the 31 did own slaves.

15. Information contributed by Daniel McConnell Watters to 8th Georgia Regiment website at http://home.earthlink.net/~larsrbl/watters.htm.

BILL ARP'S UNCIVIL WAR

He was a Confederate officer, Georgia Senator, and Presbyterian elder, but the true character of Charles Henry Smith was revealed through his down home, typically humorous, sometimes irreverent, and frequently caustic writings as Bill Arp.

MARY FRAZIER LONG

C harles Henry Smith captured my interest and imagination even though he died many years before I was born. My mother had been introduced to Smith, who wrote under the pen name Bill Arp, through newspaper articles, and she never forgot the impression that his writing made. She passed her enthusiasm along to me by frequently quoting from his amusing and sometimes acerbic commentary.

I became such a fan of Bill Arp's that I named my first son William and called him Bill. My mother called him Bill Arp, and read to him while reading from Arp's writings. I remember one poem that she sometimes quoted:

Hark, I hear a bluebird sing,
And that's a sign of coming spring.
The bull-frog bellers in the ditches.
He's throwed away his winter britches.

Charles "Bill Arp" Smith was born in Lawrenceville, Georgia, one of ten children of Asahel Reid Smith, a teacher who married one of his students, Caroline McGuire. Charles put his birth this way: "On the 15th day of June, 1826, half a million children were born into the world and I was one of them."

Charles claimed that his parents had a mixed marriage. While his mother was a Southerner through-and-through from Charleston, his father had taught school in Massachusetts. This, according to Charles, had some affect on his temperament: "My infancy was not unlike that of other children, except that sometimes I had little fits of passion and then threw myself upon

Mr & Mrs. Charles H. Smith

the floor or bumped my head against the wall, at which my mother smiled and sometimes said I could help it, for it was South Carolina fighting Massachusetts."

Many years later he would look back on the simple pleasures of his childhood. "The boys had no baseball, but they had…the best rubber balls in the world and made them themselves. Some of them could bounce thirty feet high. They were made by cutting an old rubber shoe into strings and winding the strings into a ball and covering it with buckskin. But after awhile the rubber shoes were not made out of all rubber; they were mixed with something that took some of the bounce out and our balls degenerated. There was an old man living near us who was called 'Lying Tom Turner,' and he told us boys one day that when he was a boy he had a rubber ball that he was afraid to bounce hard for fear it would go up out of sight and he would lose it. We asked him what became of his ball, and he said he bounced it one day most too hard and it went up in the clouds and was gone half an hour, and when it came down his little dog grabbed it in his mouth, and it rebounced and carried the dog up with it out of sight, and he had never seen the ball nor the little dog since."

During his youth, Charles Henry Smith attended Lawrenceville Academy and then the nearby Manual Labor Institute. Many years later he remembered his school days fondly: "I went to school three miles from Lawrenceville for three long and happy years, and carried my dinner in a bucket, and how I enjoyed those cold dinners that my good mother so carefully prepared…"

Charles' father had moved to Lawrenceville in 1822, shortly after the town was founded. He had a general store on the square and served as postmaster there for many years. "Our big northern mail came by stage from Madison, Ga., twice a week," Charles wrote. "My father hired a man to ride the mail to Roswell and back twice a week. The man got sick one day and father put me on the horse and the mail in the saddlebags behind me and I had to make the forty-eight miles in a day and kept it up all winter: I nearly froze several times, and had to be lifted off the horse when I got home."

One custom of the time was that postage was paid by the recipient of a letter, and the charge was based on distance. This prompted some patrons to cautiously inspect an envelope before accepting delivery, as Smith would later describe:

"When a countryman called for letters and got one, he would look at it and very often say, 'Where did this letter come from?' Well, I would say, 'It came from Dahlonega – don't you see Dahlonega on the corner?' Then he would say, 'Well I reckon it's from my brother. He's up there diggin' gold. Don't you reckon it's from Dick?' I reckon it is," said I. "Why don't you open it and see?"

Postal patrons sometimes asked Charles to pick up other items for them while he was carrying the mail. "The old women on the route used to crowd me with their little commissions and get me to bring them pepper, or copperas, or blueing, or pins and needles, or get me to take along some socks and sell them, and so I made friends and acquaintances all the way," he recollected. "The first trip I made, an old woman hailed me and said, 'Are you a mail boy?' Why yes mam," said I. "You dident think I was a female boy, did you? I thought that was smart, but it wasent very civil, and as she turned her back on me I heard her say, 'I'll bet he's a little stuck up town boy."

Stuck up or not, Charles accepted increasing responsibility in his father's store. "When I was 18 years of age, my good father gave me an interest in his business," he noted. "I used to sell fiddles for six dollars that cost me one dollar and a half. There was a clever old man whose name was A.Q. Simmons and once a month he brought into our store for us to sell on commission a few dozen packages of yellow powder done up in brown paper and tied with old strings. We sold the first medicine he ever put up and it got to be popular and now Simmons Liver Medicine is known all over the wide world. The old man never called it a liver medicine. I don't think he knew that folks had livers. But most everybody has a liver now and most of them are sick or diseased and we are finding out that we all have kidneys, too."

It was at this time that Charles began his courtship of Mary Octavia Hutchins, the daughter of Judge Nathan Louis Hutchins of Lawrenceville. As with most every other episode in his life, his pursuit of Octavia would be a topic for his recollections in later years: "[A] pretty, hazel-eyed lassie I had only known as a child had grown out of her pantalets and into long dresses, and was casting sly glances at the boys about town. I imagined she cast some at me, for she liked to trade at my store and was in no hurry to go, and was pleased to buy what I advised her and never asked the price."

"When I used to go courting in Lawrenceville," he detailed on another occasion, "I had to pass a graveyard in the suburbs of the village and it was a test of my devotion that I braved its terrors on the darkest night and set at defiance the wandering spirits that haunted my path. My sweetheart appreciated it, I know, for she would follow me to the door when I left and anxiously listen to my retiring footsteps; and she declares to this day she could hear me running up that hill by the graveyard like a fast trotting horse over a shell road."

Octavia and Charles married March 7, 1849, when she was 16 years old and he was 22. Their courtship and union seemed to spur him to change professions, as he later remembered. "When I got to be 21 years old," he wrote, "I suddenly took a notion that measuring off tape and calico and weighing out copperas and nails and the like was a business most too limited for my ambition." So he began reading law with Ocavia's father, Judge Nathan Louis Hutchins, and eventually went into legal practice with him.

A few yeas later, the family (by then the Smiths had two young boys) joined one of Charles' brothers, a physician, in moving to Northwest Georgia. "In 1851," he remembered, "I took the Western fever, and moved to Rome to grow up with the town and the county. I was soon associated with Judge [John W.H.] Underwood in the practice of law, and for thirteen years we were as intimate as brothers."

Charles and Octavia would have thirteen children, ten of whom lived to adulthood. Judging from the reminiscences of daughter Marian, their house was a happy one: "Always an early riser, it was [father's] habit to walk up and down the halls of the home playing the flute to waken us in the morning, or playing the piano in his own unique fashion, all on the black keys, but peculiarly sweet and effective as he did it. One of my earliest recollections is of being aroused by the strains of the flute, when climbing out of bed, nightgowned, barefooted, I toddled to his side and with the other children marched up and down the hall clinging to his dressing gown while he played."

An ardent Democrat, Smith moved in political circles and held several offices including mayor of Rome and Georgia Senator. "Pollytix is a fateegin' subject, and has got as monotonous as a one-tune hand organ," he would complain. His political beliefs were decidedly populist, as another of his folksy comments illustrates: "A poor man in the country is safer from all calamity than a rich one in the city. A poor man may lament his poverty and envy the rich, but he has no reason to. A man who makes a comfortable living on a farm has a greater security for life and liberty and happiness and long life than any other class that I know of."

Smith was also a proponent of States' Rights, and on the eve of the Civil War his views earned him both a pen name and an outlet for his literary talents. In reply to President Abraham Lincoln's call for Southern troops to disperse within 30 days, Smith addressed a facetious letter to "Abe Linkhorn" in the down-home, uneducated, common sense vernacular of a country bumpkin.

So why "Bill Arp"? "I remember writing an answer [to Lincoln's proclamation] as though I was a good Union man and a law-abiding citizen, and was willing to disperse, if I could …. But thought he had better give us a little more time for I had been out in the old field by myself and tried to disperse myself and couldn't do it," Smith later recounted. "I thought the letter was right smart, and decently sarcastic, and so read it to Dr. [H.V.M.] Miller and Judge Underwood, and they seemed to think it was right smart, too. About that time I looked around and saw Bill Arp standing at the door with his mouth open and a merry glisten in his eye. As he came forward, says he to me: 'Squire, are you gwine to print that?' 'I reckon I will, Bill,' said I. 'What name are you gwine to put to it?' said he. 'I don't know

Charles H. Smith spent most of his adult life in Cartersville, where he resided in these two homes.

yet,' said I; 'I haven't thought about a name.' Then he brightened up and said, 'Well, Squire, I wish you would put mine, for them's my sentiments;' and I promised him that I would."

During the Civil War, Smith served as a major on the staff of several Confederate generals. During the Seven Days battles near Richmond in 1862, General George T. Anderson sent Smith to Robert E. Lee's headquarters. "I found [Lee] in a large wall tent with many officers around him," Smith remembered. "I saw a man, an officer, whose head and body were underneath the right hand table and his feet were out upon the straw. His slouched hat was over his head and eyes, his sword was unbuckled, and his boots were on and spurred ... My curiosity was greatly excited, and when the adjutant handed me the instructions, I ventured to point to the sleeping man and ask, 'Who is he?' 'That is Stonewall,' he said; 'he has had no sleep for forty-eight hours and fell down there exhausted. General Lee would not suffer him to be disturbed, and so our dinner will be eaten over him and in silence.'"

After receiving a medical discharge in 1863, Smith returned to Rome, consoling himself with the reflection that he had killed as many of the Yankees as they had killed of him.

By then, the Smith family resided in a big frame house in Rome known as Rose Hill, on what is now called Clocktower Hill (their first quarters had been Oak Hill, later the home of Martha Berry). General William T. Sherman would briefly make his headquarters at Rose Hill in late October 1864.

When the Union army approached Rome in May 1864, the Smith family joined the exodus from town: "Out retreat was conducted in excellent order, after the bridge was burnt," he detailed. "If there was any straggling at all, they straggled ahead. It would have delighted General [Joseph] Johnston to have seen the alacrity of our movements. P.S. Tip (family servant) is still faithful unto the end. He says the old turkey was left behind and has been setting for fourteen weeks, and the fowl invaders are welcome to her. Furthermore, he threw a dead cat into the well, and they are welcome to that."

Charles Smith and his family returned to Rome in January 1865 as the bitter war drew to a close. Union troops had wrecked the grounds and stolen or destroyed most of the

Charles Henry Smith's granddaughter Caroline died on the day of his funeral, so they were buried together in a Cartersville cemetery.

Smith's possessions, but Rose Hill was still standing. Many years later, a still-defiant Smith would say of the Yankees: "In the long run they got even with us and a little ahead and the Grand Army is still bragging how four of them whipped one of us in four years."

After the war, Smith became the editor of the *Rome Commercial*, a newspaper established by a young Henry Grady. When Grady later became editor of the *Atlanta Constitution*, Smith occasionally contributed letters under his Bill Arp nom de plume. These letters became a popular feature, so starting in 1878 Bill Arp became a regular contributor to the *Constitution*.

Henry Grady welcomed Bill aboard with this announcement: "Major Smith has commenced a new career and the readers of the *Constitution* will be able to see what he can do, which is a great deal more interesting than what he has done." A lot, as it turned out, for Bill Arp's column remained a regular part of the Sunday *Constitution* for 25 years. In 1877 the Smith family moved from Rome to a place known as the old Fontaine Farm near Cartersville. They would spend ten agreeable years there, as evidenced by one Arp letter: "I like farmin.' It's an honest, quiet life, and it does me so much good to work and git all over in a swet of perspiration. I enjoy my umble food and my repose and get up every mornin' renewed and rejuvenated like an eagle in his flight, or words to that effect."

Charles was a faithful Presbyterian who remained active in church throughout his life. He was chosen by Cartersville First Presbyterian Church in 1866 to travel to Atlanta to purchase a new bell because he had a pass on the Western & Atlantic Railroad. That bell is still used today to call members of the church to worship services.

Despite his faith, Smith wasn't above poking fun at the religious practices of his day. In one letter titled "The Harrangue of a Flatboat Parson" he wrote: "Now as there are many kinds of sperits and many kinds of fire, ha! In the world, ah! Jest so there are many kinds of Christians, ah! In the fuss place we have the Piscopalians, and they are a high-sailin', high roostin' hifalutin set, ah! And they may be likened unto a turkey buzzard that flies up into the air, ah! And he goes up, and up, and up, till he looks no bigger than your finger nail, and the fust thing you know, he comes down, and down, and down, and goes to fillin' hisself on the carkiss of a dead hoss by the side of the road, ah! And then, my brethering, thar's the Baptists, ah! And they have been likened to a 'possum on a simmon tree, and the thunders may roll and the earth may quake, and the lions roar and the whangdoodle mourn, but the 'possum clings thar still, ah! And you may shake one foot loose and the other's that and you may shake all feet loose, and he laps his tail around the limb, and he clings and he clings furever, ah!"

In one of his last columns, Smith reflected on mortality: "'I still live.' I was ruminating about the last words of great men, and those of Daniel Webster always impress me with peculiar force. On the very confines of eternity, on the brink of everlasting change that he knew was at hand his great mind seemed to be studying and waiting for the moment of his departure – waiting and watching for the separation of the soul from the body, and there was no fear, no dread, as he calmly whispered, 'I still live,' and immediately died...I thought of all this not long ago as I seemed to be drawing near the end and approached the confines of that undiscovered country from whose bourne no traveler returns."

A month after writing his last column for the *Constitution*, Charles Henry Smith died in Cartersville, August 24, 1903. On the day of his funeral, his youngest grandchild, eight-month-old Sarah Hutchins Smith died and her body was placed in the same grave with her grandfather.

I think back to my childhood and my mother's fascination with Bill Arp, a fascination that she passed down to me. I can leaf through an atlas and find towns named Bill Arp in Douglas County, Georgia, and in northeastern Texas. I'd wager there are few people who recognize that name today, and even fewer who are familiar with his writings. But my mother was right – Bill Arp was a talented and interesting man.

SEARCHING FOR PRIVATE JEMISON

For decades the haunting photograph of a young Confederate soldier has captured the imagination of many Americans interested in the Civil War. We know the soldier in the photograph was Private Edwin Jemison, but the location of his last remains is a mystery that has intrigued researchers for generations. . . and the search continues today.

ALEXANDRA FILIPOWSKA & HUGH T. HARRINGTON

In a quiet cemetery in the center of what once was Georgia's state capital, a monument has stood for well over a hundred years which commemorates the life of a young Confederate soldier who courageously lost his life in the Civil War. Private Edwin Francis Jemison was just 17 years of age when he was cut down on the battlefield, and questions about his life and death pervade to this very day.

The questions first arose 44 years ago after the publication of an old family photograph in *The American Heritage Picture History of the Civil War*. The unforgettable and haunting image immortalized the youthful Pvt. Jemison who symbolized the tragic losses involved in our most costly war. The photograph graphically conveys what so many soldiers of that period must have felt: sadness, fear, strength, courage, and an abject resignation to one's fate.

Although no one can tell what Pvt. Jemison was thinking or feeling at the time the photograph was taken, his recorded actions reflect a soldier with strength, courage, and character. One can only imagine today the awesome bravery required for a young boy of that tender age to join an army which he knew would be engaged in one of the most horrible and bloody conflicts in the history of mankind.

Jemison enlisted into the 2nd Louisiana Infantry, Company C, at the age of 16 during the first wave of recruitment in that state, a fact which further emphasizes his courage. The clearest indication of his bravery, however, comes from his obituary in which an eye-witness described him as "bounding forward at the order 'Charge!' [when] he was stricken down in the front rank...."

But what happened to the remains of Pvt. Jemison? Some time after the war ended, his parents erected a monument in his memory at Memory Hill Cemetery in Milledgeville, Georgia, which people today believe to be Pvt. Jemison's final resting-place. However, when examining the cemetery lot in conjunction with the burial practices of the Confederacy at the time of his death, and considering the severity of his wounds and his obituary, the question arises: Is Pvt. Jemison really buried at Memory Hill, as believed, or is he actually buried elsewhere?

Private Edwin Francis Jemison, 2nd Louisiana Regiment.

Early Life

Pvt. Jemison came from a long line of distinguished ancestors. His mother, Sarah Stubbs Jemison, was the daughter of a merchant and justice of the peace, and the granddaughter of a Revolutionary War hero. His father Robert was a man of many means, including landowner, lawyer, and newspaper editor. His heritage also included a Revolutionary War hero, a Georgia State Congressman, and prominent doctors and lawyers. In fact, both the Jemisons and the Stubbses are among Georgia's founding families.

Shortly after the birth of their third child, Robert and Sarah moved their family from Georgia to Monroe, Louisiana, in Ouachita Parish where they were able to

The Battle of Malvern Hill was depicted in this illustration (and two subsequent ones) published in *Harper's Illustrated Magazine* in the 1860s.

build successful lives for themselves over the next decade. Those happy days, however, were short-lived.

With the secession of Louisiana on January 26, 1861, and the subsequent fall of Fort Sumter on April 14, Louisiana was pulled inexorably into the conflict between the Northern and Southern states. A call to arms was raised across the South and men in many Southern towns formed companies that enlisted en masse into the Confederate Army. This, in all likelihood, is how Company C of the 2nd Louisiana was formed. Known as the Pelican Grays, the men of this outfit, including Pvt. Jemison, enlisted at Camp Walker in New Orleans on May 11, 1861. The unit left New Orleans for Virginia, where it fell under the command of General John Bankhead Magruder.

The first 11 months after enlistment were relatively quiet for the men of the 2nd Louisiana. Shortly after signing on, the regiment was transported from New Orleans to Richmond, and from there moved to Yorktown where they were commissioned with the job of building fortifications. For a short time the men were sent to Williamsburg, again to build fortifications, but returned to Yorktown for the winter. Other than a skirmish in April of 1862 at Dam No. 1 (also known as Lee's Mill), the 2nd Louisiana did not see heavy action until Malvern Hill.

Deadly Malvern Hill

Malvern was the last of the Seven Days battles in which General McClellan's Army of the Potomac attempted to take Richmond. This engagement was one of the bloodiest fought by the Confederate army up to that point. D.H. Hill, one of General Lee's commanding officers later recalled, "It was not war, it was murder."

Despite the bloodshed, General Lee was able to defeat General McClellan in this most important initial battle, and avoid the capture of the Confederacy's capitol —

Richmond. Despite his ultimate victory Lee's army suffered such large casualties during the campaign that the engagements could hardly be characterized as successful. The July 1, 1862, Battle of Malvern Hill alone saw the loss of 5,500 Confederate soldiers, nearly twice the number of Union losses. One of those soldiers was Pvt. Edwin Jemison, who lost his life when he was horribly cut down by an artillery round.

On July 2, 1862, the Confederate Army buried the dead on the battlefield where they had fallen, leaving those haunted by his photograph to wonder if Pvt. Jemison's last remains lie in a plot on a rolling Virginia battlefield, or, if he was – as later assumed – transported back to Georgia to be buried in his family's lot at Memory Hill Cemetery in Milledgeville.

It would have been quite possible to have been killed in Virginia in July of 1862, and have a final resting place in Georgia. Less than a year earlier Milledgeville's first battle casualty of the war – who had been killed at Pensacola on November 20th – was returned to Milledgeville and buried November 30, 1861.

Even after the war, bodies were disinterred and brought back for reburial in home states. In March 1866 the remains of a soldier killed at Knoxville, Tennessee, in November 1863, were returned to Milledgeville. In November 1866, the remains of a second soldier, killed at Sharpsburg on September 17, 1862, were also returned to Milledgeville.

Decomposing Bodies

The details involved in moving a dead body during the Civil War (in the days prior to refrigeration) are not commonly known today. However, according to an article entitled "Disinterment of Dead Bodies" in the August 13, 1862, *Georgia Journal & Messenger* (Macon, Georgia), the problems inherent with such as action are vividly described. The article was written six weeks after Malvern Hill:

"Our [the newspaper editors'] attention was called particularly to this subject, while on a visit to our Cemetery one day last week. A body had been brought here by railroad, we believe, from Atlanta, on its way to Dooly county, and had become so offensive that further transportation was refused. After remaining at the depot some time, a guard was detailed from Col. Brown's encampment for that purpose and the body buried."

The editors of the newspaper article elaborated on the distasteful topic by quoting from the *Richmond Dispatch and Whig*. The quote, in full, is as follows:

"We daily observe at the railway stations boxes containing the bodies of deceased soldiers, which have been disinterred by their friends, under the belief that they can be sent off without delay either by mail train or express. This, however, is an error. Freight trains only carry them, and the detention frequently causes the bodies to become offensive, when their immediate burial by the wayside is a matter of necessity. It would be better to postpone disinterment until cold weather, when it can be accomplished with less trouble and more certainty of getting the remains of the departed to their destination. Metallic coffins are difficult to obtain, and wooden ones can only be procured by the payment of a large sum. In these the dead bodies are packed with sawdust, and in warm weather their transportation to a distant point is uncertain, if not absolutely impossible."

In their editorial, the newspaper editors disagreed with the commonly accepted (and essentially horrible) method of removing decaying bodies from the battlefield, and offered an ironically simple method to successfully (and aesthetically) achieve the goal of transporting the dead:

"To the above we have to add (and that from personal knowledge), that nothing is more easy, convenient, or cheap than transporting bodies at any season of the year, to any distance. Any common coffin will answer. Have a piece of cotton osnaburgs or other cloth of the necessary size – dip it in boiling tar, and wrap the coffin in it and it is sealed tighter than it can be done in a metallic case. Place it in a box with some kind of packing to keep it from moving, and the work is complete. No charcoal, or disinfectant is necessary."

As in the cases of the soldiers' remains moved to Milledgeville after the war ended, it is possible that Pvt. Jemison's body could have been taken from a burial site on the battlefield in Virginia to Milledgeville after a period of several years. Or, the body could have been taken directly from the battlefield to Milledgeville for burial. However, the question remains as to whether or not either of these steps was taken, and if Edwin Jemison's body is actually under the obelisk in Memory Hill.

A Single Grave?

The obelisk upon which Edwin Jemison's name is engraved stands over a single grave and also carries the name of Edwin's elder brother Henry who died in 1859. Edwin's name is engraved into the South side of the obelisk, while Henry's is carved into the North side. However, it is clear that the obelisk was not put up at the time of Henry's death with Edwin's name engraved upon it at a later date, because a separate portion of the obelisk contains the names of both men engraved in relief.

While it is not known exactly when the monument was erected, a rough idea can be obtained from the inscription of the name of the stonemason at the base of the monument, "J. Artope & Son, Macon." The only monuments in Memory Hill that bear the company name with this exact verbiage bear death dates from the 1860s. Prior to that time (in the 1840s and 1850s), the company name found on the monuments is "J. Artope, Macon, Ga." Also, the Macon City Directory listed the company periodically as "J. Artope & Son" between 1860 and 1872. By 1877, the company was listed as "Tom B. Artope" and the monuments in Memory Hill made by the company from that time forward reflect that name change. It can therefore be safely assumed that the obelisk was erected between 1860 and 1877.

In addition, a marble Confederate soldier marker implanted on the west side of the obelisk bears the inscription "E.F. Jemison." This stone, and ones like it, were installed by the City of Milledgeville in 1896. In the *Union-Recorder* of February

4, 11, and 18, 1896, the names of Confederate soldiers were being solicited for the Milledgeville program in order that the graves might be marked. The newspaper was calling upon the citizens to respond with the names of servicemen buried in Memory Hill, but in the case of Jemison the fact that he was killed at Malvern Hill is carved on the obelisk so no person needed to come forward to provide information that a burial had taken place.

The obelisk stands on top of a stone slab that covers the grave and measures three-and-a-half feet wide by just over six-and-a-half feet long. The grave appears to have been created in the customary Memory Hill manner. These graves were not simple holes where a coffin was placed in the ground with the dirt then thrown in on top. They consist of an underground brick vault the length of the grave and about three feet wide. There is an arched or vaulted roof built of bricks that comes almost to the surface of the ground. Slabs rest on the top of the vault much like a capstone. After the burial service, the coffin was lowered into the ground surrounded by the brick sides of the vault. Then the brick mason constructed the vaulted roof over the top thus completing the vault. There is no door or opening, the entire underground structure being sealed with brick and mortar. Each one of these tombs is the size of one coffin.

As the top of the vault is so near the surface of the ground one may determine its dimensions by inserting a thin metal probe into the ground and within a few inches touch the top of the vault. The vault under the Edwin and Henry Jemison obelisk appears to be of normal size for one burial. Therefore, there is no opportunity for another grave to have been squeezed into the space designed for one person.

Other Plot Possibilities

However, the possibility of Pvt. Jemison's remains being placed in a grave alongside the obelisk should not be ignored. The grave to the north side of the Jemison obelisk is that of Robert Small Pratt who died in 1857. His was the first burial on this lot. To the west of the obelisk is a pallbearers' path containing no graves. On the south side of the obelisk is the grave of W.B. Stubbs who died in 1864. To the east of the obelisk is the grave of Robert W. Jemison who died in 1879. Each bur-

ial spot surrounding the obelisk is occupied and thus graphically reduces the possibility of Edwin's last remains being contained anywhere on the lot.

A thoughtful examination of the graves in the Jemison lot indicates that there is, in fact, no spot for the grave of Edwin Jemison. There were available spaces in 1862 but since that time, all have been used. As his brother Henry was buried in the space under the present obelisk in 1859, Edwin would have to have been placed elsewhere.

The grave to the north was already filled before Henry was buried. The grave to the south was available in 1862 for Edwin's remains but if Edwin was buried there then the remains of W.B. Stubbs could not have been placed there in 1864 (as indicated by the date engraved on the Stubbs stone). Similarly, Edwin's remains could have been placed to the East, but that grave was used in 1879 for Robert W. Jemison, so it, as well, could not have been used for Edwin Jemison. Edwin could not have been placed to the west as that area is a pallbearers' path and is clear of burials.

The only possibility for the grave containing the last remains of Pvt. Edwin Jemison, is an unmarked plot to the north of Robert Small Pratt. It is covered with bricks that today are barely visible above the soil line. However, in the 1930s when the cemetery was first indexed, this site was believed to be an infant's grave. Today, the bricks are exposed over a larger area, a fact which may indicate an adult grave at this site. However, it would seem that in the 1930s, the bricks would have been even more visible and the impression of an infant grave may therefore be accurate.

In all likelihood, if Pvt. Jemison was buried at Memory Hill in his own grave, his family would have given him a monument separate from that of his brother Henry. The obelisk dedicated to the brothers has several loving inscriptions to Pvt. Jemison carved on it from his mother and father. The one from his father states in Latin, "Sweet is the reward for those who die for their country," while the one from his mother says "A more dutiful son never lived. A braver soldier never died. Peace to his ashes." These simple words were obviously included on the monument to a son by parents who thought of him both highly and dearly. If Pvt. Jemison was buried in the unmarked grave to the north of Robert Small Pratt, or in any other plot for that matter, it is quite probable those loving words would be placed on top of that grave, and not upon the one for Henry.

Another piece of evidence placing Pvt. Jemison's remains elsewhere is his obituary. During the Civil War, the newspapers of Milledgeville printed few obituaries and the ones that *were* printed are very short. Most of the obituaries are for officers, and therefore it is surprising to find an obituary, and a long one at that, for Private Edwin F. Jemison. Regarding his burial the obituary states that, "May He who maketh wars to cease, comfort the sorrowing parents whose boy lies, buried by loving hands, on the battle field near Richmond," making it clear that at the time of his death, Pvt. Jemison was buried with his fellow soldiers on Virginia soil.

The obituary in itself is not conclusive evidence of the absence of Edwin's remains in Memory Hill. As discussed, some bodies, even several years after the War, were disinterred and shipped home. However, no record of such a shipment or reburial has been discovered in the Milledgeville newspapers. Such events were unusual, and therefore were often mentioned in the papers when they occurred.

Battlefield Grave

In addition, the Richmond National Battlefield Park – which includes Malvern Hill – has no records of the removal and subsequent relocation of the bodies of any Confederate soldiers from their graves on the battlefield. Although Union soldiers were removed for reburial between 1865 and 1866, it appears the Confederate soldiers were not accorded the same consideration, and were left where they were buried on the battlefield.

All of the above notwithstanding, it is possible that some Confederate soldiers were relocated, but if this did occur, the incidents were so few in number that they were not recorded. This, in conjunction with the absence of a newspaper account in Milledgeville of Edwin's burial at Memory Hill, the lack of actual space in the cemetery lot, and the fact there is but a single monument dedicated to the Jemison brothers, is reasonably solid evidence that the last remains of heroic Pvt. Edwin Jemison lie today in an unmarked grave somewhere on the "battle field near Richmond."

Sources
Southern Recorder (Milledgeville, GA), August 5, 1862
The Civil War, Caton, Bruce
Southern Recorder (Milledgeville, GA), December 3, 1861
Federal Union (Milledgeville, GA), March 27, 1866

REBEL LION
AT BURNSIDE'S BRIDGE

Outnumbered nearly thirty-five to one and led by a politically appointed general with little military experience, the Georgians defending a key bridge over Antietam Creek didn't stand a chance. But when the enemy finally attacked, they found a lion at Burnside's Bridge.

RAY CHANDLER

COURTESY UNIVERSITY OF GEORGIA

Robert Toombs in the 1850s

To the end of his life, Robert Toombs insisted on being called "General Toombs" in recognition of his service as a brigadier general in the Confederate Army. His rank had been a point of contention in his frequent battles with Confederate President Jefferson Davis, who Toombs thought denied him the recognition and glory – and higher rank – he earned at the Battle of Sharpsburg in 1862. Davis denied letting hard feelings play any part in his decision, but Toombs carried his grudge to the grave.

Toombs never gained the accolades he desired, and on the whole it is hard not to agree with Thomas R.R. Cobb, like Toombs a Georgian and a politically appointed general, who called Toombs' military career a "desperate failure." Perhaps, but Toombs and his Georgia Brigade would nevertheless taste glory one late summer day on a hillside overlooking a Maryland creek.

In September 1862, the fortunes of the Confederacy had never been higher. Its back to the wall just a few months earlier, the Confederacy had escaped disaster when Robert E. Lee took command of the army defending Richmond. In June, with a much larger Federal army in sight of the capital city's church spires, Lee embarked on a quick campaign of daring and costly attacks – the Seven Days battles – and threw the invaders back.

Just two months later, Lee had to turn his attention to northern Virginia to face another threat, and soon his army nearly annihilated a Union force under John Pope at the Second Battle of Manassas. Then Lee looked even further north, eying Maryland. He reckoned that dealing the Union army a crushing defeat on northern soil would fan the flames of anti-war sentiment in the North, perhaps encouraging European nations to recognize the Confederate States, and, he hoped, leading to a negotiated peace.

Confederate leaders also believed that many Marylanders harbored pro-secessionist sentiment, and that throngs of young men would join their Southern brothers in arms. In any case, there was no question that the verdant countryside, as yet untouched by war, could furnish supplies for hungry Confederate troops. Three months of hard fighting had left Lee's Army of Northern Virginia frazzled, but he held the initiative, and he advised Jefferson Davis, "The present seems the most propitious time since the beginning of the war for the Confederate Army to enter Maryland."

Kind to His Men

Lee entered Maryland with forty-one infantry brigades, none of which had a more politically advanced, or militarily inexperienced, commander than did Toombs' Brigade of Georgians. Robert Toombs' only previous military service had been as a militia officer during the Creek War of 1836, when he likely never even saw a hostile Indian. Afterwards he spent years in the Georgia General Assembly and United States Congress; thereafter, he narrowly missed becoming president of the Confederate States of America. Early in the war, he served as the Confederate Secretary of State for five contentious months, getting more than his fill of Jefferson Davis, a bitter political foe from the time of their positions in the U.S. government before the war.

By the time Toombs led his troops across the Potomac River into Maryland in 1862, he had commanded his brigade for nearly a year. He had just been released from arrest on charges of insubordination leveled by Gen. James Longstreet, his superior whose direct order Toombs had countermanded early in the Second Manassas campaign. Edward Porter Alexander, like Toombs a native of Washington, Georgia, described Toombs as "not entirely a respectful and subordinate brigadier." In fact, respect for any authority but his own was almost alien to Robert Toombs' character.

West Point-trained officers were his special bugbear. To Toombs, they either failed to fight when they should or they made costly mistakes. Toombs' Brigade had suffered nearly 30% casualties in three months of fighting, and he chalked up much of the damage to rash decisions by West Point-educated officers, including Lee's last ditch attempt to crush General George McClellan's army by attacking a strongly fortified Union position at Malvern Hill. West Point officers returned his disdain, regarding Toombs as a mere political appointee.

But Toombs' men loved him. Private Ivey Duggan of the 15th Georgia Infantry Regiment wrote, "General Toombs is always kind to his men and we love him for it...We would not willingly exchange him for any other officer."

Four veteran Georgia infantry regiments – the 2nd, 15th, 17th and 20th – comprised Toombs' Brigade. These men were hardened veterans who understood the human cost of war. Private Harvey Hightower of the 20th Georgia wrote that he had been in two battles and had no desire to see a third: "I have seen dead men so thick you could walk on them hundreds of yards and never tutch [sic] the ground."

Letters and diaries suggest that Toombs' men were worn and lice-ridden, many were shoeless, and nearly all were hungry. As Private George Abercrombie of the 2nd Georgia feasted on ripening corn in Maryland, he cursed the civilian officials that failed to properly provide for the soldiers: "Damn a government that won't furnish fodder," he grumbled.

Colonel Henry Lewis Benning

Critical Salient

Lee's Maryland campaign got off to a halting, discouraging start. Many of his soldiers were exhausted, and a sizeable number were reluctant to serve in an army invading another state. Straggling seriously reduced the number of men in the ranks, and Maryland, especially the central and western sections occupied by the Confederates, proved no hotbed of secession. As if that wasn't enough, a copy of Lee's orders fell into the hands of General McClellan at a moment when the Southern army was scattered over the countryside. Thus informed, McClellan was hot on the Southern army's trail.

Lee decided to make a stand near the village of Sharpsburg, Maryland, on a series of hills overlooking the bucolic countryside along Antietam Creek. There he began gathering the scattered elements of his army to face the enemy, which outnumbered the Confederates five to two.

On September 14, 1862, Toombs received orders to move his brigade toward Sharpsburg. Two of his regiments, the 15th and 17th, were sent to guard the Army of Northern Virginia's supply wagon trains near the Potomac River crossings, but Toombs led the other two regiments to a position guarding the lower crossings of Antietam Creek. The key crossings were a stone bridge known locally as Rohrbach

Bridge and two fords. Collectively, these points were a backdoor to the rear of the outnumbered Confederate army.

Toombs' Brigade was in David Jones' division, but in actuality Toombs was on his own for much of the ensuing battle. His troops occupied a critical salient near the right end of a line of battle nearly four miles long. This salient would soon be a focal point of General George McClellan's effort to turn Lee's right flank.

Old Rock

Before dawn on Wednesday September 17, McClellan uncoiled his army and struck Lee. The battle unfolded from north to south in a series of disjointed attacks, and for a time it seemed that the men guarding Rohrbach Bridge would be bystanders. But McClellan's plan called for his IX Corps, 12,000 infantry and artillery under the command of General Ambrose Burnside, to seize the vital 125-foot long stone bridge that spanned the usually placid and shallow waters of Antietam Creek.

One of Toombs' subordinates that day was Colonel Henry Lewis Benning, a 49-year-old Columbus lawyer and former justice of the Georgia Supreme Court.

Frank Leslie's illustration of the Federal attack across Burnside's Bridge appeared in the October 11, 1862 edition of Frank Leslie's illustrated newspaper.

Burnside's Bridge circa 1880.

Benning was the officer who had assumed command of the brigade while Toombs was under arrest at Second Manassas, and there Benning earned the nickname "Old Rock." Benning's account of the events at Rohrbach Bridge on September 17, 1862, details how a small, resolute troop came to face an overwhelming enemy force:

HEADQUARTERS TOOMBS' BRIGADE
Camp near Winchester, October 13, 1862

On the morning of [September]15th I was ordered by General Toombs to place the brigade across the road leading from Sharpsburg to Rohrersville at the Stone Bridge over Antietam Creek and to defend the bridge.

The men of the two small Georgia regiments deployed on the side and crest of a steep, rocky, thinly forested hill looming above the bridge and quickly built "rude barricades" of fence rails. Benning, who would command the contingent when Toombs was absent attending matters elsewhere on the battlefield, sent pickets and skirmishers across the creek and awaited the enemy.

It proved a long wait, because the Union IX Corps did not advance on the bridge until the morning of September 17, nearly two days later. Benning noted that the skirmishing grew heavier the morning of the 17th, "till about 9 o'clock, when our skirmishers were driven in." A Confederate battery then opened fire and drove back the Union troops, but the cannoneers were soon ordered elsewhere. "Thus," Benning lamented, "the two regiments were left at the bridge without army artillery supports whatever."

DAN ROPER

The bridge today.

Benning worried that there were no other Confederate infantry units in the area and that his men were "without the expectation of receiving any re-enforcements." In fact, there were a few other units nearby – the 50th Georgia and a company of South Carolinians positioned downstream to guard a ford, and a Virginia battery within supporting distance – but from his perspective, the situation looked grim:

The two [regiments] together numbered not more than 350 men and officers, the Second having only 97, and the Twentieth not more than 250. In their front was Burnside's whole corps of not fewer than 12,000 or 15,000 of the enemy's best men, with numerous artillery. In this forlorn condition were the two regiments at about 9 o'clock, when the fight opened in earnest. At this time the enemy's infantry, aided by the fire of many pieces of artillery, advanced in heavy force to the attack; and soon the attack opened on our whole line as far up as the bridge. It was bold and persevering.

The Southerners faced three waves of attacks in which the fire from the Union infantry and artillery was "incessant." But the Georgians were up to the challenge and the enemy assaults were "met by a rapid, well-directed, and unflinching fire from our men, under which the enemy, after a vain struggle, broke and fell back."

At noon, the Federals prepared to unleash a still greater force to seize the bridge. A Union artillery battery occupied a position "from which it could command...the whole face of the hill occupied by our troops," Old Rock recorded. "Soon it opened fire, and the infantry, in much heavier force than at any time before, extending far above as well as below the bridge, again advanced to the attack. The combined fire of infantry and artillery was terrific."

The beleaguered Confederates stood steady for a time, but eventually had to withdraw. "[The attack was] withstood by our men until their ammunition was quite exhausted," Benning detailed. Finally, when "the enemy had got upon the

The flag of the 15th Georgia regiment.

bridge and were above and below it fording the creek," Benning gave the order to fall back.

"Under an order received from General Toombs," he continued, the men of the 2nd and 20th Georgia Regiments "retired to a position near the right of the general line of battle." Although the Georgians had pulled back, Benning rightly emphasized the importance of their stand: "Thus at near 1 o'clock we were driven from the bridge, but we had held it long enough to enable the advance troops of General A. P. Hill to reach their position in the line of battle; and this, I suppose, was attaining the great object of defending a place so far in front of that line – a place so untenable as was the bridge."

In defending the Rohrbach Bridge – known thereafter as Burnside's Bridge – the Georgians suffered 110 casualties including Lieutenant-Colonel Holmes, who, Benning eulogized, was as "good officer, and as gallant a man, I think, as my eyes ever beheld." He lauded his men similarly:

No words of mine in praise of officers and men are needed. The simple story is eulogy enough. I must, however, bear witness to one fact: During that long and terrible fire not a man, except a wounded one, fell out and went to the rear - not a man. The loss of the enemy was heavy. Near the bridge they lay in heaps. Their own estimate, as a paroled sergeant of ours taken at the bridge told me, was at from 500 to 1,000 men killed. He also told me that they informed him that at about 12 o'clock an order came from General McClellan to take the bridge, cost what it might, and that then the whole corps advanced to the attack…"

His Only Reward

While "Old Rock" Benning directed the two regiments, Toombs was doing what he did best – he was seemingly everywhere, exhorting and encouraging his Georgians by the sheer force of his personality. Accounts of his actions by his own men are sketchy, in part because the soldiers were so busy fighting that they had little opportunity to observe what was happening even close by. In fact, they were loading and firing so fast that several were wounded when their powder exploded in their faces as they poured it down hot musket barrels.

But Toombs captured the eye of other observers. Private John Dooley of Kemper's Virginia Brigade, which arrived near the close of the fight, observed Toombs galloping "up and down the line like one frantic, telling the men to stand firm…" This account is consistent with Toombs' demeanor at Second Manassas, where just released from arrest, he had arrived right before the final attack against the Federal defenses and galloped along his brigade line, cursing, urging his men to victory, and waving his sword while his men cheered.

By blunting the Union attack against Lee's right flank, Toombs' Brigade helped the Army of Northern Virginia survive a battle in which it was greatly outnumbered. Afterwards, Toombs queried Captain Charles Squires, an artillery officer: "Squires, what is being said of me at headquarters?" The captain replied that it was said that with two regiments Toombs had stood off an entire Federal corps. That seemed to satisfy the normally irascible Toombs.

Other accounts, both official and in the press, gave Toombs and his Georgians their due, but in the end that proved to be Toombs' only reward for the gallant stand by his little brigade at Antietam Creek. He soon resigned from the army, spent the rest of the war contending with various Confederate officials, and thereafter remained a self-proclaimed "un-reconstructed Rebel." He died in Washington, Georgia, in 1885.

Sources

R.E. Lee letter to Jefferson Davis, Sept. 3, 1862 quoted by Tucker, Phillip, *Burnside's Bridge: The Climactic Struggle of the 2nd and 20th Georgia at Antietam Creek*, 2000. Stackpole Books, Mechanicsburg, Pa., p. 2.

Letter from Ivey Duggan of 15th Ga. published in October 14, 1862 issue of *Central Georgian* newspaper.

September 1862 letter from George Hightower to his family quoted in *Burnside's Bridge* (See Note 1) at pg. 42.

Letter from Henry Abercrombie published in a September 1862 issue of the *Daily Columbus Enquirer* newspaper and quoted in Burnside's Bridge (See Note 1) at p. 41.

All quotes from Benning come from his after action report found in *The War of the Rebellion: a Compilation of the Official Records of the Union and Confederate Armies*, Vol. 51, Part1 (Ser #107), pp. 161-165.

Durkin, Joseph (Editor), *John Dooley, Confederate Soldier: His War Journal*, 1945. Georgetown Press, p. 47.

REBEL LION REDUX

Robert Toombs was a giant of a man who roared against friend and foe alike. His prodigious talent led to great political stature, but his personal vices possibly cost him the presidency of the Confederate States of America.

RAY CHANDLER

Robert Toombs in 1885.

In May 1865, the guns of the Civil War had fallen silent, but not Georgia's Robert Toombs. If there was a chance to denounce his enemies – in blue, in gray, or in neither – Robert Augustus Toombs was never silent.

As the ragged and hungry veterans of the surrendered Army of Northern Virginia and other Confederate forces streamed through his hometown of Washington, Georgia, Toombs moved among them, letting roll the oratory that made him one of the most formidable politicians of his day. In an "ill-cut Websterian coat, the worse for wear, his face concealed under a broad-brimmed black hat," he stood in an old buggy pulled by a spavined horse and made the air "murky with blasphemies and denunciations of Yankees."

That was the last glimpse Varina Davis, first lady of the Confederacy, had of Toombs when she fled the Wilkes County seat in the spring of 1865. On her arrival Toombs, ever the gentleman to a lady, had offered her whatever help he could give. Days later, when her husband Confederate President Jefferson Davis arrived in Washington in flight from Union forces, Toombs refused to even meet with him.

Never really friends, Toombs and Jeff Davis had been rivals for the Confederate presidency in 1861. Then, as Davis's secretary of state, Toombs had wasted little time in coming to loggerheads with the president over the conduct of the war.

Toombs left the government to take a field command, but resigned after Davis denied him a promotion he felt he had earned at the Battle of Sharpsburg. He returned to Washington to sulk and denounce Davis and the Confederate government for the rest of the war.

Toombs never lost his distaste for either Yankees or Jefferson Davis. In 1881, after Davis published his *The Rise and Fall of the Confederate Government*, Toombs answered the question of whether he had read it with, "No sir! I never intend to…The trouble with Davis was and is that he has an exalted idea of his own importance."

Many of Toomb's critics said the same of him. But for all that, the life of Robert Toombs, with its personal and political turmoil and tribulations, embodies the society Toombs so ably defended in peace, in war, and in defeat – a tenuous peace in a stratified society, followed by a war that quickly lost its grandeur, succeeded by his stubborn determination to remain "unreconstructed" despite defeat and during the Reconstruction era.

Jefferson Davis

Boys will be Boys

Toombs was born July 2, 1810, about four miles outside of Washington, Georgia, the fifth child of Robert Toombs and his third wife, Catherine Huling. The elder Toombs, a veteran of the American Revolution, came to Georgia from Virginia shortly after independence. He died when the future Georgia firebrand was only five years old, but left his family well provided for. Records show that all the Toombs children received as fine an education as was available in the region at the time.

In 1824, when he was 14, young Robert, already well versed in the classics, entered Franklin College in Athens (later the University of

Alexander H. Stephens

Georgia). Soon, the Robert Toombs who for the rest of his life would make men shake with anger, fear, or mirth began to emerge.

Early in his second year, Toombs developed a feud with two brothers, Granby and Junius Hillyer. By some accounts the dispute was over a card game and by others it was over obscene name-calling by Toombs; whichever it was, the brothers "thrashed" Toombs.

A short time later, Toombs attacked the Hillyer brothers, the first with a pistol and the second with a knife and a hatchet. In both cases, other students intervened and pre-vented bloodshed. The next morning, Toombs tried to ambush them again, this time armed with a club and a pistol. Again, the brothers escaped harm, but the incidents did not go unnoticed.

The Franklin College faculty was shocked by the violent behavior. While the Hillyer brothers got off with a public admonishment, Toombs was expelled. Later, after he wrote a contrite letter to the college president and submitted a petition in his support signed by both the Demosthenian and Phi Kappa literary societies, he was readmitted.

"Toombs should have learned his lesson, but he did not," writes his biographer, William Thompson, of the incidents. "In a sense, he never did. Contempt for authority remained a lifelong characteristic."

Toombs's college records reveal that he often received warnings or fines for swearing – another lifelong habit – as well as "boisterous conversation" – probably an understatement – in his room; other evidence points to episodes of drinking and gambling. In Athens then, as now, boys would be boys.

One account tells of a drunken Toombs and cohorts confronted by a proctor while returning to their rooms. His companions fled, but Toombs stood his ground. "The guilty flee where no man pursueth," he is quoted as saying, "but the righteous are as bold as a lion." The story has the ring of truth, because it sounds like the Toombs who would be seen over and over again in years to come.

This was one of the first accounts of Toombs the worse for drinking, a weakness that would frequently surface during his public career, often with costly consequences, most notably his being passed over for the presidency of the Confederacy. By January 1828, however, the Franklin faculty had seen enough. Toombs was expelled, without reprieve.

Almost immediately, Toombs enrolled in Union College in Schenectady, New York, where he completed his degree without apparent incident. Then he studied law at the University of Virginia where minor infractions whispered of his past. After a year in Charlottesville he returned to Georgia, ranked last in his law school class of 14. Nevertheless, he was admitted to the bar and entered practice in Elberton in March 1830, his license signed by the celebrated jurist and politician Judge William H. Crawford.

The Vilest Poltroon

About eight months later, the 20-year-old Toombs married 17-year-old Julia Dubose, the daughter of a Lincoln County planter. She is described as quiet and pious – the opposite of her loud and profane husband – but it seems a true love match that endured for 53 years through peaks and troughs of fortune that included the deaths of their three children. She and future Confederate Vice-President Alexander H. Stephens of nearby Crawfordville were the only people able to sway the headstrong and difficult Toombs.

Bored by the paperwork of the legal profession, Toombs was not an immediate success as a lawyer, but with practice he shaped his natural bent for oratory into an overpowering courtroom demeanor. He could hone in on the relevant issues and hold his audiences spellbound. Alexander Stephens, possessing a fine legal mind himself, described his friend as a "close and hard student of the law," adding that he had "never seen his superior before judge or jury."

Toombs's income rose with his reputation and the demand for his services, and he began to acquire land. By the 1850s, he owned several thousand acres in Georgia, Mississippi, Arkansas, and Texas, including the site of present day Fort Worth, Texas. He also owned nearly 200 slaves who worked his Georgia plantation lands.

Politics beckoned Toombs, and in 1836 he was elected to the Georgia House of Representatives as a Whig. He was a natural politician in the opinion of press observers of the day, described during one day-long political rally in Elberton in 1840 as "fastening the attention of the crowd for between one and two hours by the brilliancy of his wit, humor, anecdote and argument." He was honing his talents for higher office.

In 1844, Toombs was elected to the U.S. House of Representatives, joining his friend Alex Stephens. Again, Toombs and controversy seemed natural companions. In his maiden speech to the House he attacked the Polk Administration's plans to assert control over the Oregon Territory, long a sore spot between the United States and Great Britain. Polk, he thundered, "was the vilest poltroon that ever disgraced our Government," and was determined to bring on a war.

To Toombs, Democrats who favored war with Britain were themselves "common sewers to pass those denunciations through this House to the country." In his campaign he had supported the Whig platform opposing the annexation of Texas for the same reason and, ironically, had been accused of being "soft on slavery" in a time when the battle between free and slave states was already shaping up. Later he, along with Stephens, joined a young congressman from Illinois named Abraham Lincoln in opposing the war with Mexico, bitterly contesting what he viewed as the Polk Administration's imperialism.

Eternal Hostility

Despite his gift for acrimony, Toombs thrived in Congress; mainly, his biographer Thompson holds, because he was "an excellent raconteur" who intrigued by "spinning his web of charm, bombast and earthiness." Alex Stephens thought his friend a better speaker than Henry Clay, Daniel Webster, or John C. Calhoun, "surpassed for raw power only by Niagara Falls."

One of Toombs's chief enemies in the debate over the Compromise of 1850 was Jefferson Davis of Mississippi, yet Toombs managed to make a good impression on Varina Davis. "One could scarcely imagine a wittier and more agreeable companion," she recorded. He was a "university man, and had kept up his classics. He had the personal habits of a gentleman, and talked such grammar determinately, not ignorantly, as the negroes of this day eschew – unless he became excited, and then his diction is good, his wit keen and his audacity made him equal to anything in the heat of debate. ...His eyes were magnificent, dark and flashing, and they had a certain lawless way of ranging about that was indicative of his character." As for Toombs and her husband, however, they were "never congenial ... but we all went on amicable enough."

The Compromise of 1850 was a benchmark for Toombs. An ardent unionist to that point, he joined with Stephens and Howell Cobb of Athens in supporting the Georgia Platform, which – it was hoped – would put an end to the sectional questions over the spread of slavery to the western territories. Toombs was on firm political ground since pro-union votes had swamped those for secession in Georgia.

In the midst of this fight, Toombs foreshadowed his coming shift in ideology to support of states' rights and the spread of slavery. If, he said, the South were driven from the western territories, then he favored disunion. Deprive the South of its rights and "it is your government, not mine. Then I am its enemy...I would swear eternal hostility to your foul domination...I will strike for independence."

The results were not long in coming. Toombs's power had grown and the next year he was appointed to one of Georgia's U.S. Senate seats (prior to ratification of the 17th Amendment in 1913, Senators were appointed by state legislatures). In

Mississippi, Jefferson Davis lost his bid for the governorship and eventually accepted appointment as Secretary of War in the Franklin Pierce Administration. Toombs continued to jab at Davis, calling him "a disunionist sitting in the councils of the nation," a course Toombs claimed would be taken only by "swaggering braggarts and poltroons."

The Compromise of 1850 failed to end tension over slavery, and the wounds between the sections grew rawer. With the Whig Party in disarray and nearing collapse, Toombs reluctantly became a Democrat. Many Southerners, Toombs included, considered the 1860 election of Abraham Lincoln to the presidency as intolerable. In mid-November 1860, in a speech in Milledgeville, Toombs advocated secession.

"The door of conciliation and compromise is finally closed by our adversaries," he said, "and it remains only to meet the conflict with the dignity and firmness of men worthy of freedom." After South Carolina seceded in December 1860, Toombs urged Georgia to follow suit. For the first time, a rift developed between him and Alexander Stephens, who opposed secession. In a statehouse debate over secession in Milledgeville, the two friends exchanged barbs, but in the end Toombs's view prevailed and Georgia seceded.

Too Tight by Far

When delegates from the seceded states met in Montgomery, Alabama, in February 1861 to form a government, Toombs and Stephens were two of Georgia's ten delegates. According to some sources, Toombs believed the presidency of the new country was his although he publicly disdained it. But it was Jefferson Davis who emerged from the wrangling to become the Confederate chief executive.

Why Davis was chosen rather than Toombs is still debated. Some historians maintain that Toombs's political enemies, the Cobb brothers of Athens, undermined his candidacy. Alexander Stephens, another target of the Cobbs, considered Toombs the most qualified, but believed that Toombs's recurrent drinking was the reason.

Toombs was "in the habit of getting tight every day at dinner," Stephens wrote his brother. "One day in particular about two days before the election he got quite tight at dinner and went to a party in town tighter than I have ever seen him – too tight for his reputation and character by far. I think that evening's exhibition settled the Presidency where it fell." In the end, Stephens became vice-president and urged Toombs to accept Davis's offer to become secretary of state.

At first, Toombs seemed to take his new role to heart. He advocated shipping as much cotton abroad as possible to secure needed weapons and military materiel for the Confederacy. He also pointedly warned against firing on United States troops at Fort Sumter in Charleston Harbor. "It would stir up a hornet's nest," he said. "Legions now quiet, will swarm out and sting us to death ... it puts us in the wrong; it is fatal."

The long-standing rift between the president and his chief diplomat continued to grow. Of Toombs, one observer noted that "he curses freely everything Confederate from a president down to a houseboy." Vice-President Stephens also became disillusioned with Davis, and Richmond swirled with speculation that Toombs might lead a coup d'etat. (Indeed, during the final years of the war while he sulked in Washington, Georgia, Toombs urged that Davis be deposed.)

On July 19, 1861, Davis granted Toombs's oft-made request for an army commission, appointing him brigadier general. On July 24, Toombs resigned as Secretary of State.

Toombs's military career lasted until early 1863, when he resigned because Davis declined to give him a promotion. Toombs took this as a personal affront, especially after what he – and others in the Army of Northern Virginia – regarded as a display of determined gallantry at the Battle of Sharpsburg on September 17, 1862 [see "A Rebel Lion at Burnside's Bridge," preceding chapter]. Toombs returned to Georgia and never missed an opportunity to denounce the Confederacy and Jefferson Davis, especially decisions to suspend habeas corpus and to impose a military draft.

Toombs was not content with that alone, however. He made a bid for a Confederate Senate seat, but lost. He also served in the state militia, commanding a cavalry regiment and later serving as a staff officer with militia forces during the battles around Atlanta. The last days of the Confederacy found him back home in Washington, Georgia.

A few days after Jefferson Davis fled Washington, Toombs left to avoid arrest by Union troops. After dodging about north Georgia, he made his way to Cuba, then England and France, where his wife later joined him. Even on the run, he remained a wealthy man, though he had to sell some of his Texas land to support his lifestyle. He later joked that in France he had "eaten an acre of Texas a day."

The Worst that can Happen

In October 1866, Toombs's last surviving child, his daughter Sallie, died in Washington, Georgia. "This blow is insupportable," he wrote Stephens. "It has crushed my heart and buried my hopes in the grave." Brokenhearted and weary of life abroad, he decided to return to Georgia in early 1867. "The worst that can happen to me is prison," he wrote Julia, who returned home before he did, "and I don't see much to choose between my present condition and any decent fort."

After his return, Toombs traveled to Washington, D.C., where he had an interview with President Andrew Johnson. Apparently, the interview ended whatever thoughts Johnson might have had of having the former Confederate officer and government official arrested. Toombs returned home to Georgia, and was never molested by federal authorities again.

Yet Toombs never applied for a pardon – "I am not loyal to the existing government of the United States and do not wish to be suspected of loyalty," he proclaimed. He resumed his law practice with his son-in-law, Dudley Dubose, specializing in railroad cases, and his income soon reached an estimated $40,000 per year. He remained active in banking, railroads, and politics.

Toombs favored adopting a new state constitution to replace the one ratified in 1868, calling it a "nigger constitution constructed by knaves and carpet baggers." At rallies, he urged crowds, "I can make you a constitution by which the people will rule and the nigger will never be heard from." The statements only served to further galvanize northern Republicans and vexed southern and northern Democrats who hoped the Democrat candidate might win the presidency in 1876. The Georgia General Assembly hastily declared it had no intention of disenfranchising blacks.

Nevertheless, a new state constitution was ratified in 1877, and Toombs emerged from the debate a populist hero, having helped craft a constitution that dealt with state aid to railroads, regulation of railroad tariffs, and taxation of corporations. As it turned out, this would be his final hurrah in the public arena.

In 1881, Toombs lost two people he held most dear, his beloved Julia and his lifelong friend Alexander Stephens. Afterwards, according to acquaintances, Toombs's drinking increased and he seldom left home. In the words of one observer, "he deliberately chose to drain bitter cups of purpose to sweeten bitter memories…During this time he was dying by inches."

Robert Toombs died December 15, 1885 in Washington, ending a talented but tumultuous life. One of the clergy officiating at his funeral was Granby Hillyer, whom Toombs had assaulted sixty years before during their university days. The *Atlanta Constitution* noted that the day was "calm and bright, in strange contrast with [Toombs's] stormy life." The storm had finally blown out, and an unnatural quiet settled over Washington for the first time in some 70 years.

Note: *Robert Toombs's magnificent ante bellum plantation house at 216 E. Toombs Avenue, Washington, Georgia, is a State Historic Site operated by the Georgia Department of Natural Resources. It is open Tuesday through Saturday 9 a.m. to 5 p.m. and on Sunday 2 to 5:30 p.m. The Site includes a museum.*

Sources

Robert Toombs of Georgia, by William Y. Thompson, Southern Biography Series, Louisiana State University Press, 1966.

Burnside's Bridge: The Climactic Struggle of the 2nd and 20th Georgia at Antietam Creek, Phillip Thomas Tucker, Stackpole Books, Mechanicsburg, Pa., 2000

The Long Surrender, Burke Davis, Vintage Books, 1985.

THE STORY OF CASSVILLE'S EMORY BEST

A young Confederate officer is wounded in battle and taken prisoner by Union troops during the Civil War. But his greatest suffering proves to be at the hands of his own men.

DANIEL M. ROPER

In the summer of 1861, 21-year-old Emory Best left Cassville, Georgia, to join the Confederate Army. He must have been a natural leader, for despite his youthfulness and lack of a military education, Best quickly advanced in rank. Just 14 months after joining the army, he was promoted to the rank of colonel and given command of the 23rd Georgia Infantry Regiment. Six months later, Best and his regiment would play a crucial role in the South's decisive victory at Chancellorsville, Virginia, but the cost to Best would be steep.

For all intents and purposes, Best's promising career in the military abruptly ended on that bloody Virginia battlefield in May 1863. Under circumstances that still would be debated a half-century later, he was accused by his own men of cowardice and was court-martialled and stripped of his rank. This experience left Best so embittered that when he died in 1912, references to his military service were omitted from his funeral and from his epitaph.

Following Best's death, his ordeal at Chancellorsville was all but forgotten. While historians were concentrating on more well-known aspects of the battle, Best's family understandably did not wish to perpetuate memories of this unpleasant chapter in their ancestor's life.

But National Archives records of the court-martial include information suggesting that those who pressed charges against Best may have done so in order to enhance their own prospects for promotion. If that is the case, the first seeds of ill will towards Best were likely sown in northwest Georgia long before that fateful day in Virginia in 1863.

First a Gentleman

After graduating from Lebanon College in Tennessee in 1860, Emory Best returned to his parents' home in Cassville, Georgia, to practice law. His prospects for a long and distinguished career were bright. Best apprenticed under Warren Akin, a noted lawyer who had established his practice in Cassville in 1836 and who had argued the first case reported by the Georgia Supreme Court. Best's choice of a mentor was fortuitous, because Akin was later elected to the Confederate Congress, a position from which he would play an instrumental role in an effort to obtain a presidential pardon for Best after the court-martial.

In 1860, Cassville was one of north Georgia's principal cities. It was the seat of

Emory F. Best (1840 - 1912) – This photograph was taken in 1862, while Best was a prisoner of war.

Cass (now Bartow) County and had more than 3,000 residents. The growing city also housed Cherokee Baptist College and Cassville Female College. But two events combined to ensure that Cassville's prominence in 1860 would be short-

COURTESY HUGH BEST, WAYNE, PENNSYLVANIA

The Robert Best family, circa 1900, at Grassdale Plantation near Cassville. From Left to Right, Robert Best Jr., Hugh H. Best, and Orianna Best seated on steps; Aileen Best, Robin Best (grandson) and Waring Best seated on porch; Robert Best and wife Orianna seated in chairs. Like his younger brother Emory, Robert Best served in the Confederate Army. The Robert Best family was the last of the Bests to reside in old Cass County.

lived – the recently constructed Western & Atlantic Railroad had by-passed Cassville and, in 1864, General William T. Sherman's troops would not.

Emory Best came from a prominent Cassville family. His father, Reverend Hezekiah Best, moved his family from Virginia to the old Cherokee country of northwest Georgia in 1857. There Hezekiah had purchased a magnificent plantation called Forrest Home for $30,000 in gold. Located a mile west of Cassville, Forrest Home had a grist mill, a saw mill, and more than 1,000 acres of land in the fertile and scenic valley of Two Run Creek.

In 1860 census records, Hezekiah is listed as a "Farmer and Methodist Minister" while each of his sons Albert (25 years old), Robert (20), and Emory (19) is listed as "gentleman." The Best household also included Hezekiah's wife, Adaline, his daughter Louisa Phillips, and his grandson William Phillips.

Although Hezekiah was an ordained Methodist minister, he retired from the ministry so that he and his sons could attend to the land and operate his mills. He was also a philanthropist of sorts, donating funds to build several churches in Cass County. (One of these – Best's Chapel in the Crowe Springs community – is still standing today.)

By late 1860, tension between the North and South was increasing and there was talk in Cassville and throughout the South of secession and war. It was in this atmosphere that Emory Best made the decision that may have initiated the events that would ultimately lead to his discharge from the Confederate Army: the seemingly harmless decision of establishing his law practice in nearby Rome, Georgia.

Next an Officer

Following Georgia's secession from the Union in January 1861, military companies began forming throughout the state. Although several were organized in the Cassville area, Emory Best decided to join the Floyd Springs Guards, a company from a small community 12 miles north of Rome. This decision is curious since Best had no known family or business ties to Floyd Springs. But perhaps while practicing law in Rome, Best learned that the Guards were seeking men with leadership capabilities.

Best joined the Floyd Springs Guards and was elected first lieutenant despite his youthfulness and lack of military training. He was second in command to Captain Marcus R. Ballenger, a Floyd Springs physician who would later play a prominent role in the court-martial proceedings against Best.

The Floyd Springs Guards left Rome in August 1861 and spent three months training at Camp McDonald near Marietta, Georgia. Here the Guards were assigned to the 23rd Georgia Infantry Regiment as Company C. Most of the ten companies in the 23rd were from north Georgia. Each had distinctive and colorful names including Bartow Yankee Killers, Bartow Invincibles, and Cherokee Field Guards.

While at Camp McDonald, the 23rd Regiment drilled in preparation for the fighting to come and also elected officers. For reasons lost through time, Emory Best was elected major, leap-frogging Marcus Ballenger in rank. In light of their future difficulties, one wonders if this proved to be a source of resentment between the two officers.

A Red Badge of Courage

In November 1861, the 23rd Ga. Regiment was transported by train from Camp McDonald to Virginia. During the ensuing six months, the regiment participated in a series of major battles near Richmond, suffering heavy losses. In one engagement, the 23rd Regiment suffered 80 casualties. By the end of June 1862, more than 140 of its 400 officers and soldiers had been either killed or wounded in action. But its darkest days were yet to come.

In September 1862, the 23rd Ga. accompanied the Army of Northern Virginia and its legendary leader, General Robert E. Lee, marching north into Maryland. The Union Army moved to head off the invading Southerners, and the two armies collided near the little town of Sharpsburg, beside Antietam Creek. The resulting battle proved to be the bloodiest single day in United States history.

Positioned at The Cornfield and Bloody Lane – two locations where the fighting was particularly ferocious - the 23rd Ga. helped repulse numerous charges by the Union Army and suffered severe losses: 62 killed and wounded. Included among that number was its leader, Colonel William T. Barclay, who was killed, and Emory Best, who assumed command only to be severely wounded and then captured. Later, Best's supporters would cite his injury as evidence of his bravery under fire.

After two months in captivity, Best was exchanged for a Federal officer. In November 1862, he was promoted, given command of his old regiment, and received a 60-day furlough to recuperate from the injury he had suffered at Sharpsburg.

Position of Honor

By the time Emory Best returned to his command in the spring of 1863, a major confrontation was developing. In April of that year, the Union Army launched an offensive against the Army of Northern Virginia, which was entrenched at Fredricksburg, Virginia. In a move that threatened to surround and destroy the badly outnumbered Southerners, General Joseph Hooker divided his army into two forces, each of which outnumbered the Confederates. While one Union force held the Confederate Army in check, the other swung west, crossed the Rappahannock River, and prepared to pounce upon the Confederate flank near a crossroads settlement named Chancellorsville.

Robert E. Lee recognized that his army was about to be trapped between the two Federal forces. In a risky but brilliant move that is still analyzed in military schools today, Lee divided his already outnumbered army into two bodies. While the first, commanded by Lee, would try and hold the line at Fredricksburg, the second, commanded by Stonewall Jackson, would march west to attack the Federal force moving on Chancellorsville.

Lee's plan called for Jackson to strike the right wing of the Federal army from the rear. But this strategy was risky for several reasons. First, if it was discovered that Lee had divided his army, the Union Army could destroy it piecemeal. Morover, while in transit Stonewall Jackson's Corps would pass close to the Union lines and would be vulnerable to attack. For several hours, Jackson's men, artillery, and supply wagons would be strung out for miles, exposed to enemy artillery and infantry fire.

Jackson was concerned about one place in particular: the point where his men would pass closest to the Federal line. In order to protect his soldiers from a flank attack here, Jackson issued orders for a regiment to be placed between the road and the enemy. That regiment was the 23rd Georgia.

Into the Furnace

Positioned in broken woods about one-half mile north of the road on which Jackson's Corps was passing, the 23rd Ga. was all that stood between the exposed Confederate column and the Union Army's III Corps. The role of the 23rd Ga.

This flag was carried by the 23rd Georgia Regiment during the Civil War. After the war it remained in the personal collection of Col. Emory F. Best and family. Later the flag was sold to a private collector in Florida.

was so important that General J.E.B. Stuart personally supervised the positioning of the regiment and cautioned Col. Best to refrain from advancing or otherwise provoking an attack by the Union infantry. With less than 300 soldiers to oppose 18,000, the mission of the 23rd Ga. was to give warning in the event of an enemy attack and to do whatever was within its power to hinder the enemy's advance.

For two hours that morning everything was quiet. But at about noon, General David Birney's division of 6,000 Union infantrymen began an advance towards the Confederate position. Outnumbered nearly twenty to one, the 23rd Ga. fell back slowly – first to a foundry known as Catherine's Furnace and then to the protection afforded by the cut of an unfinished railroad. During this retreat, Marcus Ballenger and about 40 men were captured. But the 23rd Ga., with some assistance from passing artillery and infantry units, successfully held off the advancing Federals until all of Jackson's troops had safely passed.

Then calamity struck. A general withdrew the supporting troops and ordered the 23rd Ga. to retreat. Best, who was standing near the left side of his line, later claimed that he relayed the order by shouting to the nearest company commander. But if he did so, there must have been some breakdown in communications, because it evidently was not passed along to the other eight companies.

Instead of remaining to see that his order was carried out, Best immediately left the railroad cut. He and 40 men escaped, but the remainder of the leaderless 23rd Ga. was captured. Although Best justifiably reported to his superiors that his mission had been accomplished, his own escape would prove to be his downfall.

Specifications of Cowardice

Within a month of their capture, the soldiers of 23rd Ga. were exchanged and transported back to Virginia. One of the freed captives, Captain J. J. Sharp, promptly filed charges against Best including an allegation that he had abandoned the regiment at the railroad cut near Catherine's Furnace.

Acting upon Sharp's accusations, General Alfred H. Colquitt had Best arrested and gave Marcus Ballenger command of the 23rd Ga. Judging by his report of the arrest, Colquitt may have had doubts about the accuser's motives: "Colonel Best...is a good drill officer, and strict in discipline, without judgment in its exercise; this may have some influence in making his officers bitter against him, but he has rendered himself liable to distrust, and I should have ordered no investigation if it had not been made necessary by the charges sent forward."

Before the trial could be conducted, the 23rd Ga. received orders to move to North Carolina and then to Charleston, South Carolina. As a result of these moves, Best's trial was repeatedly postponed. Left in limbo, the accused grew exasperated. In September 1863, a frustrated Best finally appealed to the Army for an immediate hearing. "There is certainly great injustice done either to myself or the Service in retaining me so long under arrest without a trial and I now respectfully request that a Court be convened for my trial," Best wrote. It would be two more months, however, before he would be given an opportunity to face his accusers.

The Court-Martial

The trial, which finally began on November 23, 1863, lasted seven days with 27 witnesses giving testimony, 14 for the prosecution and 13 for the defense. Although there were several charges proffered against Best, most of the testimony would focus upon his "unusual" conduct during the Battle of Chancellorsville.

Even before the incident at the railroad cut, Marcus Ballenger testified, he had urged Best not to leave the regiment: "I told him I did not think he ought to go [to the rear to get reinforcements]... I said to him, that if he went and we got into a fight, he would be sorry for it."

Corroborating Ballenger's testimony, another officer from the regiment recalled: "Someone asked the accused what he was going to do. He replied that he was 'going to take his Regiment to the rear, and that by the nearest way.' I said that that would not do – that it would be shameful – that the wagon train was just on the top of the hill, and we had been put there to guard it, and that we ought to do it."

But the most damning testimony against Best concerned his conduct at the railroad cut. Captain Sharp testified that he had "received no notice from the accused of his intention to leave the command there. Nor did I receive any order from the accused for retreat from there." Several others – including a defense witness who testified later – said that Best had failed to order the regiment to retreat before he made his escape. Lieutenant T. B. Davis testified that Best walked "pretty fast" out of the railroad cut but, after the enemy fired a volley, "moved faster than a double quick – I would call it a run."

Not everyone thought that Best had acted cowardly. Lieutenant M. A. Collins testified that he "saw nothing unusual in the conduct of the accused." Even a witness for the prosecution conceded that Best "did about as well as could be done, as far as I noticed him." And as far as his conduct at the railroad cut was concerned, several officers testified that Best had, in fact, issued orders for the regiment to leave.

But the prosecutor countered that even if such an order had been issued, Best had abandoned his men by failing to remain to see that it was carried out. "An officer's responsibility," the prosecutor argued, "does not cease with the issuing of an order. He is bound to superintend its execution..." Had Best not run away in "a disgraceful flight," he continued, "he would have discovered before he had run a half a mile that but two or three of his officers and some twenty men were following him." The prosecutor concluded by noting that "an officer who quits his post or command in danger, without justification or excuse, quits it shamefully..."

In his own defense, Best told the court that he had issued an order to leave the railroad cut and that those who had failed to follow him "must have preferred to halt behind a large bank [the railroad cut], perfectly secure, than to risk the danger from a heavy fire in passing out." Had he been a coward, Best argued, he would have remained in the cut rather than passing through heavy fire to escape.

In his closing argument, Best urged the court to consider the prosecutor's motives: "In conclusion, I would ask the Court to look at the spirit of this prosecution. No efforts have been spared to make the way clear for his promotion; he knows full well that while I have the command of the Regiment he can never receive my recommendation for promotion. My misfortune is not that these charges have been preferred, but that they are preferred by a man with such a record."

Disgraced and Ruined

On December 7, 1863, the military court issued its verdict. Best was acquitted on four of the five specifications of wrongdoing, but on the specification addressing his conduct at the railroad cut, the court found that Best did "shamefully run away and shamefully abandon and leave his Regiment upon the approach of the enemy." The court then sentenced Best to dismissal from the service.

Best must have been stunned by the outcome of the trial. He was stripped of his rank and was, undoubtedly, humiliated and embarrassed. In desperation, he asked for a new trial, but his request was denied.

Then Best turned to his old friend from Cassville, Warren Akin, for assistance. Akin, who was by then a Confederate Congressman, appealed to Confederate President Jefferson Davis for a pardon. "Can no other conclusion be drawn from the facts in this case than that arrived at by the Court?" Akin wrote. "May there not be a reasonable doubt as to the correctness of the decision of the Court in this case? If so, is it right? Does the good of the Country require it? That a high minded, honorable young man, whose blood has been poured out on the battlefield in defense of his country should remained [sic] disgraced, ruined, by the decision of the Court?"

Whether Best was ever pardoned is uncertain. In December 1864, just four months before the war ended, Warren Akin wrote to his wife that he had seen Emory Best several times and that Best had "not yet had his case heard by the President." The final entry in Best's military service record – a document signed by Best without any notation of rank – suggests that at the end of the war he was training young soldiers in Richmond.

After the War

After the Civil War ended, the debate whether Emory Best was guilty of cowardice continued for many years. On the one hand, the veterans of the Floyd Springs Guards, his old company, did not even see fit to include Best in a roster of the unit prepared at the turn of the century.

On the other hand, several veterans of the 23rd Ga. defended Best in magazine and newspaper stories. In one such article published in *Confederate Veteran* magazine in 1918, H. S. Fuller cast aspersions at Best's accusers: "The captains who stood next in line for promotion, to make it appear that they did their duty in refusing to retreat when ordered to do so by the Colonel, preferred charges... I know he remained at his post as long as good judgment and bravery required. I have never seen or heard of him since. He may be living, or he may be dead; but in either case it is but justice to him that it should be known that he was made a martyr."

Although Emory Best was undoubtedly embarrassed by his court-martial, he became a successful businessman after the war. For more than 20 years, he practiced law and served as a city judge in Macon. Then, in 1887, the Akin family came to his assistance for a third time. A son of Best's old benefactor, Warren Akin, held an influential position in the Federal government. With his assistance, Emory Best received an appointment from President Grover Cleveland to the Interior Department in Washington, D. C. where he would work for the remainder of his life.

Emory Best died in Washington, D.C. in April 1912, and his body was carried to Macon where it was buried in Rose Hill Cemetery. At his funeral, there were neither military salutes nor stirring eulogies recalling his Civil War experiences. There was just a simple ceremony that even his wife failed to attend. Even today, there is nothing at Best's gravesite to indicate to a visitor that the old soldier had once served under Stonewall Jackson and had played an important role in the South's victory at Chancellorsville.

Emory Best did not have any children, but he did have a namesake that this writer spoke to in 1996. Emory Fred Best, the grandson of Col. Best's brother, was then a 76-year-old California resident who recalled that his great-uncle's court martial was never mentioned by the family. In fact, he did not even learn of it until the 1960s when he had received his ancestor's military records from the National Archives.

Protesting the blemish he found in Emory Best's record, Fred Best wrote the National Archives in 1967: "I was surprised to learn of a court martial as our family had no knowledge of this. Mr. Best held a responsible position as Commissioner of the Land Office in Washington, D.C. after the Civil War. He also held a high office in the Confederate Veterans organization. These two positions would not be forthcoming to a man who had been court martialled by the military."

It is a testimony to the Civil War's lasting impact on America that even 130 years later there were those who still had a personal interest in the affairs of that great war. Three-quarters of a century after the last veterans of the 23rd Ga. Regiment had passed away, the court-martial of Emory Best still troubled Fred Best. When I asked him whether he believed that the charges against his great-uncle were true, Fred Best replied softly, "Oh, that can't be. I would like to think not." But there are none left today to testify to his record.

Sources

Georgia Reports, 1846. The Harrison Co., Atlanta, Ga. (Vol. 1, p. 1).

The Battle of Seven Pines on May 31, 1863.

Testimony of Cpt. J. J. Sharp, Best Compiled Service Record (hereafter "Best CSR").

Davis, Maj. George (Ed.), 1897. *Official Records, War of the Rebellion* (Government Printing Office, Washington, D.C.). Series I, Vol. 27, Part III, p. 918.

September 17, 1863 letter in Best CSR.

Testimony of Cpt. W. J. Boston, Best CSR.

Testimony of Lt. William A. Smith, Best CSR.

Testimony of Cpt. P. Patton, Best CSR.

Testimony of Cpt. W. Butt and Lt. W. Keown, Best CSR.

June 28, 1864 letter of Warren Akin, Best CSR.

The Letters of Warren Akin, Confederate Congressman. *The Georgia Historical Quarterly*, Vol. 42, p. 39.

Roster of Company C, 23rd Georgia Regiment in the Floyd County Records Retention Center, Rome, Georgia.

Fuller, H. S., 1918. "Narrowly Escaped Prison", Confederate Veteran, Vol. 26, p. 473.

Obituary of Emory F. Best; April 25, 1912 issue of *Macon Telegraph*, p. 16A.

GARTRELL'S GEORGIANS:
NATHAN BEDFORD FORREST'S TEENAGED WARRIORS

When Nathan Bedford Forrest rode to the rescue of Rome, Georgia, during the Civil War, he earned the everlasting gratitude and loyalty of young Romans who pledged to serve "that Devil Forrest."

ZACK C. WATERS

Nathan Bedford Forrest

Near mid-afternoon, General Nathan Bedford Forrest sensed that the critical moment had arrived in the Battle of Brice's Crossroads. Outnumbered two to one, Forrest's Confederates had been fighting since mid-morning. For hours the Southerners had slugged it out against Union General Benjamin H. Grierson's cavalry, and just as the Yankee horse soldiers began to give way, blue-coated infantry came trotting through the Mississippi heat to reinforce Grierson's faltering troopers. With sleeves rolled up, coat across his saddle, and pistol in hand, the fiery Rebel general spurred his horse up and down the line urging his men to press the attack and drive the enemy into nearby Tishomingo Creek.

Trailing behind the Confederate "Wizard of the Saddle" rode Captain Henry A. Gartrell and 65 young men from Rome, Georgia. Gartrell's Georgians had only been in camp ten days, but Forrest had given the youngsters a place of honor as part of his personal escort. It was a tribute to these teenaged warriors, but also a post of extreme danger. Forrest always led his bodyguards into "the thickest of the fray," for as historian Edwin C. Bearss explained: "Forrest's escort was composed of men with similar character to Old Bedford, men who knew that 'war means fighting, and fighting means killing.' Forrest always kept these men close by."

William M. Towers, a 17-year-old resident of Cave Spring, a small town near Rome, summed up his experience as a member of the general's personal escort: "We were…entitled to many privileges, but [we were] required to do some of the most dangerous service, and probably more hard fighting than any other part of the command."

When Forrest reached the southern end of his battle line at Brice's Crossroads, Mississippi, on June 10, 1864, he ordered two companies of Kentucky cavalry and his escort to turn the flank of the Union defenses. Screeching the eerie Rebel yell and with Jacob Gaus, the bugler, sounding "Charge!" the men followed Old Bedford into the undefended area while some Tennessee troopers repeated the tactic to the north.

Forty years later, Billy Towers vividly recalled this moment: "Some of the [other Southern] troops were lying on the ground for protection, while [Forrest] with his staff and part of his escort were mounted. I remember distinctly Gen. Forrest's looks and words as he sat on his noble sorrel and gave the command to charge. It was here that I heard the first shell and saw the first man struck with a bullet."

With six-shooters blazing, the gray-coats rode over the Unionists, creating havoc. "The fight," Towers recalled, "was very bloody." Exhausted from running for miles, the shock of combat, and undergoing attack from both front and back, the Yankee foot soldiers finally broke, scattering in complete and utter rout. Frightened teamsters overturned wagons, thus blocking the only bridge over Tishomingo Creek, and the panic-stricken Federals splashed and floundered through the stream in their haste to escape.

Keep them Skeered!

Unlike most Civil War generals, Forrest despised the West Point rules of civilized warfare. Raised poor on the frontier and thrust into the role of provider for a large family by the untimely death of his father, Forrest's credo was to win at any cost. Bearss wrote: "Although his men had been in the saddle or fighting for more than twelve hours [at Brice's Crossroads], he resolved to pursue the Yankees relentlessly. His way of war was to put the "skeer" in the enemy and keep them "skeered."

One of Captain Gartrell's young Georgians graphically described the pursuit at Brice's Crossroads. "After several hours of hard fighting the fun began, and we had the enemy in full retreat, so demoralized that no man on earth could have checked them. We followed them all night, with only a short rest, and the next two days we ran across them scattered through the woods like sheep…They were a badly scattered and scared lot of troops, and, with no organization whatever – [they] were making for Memphis, a hundred miles away. They had bent their guns around trees to make them useless, and had thrown away their cartridge boxes, knapsacks, and hats, and had cut off their pantaloons at the knees, so as to get rid of the accumulation of mud."

Gartrell's small company had "seen the elephant" in this severe, gory engagement. While yet "green," these young soldiers from Rome had exceeded even Forrest's demanding standards, and they would remain an integral part of Forrest's escort until the final days of the War Between the States.

No Young Men Left

The organization of Gartrell's Georgians had begun almost a year before the Battle of Brice's Crossroads. On the evening of May 3, 1863, Forrest had arrived in Rome with a large contingent of Federal prisoners of war – Union Colonel Abel D. Streight's raiders, captured just two days before near Gaylesville, Alabama.

The citizens of Rome threw a gigantic party for the troops that had saved their town from the torch. "Old Bedford" and his men were given a "triumphal procession," the weary gray-coats "were royally entertained," and the ladies of Rome presented Forrest the "finest saddle-horse their country could afford." Sometime during his brief stopover in Rome, the Rebel general met with Henry A. Gartrell, a local lawyer and newspaper editor, and planted the seeds for the creation of the cavalry troop.

A jolly, chubby bachelor who had been elected mayor of Rome in 1860, Gartrell didn't want to just cobble together a company. Instead, he wrote Confederate Secretary of War James A. Seddon in Richmond seeking permission to organize a cavalry troop and requesting help in outfitting the unit. In his letter to Seddon, Gartrell noted that as a journalist he was not subject to the draft laws, but that he planned to enroll teens because "there are no young men left in this country, except …[those who] are not subject to conscription."

Friends or family of another prominent Roman, Charles Wood Hooper, later claimed the he actually raised the company and that Gartrell attached his name to the unit by furnishing horses and money to the men. Confederate records and contemporary newspaper articles indicate, however, that Gartrell was the moving force in creating the troop.

On October 5, 1863, Gartrell's Georgians were sworn into Confederate service as an independent cavalry company. Almost all of the new Rebel troopers were teenagers between the ages of 15 and 17 from Floyd and surrounding counties, though a handful of veteran soldiers from the Virginia and Tennessee armies, including Charles Hooper, also joined. A *Rome Tri-Weekly Courier* article, full of flowery prose, announced that the squad came "from the first families in Upper Georgia. They are well mounted, buoyant and hopeful, and a brilliant career is confidently expected. May…they all return with their brows enwreathed with chaplets of victory."

For five months the unit remained in Rome, where they helped "guard the town

Citizens of Rome welcome a victorious Nathan Bedford Forrest into town in May 1863.

against a growing number of roving deserters and outlaws as Confederate forces moved in and out, preparing for the inevitable Union advance." Finally, they moved "by way of Cedar Town to LaGrange," halting there for a month. They received new weapons and a few more recruits in LaGrange, then headed west, joining Forrest's command in Tupelo, Mississippi, on June 1, 1864. Old Bedford remembered Gartrell from his triumphal stay in Rome, and assigned this troop to serve as his escort.

Why Forrest selected the Romans to serve as his personal bodyguard remains a mystery. The Hooper family believed the Wizard of the Saddle had promised their sire, Charles Hooper, the plum position for his help in capturing Streight's raiders (though the nature of his assistance has somehow escaped the attention of historians). Billy Towers offered another explanation: Forrest, he said, "was struck by the youthfulness of the members of our company, and as he had quite a tender feeling for Rome, as the ladies of that place had presented him with a fine horse, he assigned us as a part of his personal escort."

There may be an element of truth in both explanations. Old Bedford may have promised Gartrell the high profile position as a reward for raising the company, and he almost certainly recalled the regal reception he received in the City of Seven Hills. More likely, with Forrest's keen insight of human nature, he knew the reckless, devil-may-care attitude of young males – two traits needed by his personal bodyguards.

The Devil Comes to Memphis

After Brice's Crossroads, Gartrell's troops may have become battle-tested soldiers, but they also retained the habits of teenaged boys. They enjoyed giving nicknames

FOR LIFE OR DEATH.

designed to irritate their friends and were often quick to take offense. Bird Greenwood's dark complexion thus earned him the unfortunate moniker "Yaller Henry." When he could stand the name calling no longer, he drew his pistol and chased his tormentor into the woods, firing as he went. "It is needless to say," Towers wrote, "that we never heard the name of 'Yaller Henry' after this little affair."

On another occasion, Towers and Tom Rentz became so angry that they drew their weapons to settle a dispute. Luckily, Rentz drew his saber while Towers pulled his pistol. Seeing the disparity of the situation, the combatants called a truce and were soon better friends than before.

Respect for Old Bedford's ability and nerve haunted Maj. Gen. William T. Sherman. He recognized that the Western & Atlantic Railroad, the supply line for his army in Georgia, was his Achilles' heel. If Forrest tore up the tracks in Middle Tennessee, the Union troops would be forced to retreat or face starvation. Sherman viewed "that devil Forrest" the chief threat to his ability to provision his army, and developed a plan to destroy Old Bedford. He would send several strong forces to attack the Confederates in northern Mississippi, while Sherman's army moved toward Atlanta. He publicly declared that Forrest must be killed or kept occupied "if it costs ten thousand lives and breaks the Treasury."

The ensuing Battle of Brice's Crossroads may have been Old Bedford's greatest military feat, but his raid on Memphis was a strategic masterstroke. It certainly sparked the imagination of Gartrell's youngsters, and Billy Towers wrote about it at least twice – once in his memoirs and again to correct factual errors in a story that appeared in the *Atlanta Journal* newspaper in 1902.

In August 1864, Forrest had faced a Union army numbering nearly 20,000. The Wizard of the Saddle divided his "critter command," which numbered at most 4,000 troopers. He left half his horsemen near Oxford, Mississippi, to keep the Yankees busy while he led 2,000 picked men, including Gartrell's Georgians, through 100 miles of enemy territory before unleashing his Rebels to rampage through Federally-occupied Memphis.

Gartrell's Georgia teens served in the escort, a unit commanded by Captain Bill Forrest, Old Bedford's brother. Their main objective was to capture Major General Stephen A. Hurlbut, who was visiting Memphis. The Union general, disgraced and relieved of command for letting Forrest escape from Tennessee in April, had taken rooms at the Gayoso House, a ritzy hotel.

Billy Towers described the subsequent events: "When Capt. Forrest arrived at the Gayoso House he rode his horse up the first flight of steps, which led to the rooms occupied by Gen. Washburn but found he had heard the noise and jumped out the window on top of the adjoining house, leaving his clothes lying in the room he had just vacated. Capt. Forrest thought it a good joke to remove his clothes, and carry them off as a relic."

Each of the three generals Forrest hoped to snare escaped, but the raiders made off with 600 prisoners, 300 horses, and, as Towers described it, "a lot of plunder." The incursion into Memphis did accomplish its primary purpose – the powerful Yankee army near Oxford retreated immediately, hurrying back to protect the River City. Hurlbut offered the most cogent comment on the raid. "They removed me from command," he wrote, "because I couldn't keep Forrest out of West Tennessee, and now Washburn can't keep him out of his own bedroom."

Most Ardent Devotion

By mid-September 1864, the authorities in Richmond decided to turn Old Bedford and his critter cavalry loose on North Alabama and Middle Tennessee, but the move arrived too late to halt Sherman's Atlanta Campaign. Atlanta had fallen, and Confederate General John B. Hood and the once proud Army of Tennessee were stumbling toward Gadsden, Alabama, in a desperate attempt to elude the pursuing Federals. Forrest and Hood eventually joined forces for the ensuing invasion of Tennessee, an operation that Billy Towers called "the most disastrous campaign to the South."

At this time an incident occurred that showed Forrest's concern for his youthful warriors and their high esteem for their commander. In the first week of October, Forrest offered to send Gartrell's company to Georgia where they could protect their homes and families. A committee, which included Hooper, Towers, C. W.

Fouche, and J. R. DeJournett, expressed their "most ardent devotion" to their native state, but concluded they could best serve the Confederacy as part of Forrest's escort. They wrote: "Believing as we do that his troop has accomplished more than a like number of any other command, fidelity to a glorious cause demands that we remain with him until our common country is free." Forrest gratefully accepted their resolution and assured them that only a desire to let them protect their homes, and not a lack of faith in them, had prompted his offer.

The fighting experienced by the Georgians in Mississippi paled in comparison to the horrors that awaited in Tennessee. Towers recalled: "On this trip Forrest and his troops fought almost every day for thirty days. It is true they were not all set [pitched] battles, but some were very severe; the Battle of Franklin being the most prominent and ill-advised, and was certainly the most bitter in which Forrest and his men had ever engaged."

In the Volunteer State, Lieutenant Hooper was at his best. His post-war obituary noted that his "services were dashing and brilliant, and years afterwards Forrest characterized him as one of the most reliable…men who were the eyes and ears of the army."

Gartrell's Georgians lost their commander during the Tennessee campaign. Writing from the Federal prison on Johnson's Island, Ohio, in December, 1864, Henry Gartrell reported: "I was captured near Nashville on the morning of the 17th ultimo. I was cut off, made a desperate effort to escape on the night of the 16th by running over the Federal pickets. At least 20 shots were fired at me from not more than 20 to 100 yards, but with the exception of a wound to my horse and a ball through my coat, they did no harm to me. I'm going to write to Gen. Forrest…asking him to procure a special change for me."

When his troopers heard about Gartrell's proposed letter to Forrest, they joked that Old Bedford would move heaven and earth to get Gartrell released if he fought as well as he talked.

Retreat and Defeat

After the decisive Southern defeat at Nashville in December 1864, Towers wrote "the demoralization that followed was the greatest that befell any army of the South during the war." Nevertheless, during the retreat from the Volunteer State, the Wizard of the Saddle and his cavalry did their finest service. Towers recalled: "I do not believe there is a man in Hood's army … but who would say that if it had not been for Forrest and his men the whole of Hood's army would have been captured before it reached the Tennessee River." Years after the war, an anonymous writer in *Confederate Veteran* magazine claimed Gartrell's unit "served night and day in the rear of Hood's army while on the retreat…until the Tennessee River was crossed, and it was among the very last to cross the Harpeth River."

While most of the tattered remnant of the Army of Tennessee either deserted or boarded trains to join Joseph Johnston's Confederate army in North Carolina,

FROM "THE LIFE OF LIEUTENANT-GENERAL NATHAN BEDFORD FORREST," 1908

This sketch of Forrest's cavalry capturing a Federal cannon appeared in a book authored by John A. Wyeth, a veteran who served under Forrest.

Forrest's cavalry remained in northern Alabama and Mississippi hoping to once again work their old magic against the vast number of Yankees invading the Confederate heartland.

The dream of Southern Independence might have been going up the spout, but fighting continued as if by reflex. In mid-February 1865, the Georgia Company, commanded by Hooper, suffered a serious loss near Senatobia, Mississippi. While on a scouting assignment, four of Gartrell's troop encountered a Union regiment. Towers, DeJournett, and Lieutenant Merritt's jaded horses proved no contest for fresh Federal steeds, and Sergeant Fouche, riding a mule, was totally outclassed. DeJournett escaped, but Fouche and Merritt were captured and ended the war in Federal hands. Billy Towers played possum in the high grass near a fence line, and after dark found the home of a Southern sympathizer who led the Georgia teen to Forrest's camp.

A Fit Subject for an Insane Asylum

The final campaign of the war in Dixie's heartland began March 22, 1865. General James H. Wilson led a bluecoated cavalry command mounted on fine horses and armed with Spencer repeating rifles. The primary objective of this army was to destroy Southern manufacturing facilities in Alabama and Georgia. Old Bedford and his men fought hard to slow or stop Wilson's Raiders, but for once

Grown gray with age, the soldiers in gray who served under Nathan Bedford Forrest gathered at a reunion in 1917.

the Wizard of the Saddle could not whip the Yankees. In battles at Montavello, Ebenezer Church, and Selma, Alabama, Wilson's horsemen routed Forrest's fatigued graycoats.

After the engagement at Selma, Forrest sent General Abraham Buford, a 300-pound Kentuckian and prewar breeder of thoroughbred horses, to intercept a Union cavalry division commanded by Union General Emory Upton. In order to give Buford as much help as possible, Old Bedford assigned Gartrell's company as Buford's personal bodyguards.

While Buford's outnumbered command contested every inch of ground, Upton's bluecoats slowly drove them south toward Columbus, Georgia. On the west bank of the Chattahoochee River, Buford's troopers fought a last, desperate battle to keep the Federals out of the Georgia city. The beefy Rebel commander stationed his men near the bridge spanning the Chattahoochee, and Billy Towers vividly described the scene that ensued:

"Gen. Beaufort [Buford], some of his escort, and a few [Southern] troops came across the bridge with the advance troops of the enemy. Such pandemonium one rarely sees as was witnessed on that bridge. You could not tell friend from enemy. Gen. Beaufort was recognized [by the Federals] about the time he entered the bridge, and was attacked with sabers … but he put his spurs to his horse, and cutting with his sabre managed to get away from them and come safely through." Buford, Towers recalled, was left with no troops "but our escort company amounting to thirty five men."

After a long, danger-fraught odyssey, Buford and the remnant of Gartrell's group rejoined Forrest's battered army at Gainesville, Alabama. Old Bedford apparently considered striking off to unite with General Edmund Kirby Smith in the Trans-

Mississippi region, but finally concluded: "Any man who is in favor of further prosecution of this war is a fit subject for a lunatic asylum, and ought to be sent there immediately." He and his men surrendered at Gainesville, Alabama, on May 9, 1865. Towers remembered it as "the saddest day I ever experienced."

The army immediately broke up, each man heading home the best way he could. As Towers moved through the defeated, devastated South, he passed through Rome. What he saw filled him with sorrow: "When I arrived at the city I found the bridge burned, and had to cross in a ferry boat at the forks of the river. The bridge across the Oostanaula was also burned, along with quite a number of store houses, the Old Etowah House, the depot, etc., the remaining store houses looking desolate, all the doors standing open, and the shutters flapping in the wind. None were occupied, and there was not a living thing in sight when I arrived at Broad Street. After staying a few hours I was only too glad to continue my journey."

Billy Towers soon returned to the City of Seven Hills and led a long, productive life. He married Mary Caroline Norton, managed his father's metal coating business for many years, won election to the city council several times, and served as president of the "North Georgia and Alabama Exposition held at Rome in 1888." His son John attended the United States Naval Academy, rose to the rank of admiral, and is widely acknowledged as the "Father of Naval Aviation."

Captain Henry Gartrell survived the war by only six years. He moved briefly to Athens to serve as guardian for his nephew, Henry W. Grady, who followed in Gartrell's footsteps as a journalist and orator (Grady later became editor of the *Atlanta Constitution* and widely hailed as the "Spokesman for the New South"). Henry Gartrell died in January 1871.

Sources

The author thanks Dr. Keith Bohannon, of the University of West Georgia, and the late William "Billy" Maddox, Esq. for their help.

George M. Battey, Jr., *A History of Rome and Floyd County, 1540-1922.*

Edwin C. Bearss, *Forrest at Brice's Cross Roads and in Northern Mississippi in 1864*; and Bearss, "Brice's Cross Roads: Forrest Puts the Skeer in the Yankees, *Blue & Gray Magazine*, Summer 1999.

Confederate Service Records and Record of Events for Captain Henry A. Gartrell's Company.

Confederate Veteran magazine.

Clark G. Reynolds, "Confederate Romans and Bedford Forrest: The Civil War Roots of the Towers-Norton Family," *Georgia Historical Quarterly*, Spring 1993.

William Towers Memoirs (provided to author by "Billy" Maddox) and Towers articles in *Atlanta Journal*, February 16, 1901 and April 6, 1901.

John A. Wyeth, *Life of Lieutenant-General Nathan Bedford Forrest*, 1899, Harper & Brothers, New York, 1899.

NOT BY HIS OWN HAND:
THE DIARY OF A GEORGIAN AT GETTYSBURG

After enlisting in the Confederate Army, a young farmer from Lincoln County, Georgia, kept a journal describing commonplace things like tiring marches, scant rations, and a longing for home. He also described unforgettable events like the invasion of Pennsylvania. The soldier was destined for Gettysburg, America's bloodiest battle, but the entry in his journal about this cataclysmic conflict would not be penned by his own hand.

RAY CHANDLER

Thomas Ware came to my attention while I was researching the 15th Georgia Infantry Regiment, which included three companies from my native Elbert County. My great-great uncle, William McPherson McIntosh, organized Company I, the McIntosh Volunteers, and eventually commanded the regiment. He was mortally wounded during the Seven Days battles in June 1862, and left just a few fascinating scraps of his own thoughts on the war and soldiering.

I found the diary of Thomas Ware, a sergeant in the 15th Georgia, at the University of North Carolina-Chapel Hill. I began reading it in hopes of learning more about McIntosh. I kept reading it because I got to know Ware.

Thomas Lewis Ware was born September 9, 1838, in Lincoln County, the oldest of 13 children born to Nicholas and Matilda Stovall Ware. He was 22 years old when he enlisted in the Lamar Confederates, later the 15th Georgia's Company G, in 1861.

Before joining the army, Ware worked on his father's farm. He was unmarried, but his diary is sprinkled with references to letters received from and sent to someone he refers to as "CWP;" he also sometimes wrote of dreaming about a "sartain someone." It is likely, then, that CWP was waiting anxiously in Georgia for her young soldier to return home from the war.

I can only speculate about Ware's reasons for enlisting, because he never reveals in his journal why he joined the army. There is little in his words smacking of idealism or patriotism. Two topics dear to many of the more politically inclined of the day - states' rights and slavery - are not mentioned at all.

Politics apparently held no interest whatsoever for Thomas Ware. A few days before he began the march to Gettysburg, he complained when a sermon at an army camp revival meeting strayed from fighting the devil to fighting Abe Lincoln: "Another good meeting," he grumbled, "but marred by a political speech of 15 minutes that made it worse."

Somewhere, sometime, Ware may have entertained thoughts that he was fighting for his home and Southern independence, but his diary leaves one with the

June 27 Saturday
Received orders to leave at 8 a.m.
Cool & pleasant day... go in the rear
soon in the pike & then we stopped for
2 hours & several the Stragglers & Pioneer
Corps went ahead with the Pioneers
3 miles then brought us to the
beautiful town of Greencastle on the
Harrisburg R.R. this is a fine town
larger than Washington Ga houses large
& fine shady streets this town like others
in this State I ever felt the
affect of war the R.R. runs down main
street. People strong unionist & looked
mad & sullen at our appearance a great
many closed doors; stores all closed
the streets & hotels crowded with young
men just out of service, some nice
looking girls dressed very fine as every
thing is cheap, several Federal Flags were
seen the girls had them on their bonnets
we marched through quick time with
music, the depot on the south side of town
was burnt & R.R. in several places

The diary of Thomas Ware

impression that he signed the enlistment roll and left Lincoln County mainly because his friends were doing the same.

Stepping Off

Ware "saw the elephant" with the 15th Georgia through its first trials by fire in 1862. Of the bloody attack at Malvern Hill in July of that year he wrote, "We commenced ascending a hill in front of the enemy, where we suffered awful. Men could be seen falling in every direction, the grape & bombs ... taking off a great many heads & cutting some half [in two]."

The Confederate army started on the trek to Gettysburg on June 6, 1863. Ware recorded that it rained that day, but the moisture kept down the dust ordinarily raised by tens of thousands of feet, countless horses, and a multitude of wagons and artillery pieces. The 15th Georgia, one of four regiments in Brigadier General Henry L. Benning's brigade, covered 18 miles and finally halted at 11 p.m. near Stevensburg, Virginia, at a river ford. Despite the dampness, no fires were permitted.

"Evry one so tired," Ware scribbled. "Just fell out & lie down with orders to leave in 2 hours."

Before the men of the 15th Georgia broke camp, they each received a measure of flour and were ordered to prepare three days' rations. Flour or cornmeal with salted pork or beef were the mainstays of marching provisions. Sometimes there was enough flour or meal but scarcely any meat, and other times meat without bread. At one point during the advance, Ware noted that supplies of salt, soda, and lard had been depleted, reducing rations to "biscuits dry and flint hard."

These photos of Confederate dead in and near Devil's Den graphically portray the human cost of the bitter fighting on the battle's second day.

By June 15, some of the men had become exhausted or ill from the incessant, grueling marching. Some days were long, others short, with plenty of counter-marching in response to various reports (usually inaccurate) concerning the position of enemy troops.

The Georgians endured a forced march on the 15th covering 18 more miles, "the hottest days march I ever took," Ware observed. The Culpepper Court House turnpike, he remarked, is "very good but very dusty, the day warm water scarse. We suffered very much … A great many fell out of ranks overcome by heat & several sunstroke & some died, the roadside was full."

Well-Received

Ever the farmer, Ware noticed few fields in cultivation and that the country seemed poor with most houses abandoned. Perhaps he was too tired to dwell on

the reason: northern Virginia was well acquainted with war. The regiment halted at 9 p.m. "We lie down in an open field with orders to leave by light tomorrow," the fatigued soldier griped, "but very little sleep by me."

On the morning of the June 17, drums roused the soldiers early. In their haste to depart, they didn't have time to eat and of necessity abandoned some of their food. For that reason, news that Lt. Gen. Richard S. Ewell's Second Corps had occupied Winchester, Virginia, bagging 6,000 Union prisoners and a cornucopia of commissary stores was especially welcome. This news, Ware wrote, "created great elation among the wearied soldiers."

The pace slackened somewhat, but it was still uncomfortably hot going. Ware estimated that more than 100 soldiers of the 15th Georgia fell out of ranks due to the heat. Nevertheless, he noted that water was "cool & very plentiful" and the route wound through "mountains on either side which makes it a beawtiful coun-

try…Some very fine farms & fine dwellings, a few farms in cultivation, lands very rich & was before the war the most beawtiful section in Va."

As the Confederates strode through villages with their military bands playing, cheering crowds gathered and girls waving handkerchiefs greeted the Southern soldiers. Near Piedmont Station, a woman presented the 15th Georgia with two gallons of fresh milk and a large bucket of ham biscuits. This was meager fare for over 300 hungry soldiers, but many of the locals, no matter how poor the war had left them, gave whatever they could to the boys in gray.

The 15th Georgia halted at 4 p.m. on June 17 near Upperville, Virginia, a town of "fine houses & beawtiful ladies." The strenuous march had tired the men and nightfall offered a much needed respite. "We had a good nights rest for the first time in 3 nights. Not more than half the [company] fit for duty, some quite sick from fatigue in Camps & some scattered along the road."

On June 26, Benning's Brigade was ready to break camp by first light despite a persistent drizzle. The previous day, the brigade had logged 21 miles. Now, after nearly three weeks, these Georgians would finally exit Virginia, traverse

Modern research indicates that the body of this "sharpshooter" in the rocks at Devil's Den may have been repositioned for dramatic purposes.

Maryland's narrow neck, and enter Pennsylvania, the farthest north Thomas Ware had ever been.

Ware didn't reflect on this, however, just as he didn't comment on the significance of the Confederate invasion of Pennsylvania. Perhaps his reticence stemmed from his involvement in the Maryland campaign the previous autumn when the Confederate and Union armies clashed at Sharpsburg, Maryland.

Occasionally, there were lighter moments to relieve the tedium and toil of the campaign. When the 15th Georgia crossed the Potomac River into Maryland each soldier received a dram of whiskey. "Several of the boys got quite drunk & we had a jolly set…Some past traveling & a few fights." Ware was also pleased to find that tasty ripe cherries were readily available when 16 miles of marching ended at sunset near an orchard. "We got a great many cherries & living finely," he recorded with satisfaction.

A Chilly Reception

Ware observed that this section of Maryland countryside was densely populated and untouched by war. It was a region of prosperous farms and bountiful crops of corn and wheat, but the citizens were clearly Unionists. The Stars and Stripes was displayed at many houses and girls even wore emblems of the flag on their bonnets.

Typical of the Confederate rank and file at Gettysburg, William Thomas (left) and Henry M. Bailey of Hart County served in Company C of the 16th Georgia Regiment. The 16th was in Wofford's Brigade, McLaws' Division, and was engaged just to the west of Benning's Brigade. William Bailey was furloughed home in August 1863. Henry Bailey was captured on June 1, 1864 at Cold Harbor, Virginia, and died of chicken pox in prison at Elmira, New York, on January 16, 1865.

Yet locals who watched the invading Confederates appeared frightened and sullen. Ware and his comrades had experienced a similar attitude during the Maryland campaign in 1862 and judged that the reception would grow even chillier in Pennsylvania.

The further north they went, the more Ware thought of home. He drew comparisons between Lincoln County and Pennsylvania's towns, rolling hills, and rich farms with rock barns and tidy fields bordered by stone walls. The people lived well, he surmised, and "all do their own work." This is one of the few instances in which Ware touched on slavery. He also noted with some disdain the multitude of young men in the towns who had completed their enlistments in the Union army and idly watched as the Confederates passed.

On June 27, the 15th Georgia reached Chambersburg, Pennsylvania, "as large as Atlanta Ga & as nice & fine a town as I ever saw," which "has never felt the affect of war." The town was under martial law, with provost guards on each street corner to maintain order.

General Robert E. Lee had ordered his Southerners to respect private property, but the tired, hungry soldiers were sorely tempted by what seemed, in comparison to war-torn Virginia, a land of plenty. Crops were trampled and soldiers considered beehives, orchards, and green corn fair game. They also dismantled rail fences for firewood.

Ware and his messmates also indulged in chicken stew, fresh butter and milk, and more of the abundant cherries: "This is a rich country, wheat very good & corn good, people very thickly setled & live in fine houses, nice gardens & seem to think more of their gardens & barns than anything else, as they had the largest & finest Barns I ever saw."

Benning's Brigade remained in the area several days, rounding up horses and cattle for the army as well as ripping up a section of railroad. Though it rained frequently, the troops' spirits remained undampened.

RAY CHANDLER

To Gettysburg

At the end of June, Benning's Brigade made an unhurried march east, leisurely enough for Ware to

While sharply engaged with the 124th New York Regiment, dozens of men from the 15th Georgia Regiment – including Thomas Ware – fell in this field below Devil's Den. The regiment took 335 men into the battle and suffered 51% casualties – 19 killed and 152 wounded.

enjoy an early afternoon camp. The 15th Georgia met with men from the Irwin Artillery of Washington, Georgia, and Ware gave one of the officers, who was about to return to Georgia, a letter to take to his father.

The move east by Benning's troops was part of Lee's effort to concentrate his scattered army near Cashtown, Pennsylvania, before the Army of the Potomac, under newly appointed Maj. Gen. George Meade, could attack the dispersed Southern forces. Meade intended to shield Washington, D.C. and Philadelphia from the invading Southern army, and was seeking favorable terrain and conditions to offer battle.

Benning's Brigade resumed the march at 4 p.m. and tramped eastward all night, stopping near Cashtown at 4 a.m. on July 1, 1863. With the brief diary entry of this day, the handwriting of the diary changes - for reasons that become clear later. "A cloudy day. We have orders to prepare 3 days rations & be ready to march at a moments warning. Orders came to be ready to leave at 4 O'clock. Soon the drum beat & all in lines. Our brigade (Benning's) in front. We passed through the village of Fayetteville. Here we took the Chambersburg & Baltimore turn pike. After marching all night we stoped at 4 O'clock [a.m.] and rested 3 hours."

Usually, the entries in Ware's journal are brief on the occasion of urgent or prolonged marches, but no mention is made for the haste in this instance. It is unlikely any of the soldiers of the 15th Georgia then knew that two massive armies were concentrating near Gettysburg, a small but vital town where a dozen roads intersected. Fighting began near Gettysburg on July 1 and reinforcements converged on the town until the battle reached full pitch.

Benning's Brigade was well west of town and so did not participate in the initial clash of July 1, when the Confederate army pushed the defenders back through Gettysburg. The blue soldiers occupied a long rise called Cemetery Ridge just northeast of town. The Confederate troops entered Gettysburg and took position on a parallel rise southeast of town called Seminary Ridge.

Devil's Den

As July 2 dawned, General Robert E. Lee issued orders for James Longstreet's First Corps to act as the main fist of his attack. Two of Longstreet's three divisions (Hood's and McLaws') would advance against the left of the Union line in hopes of rolling up the flank. Benning's Brigade (Hood's Division) would be in the thick of things as the Southern infantry pressed toward a pair of wooded hills called Little Round Top and Big Round Top.

Benning's Georgians began the march at 7 a.m. after just three hour's rest and halted near Gettysburg until 2 p.m. Then the Southern soldiers proceeded east and south several miles and lined up in attack formation just west of the Emmitsburg Road. Benning's men took position behind the Robertson's Brigade of Texans and Arkansans (the right flank of the first line of assault). The Georgians suffered some casualties from Union artillery fire even though they couldn't yet see their enemy.

The left flank of the Union line was well protected in a jumble of granite boulders, some the size of small houses. The boulder-strewn wasteland, known locally as Devil's Den, formed a natural barrier barring the way to the Round Tops. The 124th New York Regiment, about 220 strong and supported by two 10-pounder Parrott rifled cannon of the 4th New York Artillery, was posted at the crest of the ridge amid the rocks.

The Confederates stepped off the attack at 4 p.m. One Alabama officer in the first wave of the Confederate advance likened the rocky ridge, wreathed in sulfurous powder smoke from the Union defenders, to a volcano. When Benning's Brigade emerged from the woods southwest of the ridge, they joined the contest for Devil's Den.

The battleground was a triangular-shaped field about three acres in size enclosed by waist-high rock walls. The field descended sharply from the crest of the Devil's Den ridge. The wall on one side of the triangular field offered some cover to the 124th New York and the artillery on the crest of the ridge. It was a formidable defensive position.

The 15th Georgia advanced on the left flank of Benning's battle line, reaching the battlefield just after an attack by the 1st Texas Infantry had been repulsed and the Lone Star boys were undergoing a counterattack by New Yorkers pouring down from the heights.

A volley from the Georgians stopped the Yankee wave cold and sent the New Yorkers scampering back to the crest. While the balance of Benning's Brigade advanced further to the right, Colonel Dudley Dubose, the 15th Georgia's commanding officer, ordered an attack on the ridge.

The Georgians and Texans became hopelessly intermingled and both regiments moved toward Devil's Den. One Texan described the melee as "roaring cannon, crashing rifles, screeching shots, bursting shells, hissing bullets, cheers, shouts, shrieks and groans." The gray wave swept the New Yorkers from the ridge, but the achievement was shaky and proved to be just the first encounter in a seesaw battle that saw the hotly contested ground gained, lost, and recaptured again and again.

Final Entry

As the sun set, the 15th Georgia made its third assault on the rocky heights. The final entry in Thomas Ware's diary related the circumstances: "Here at the foot of the mountain the engagement became general & fierce & lasted until eight O'clock at night. And in the third & last charge the fatal blow was struck."

This last entry was written by Robert Ware, Thomas's brother and comrade-in-arms, to complete the story of his brother at the Battle of Gettysburg. Robert may also have written the previous entry for July 1 as well. He doesn't provide specific details of Thomas's death, only a heartfelt tribute to his fallen brother and comrade:

"My Brother: You have offered your life
as a sacrifise upon your country's Altar.
Today concludes the term of life of my Brother.
He now sleeps upon the battle field of Gettysburg
There Brothers, Fathers, small & great,
Partake the same repose
There in peace the ashes mix
Of those who once were foes."

Robert Ware had time to bury Thomas somewhere near Devil's Den, where "willows shaded his grave." The bereaved brother added, "And there we prayed that God would guard and protect that little mound."

The next day Robert Ware was captured. He spent 18 months in a Federal prison camp before being paroled. After the war, he returned to Lincoln County and became a teacher and lay preacher.

Attempts to locate Thomas Ware's resting place have continued, even in recent years, but all have failed. The triangular field is still clearly marked, however, and preserved much as it was when Thomas saw it as he encountered the withering Union fire from the Union infantry.

Indeed, it is possible to walk the very field where Ware perished. On my trips to Gettysburg over the years, I made a point of visiting Devil's Den and the triangular field where he fell. I always placed a small Confederate battle flag at the southernmost corner, near the woods.

On my last visit, there was already a flag standing at that spot. Just a small battle flag, with "15th Georgia" lettered in one corner with a felt tip marker. I have since often wondered, was this just an anonymous, coincidental tribute to the 15th Georgia? Or perhaps the words written by Thomas Ware in his diary haunt others as well.

Sources

Thomas Ware diaries, Southern Historical Collection, UNC-Chapel Hill

Nesbitt, Mark, *35 Days to Gettysburg*, 1992. Stockpole Books, Harrisburg, PA.

Details regarding the fighting at Devil's Den obtained from: Pfanz, Harry W., *Gettysburg: The Second Day*, 1987. University of North Carolina Press, Chapel Hill, NC., pp. 158-200.

McIntosh, John, *History of Elbert County*, 1935. Elbert County Historical Society, pp. 110-112.

Copies of the letters of William M. McIntosh are in the author's possession.

THE STATE OF HER UNION

She was loyal to the North but lived in the South; she thirsted for education but was limited to mundane toil; and she was devoted to her family yet frequently lamented the conduct of those closest to her. For Louisa Fletcher, the life of a mid-19th-century woman was often complicated and sometimes dismaying.

DEBORAH MALONE

"A month of anxiety & trouble has passed since I last wrote – we are once more under the Federal flag," a troubled Louisa Fletcher jotted in her diary in Marietta, Georgia, on July 25, 1864. These were the anxious meditations of a woman torn by conflicting emotions over war, her family, and her role in an era in which there was little opportunity for females to pursue matters of intellect.

Fletcher began recording her thoughts on October 29, 1857, when she was 49 years old, and penned her last words on April 7, 1883. Her journal entries provide an intimate look at the life of an intelligent, dedicated mother and wife who frequently felt trapped by the societal constraints then imposed on women.

Both bright and a gifted soloist, Louisa Fletcher's journal entries suggest that she found life as a hotel matron stultifying.

Just Arrived from Savannah

Louisa Warren Patch was born in New Salem, Massachusetts, in 1808. She married Dix Fletcher, a cabinet maker in Stow, a nearby village, when she was 23 years old. Their first three children were born in quick succession between 1832 and 1835, but none survived infancy, leading the young couple to question whether harsh New England winters contributed to their deaths.

The Fletchers were members of Stow's Unitarian Church where Louisa, an accomplished soloist, sang frequently. On one occasion, visitors from Georgia were so impressed by her voice that they invited her to sing at their church, Christ

Although a native of Massachusetts, Dix Fletcher became a slave owner after moving to Georgia. He operated the Fletcher House hotel in Marietta for many years. While he remained a Unionist during the Civil War, he never participated in clandestine activities.

Episcopal, in Savannah.

Intrigued by both the business prospects of the bustling port city and its temperate climate, Dix and Louisa moved to Savannah in 1835. For the next 14 years, Dix engaged in the lumber business and cabinetry on Factor's Walk (today a shopping enclave and historical area between River and Bay Streets). As hoped, they found the South more conducive to child-rearing. Their next child, Georgia Caroline, was born in 1838. Two more daughters followed – Eliza Hastings in 1843 and Louise Eastman in 1848.

When Louisa wasn't busy with her young family, she taught music and sang in several churches. A devoted Unitarian, she most likely attended Savannah's Unitarian Universalist Church, although for some time she was paid to sing at Christ Episcopal Church. Several entries in her journal refer to Stephen Elliott, Christ Episcopal's bishop, who later assisted the family during a time of great crisis.

In 1849, Dix's lumber yard was destroyed by fire. Once again, misfortune spurred the family to seek a fresh start far away. This time their destination was St. Louis, Missouri, but on the way they stopped in Marietta, Georgia, to visit acquaintances. There, on July 27, Dix signed the Howard House hotel registry, "just arrived from Savannah." The Fletchers liked what they saw in the fast-growing railroad town and settled there instead of Missouri.

Dix Fletcher abandoned carpentry and held a series of jobs, beginning with a position at the Howard House. In 1852 he was appointed Marshal for Cobb County. Three years later, he acquired the Breakfast House, an establishment near the railroad depot, for $12,000. He combined the Breakfast House and an adjacent 4-story cotton warehouse to create an L-shaped brick building called the Fletcher House hotel.

Louisa's inheritance was the source of the funds used to acquire and improve the Fletcher House. "Dix bought the hotel with Louisa's money because she couldn't purchase it herself," explains Connie Cox, co-editor of *Journal of a Landlady*, Louisa Fletcher's diary that was published in 1995. "In that era, women couldn't own property. Even though it was her money that bought the hotel she had to get up and work with the servants."

Cox points out that although the helpers were called servants, they were actually slaves. It is interesting to note that while Dix was a native of Massachusetts, the epicenter of abolitionism, he also became a slave owner. His son-in-law Henry Cole, a native New Yorker who married Fletcher's daughter Georgia Caroline, was also.

Louisa, Eliza and Georgia Fletcher

How Hard It Is

Louisa Fletcher had earned high marks in school, was unusually bright and well-read, and yearned to pursue her education further. "When I was young," she wrote wistfully in January 1858, "I longed for a thorough & complete education – I would willingly have waded through anything to have been an eminent scholar but that privilege would be denied me."

She had a voracious appetite for knowledge extending to subjects that few in her position would have shared. On one occasion she attended a talk about "luminous meteors," prompting her to gush: "It appears from this lecture that it is now an established fact that the Aurora Borealis & other luminous meteors [are caused by] nebulous matter in the planetary system & as the earth revolves around the sun comes in contact with this matter & produces the phenomena."

Given her eclectic interests, it comes as no surprise that Louisa's role as hotel matron brought her little satisfaction. "Saturday night & another week of toil & care is nearly closed," she noted in an 1858 entry. "How hard it is to be entirely satisfied with one's lot – I, for one, find it so & yet, I do not pine or feel unhappy because I am not situated as I would like to be."

Judging by an entry later that year, her journal does not provide a full measure of her disenchantment. "Very few of the trials of a land lady are recorded in my journal," she wrote on October 24, 1858. "For generally when I am the most tired

While a student at Ohio's Antioch College, Eliza Fletcher became acquainted with Marion Ross. When he later served as one of Andrews' Raiders and was captured by Confederate authorities, he unsuccessfully appealed to Eliza for help.

I have the least time to write – but within the last few weeks I have had so many disagreeable things to bear I am determined to record some of them so that if I should be more pleasantly situated I can refer to what I have been through recorded with pen & ink."

When her melancholy circumstances threatened to overwhelm her, Louisa knew where to turn. She often called upon her faith to sustain her spirits: "I have perfect confidence in God that He knows best what is for my good – & perhaps I should be no happier if I had everything I wanted – I am blessed with health, have a good home, enough to eat, drink & wear – I have a kind husband, good children & I believe some friends – & how many there are who have not these blessings & many I presume, would say to me what would you have more?"

Yankee Spirit

As proprietors of a busy hotel, the Fletchers on occasion had to mollify irate customers. Sometimes, though, their no-nonsense New England natures rebelled at the haughty airs of their guests. "We have a party stopping with us numbering 14, whose manners are such that one might infer they thought the Hotel was expressly for their accommodation & that everybody & everything should be subservient to their comfort & convenience," Louisa noted in one instance. "Both Mari [Louisa's nickname for Dix] & myself have still the independent spirit of Yankees

82

Fletcher House ca. 1860

although compelled by circumstances to serve the public – Mari has shewn them that he is not to be trampled upon nor insulted with impunity."

Over the years, it seems that Louisa's appreciation for Dix increased, though she regretted that she had not always been a perfect help-mate. "I have learned to be not only content with my lot, but to be thankful for the many blessings I have & I trust also that I make Mari happier by my present conduct than when I indulged in melancholy & repining – O! That I had considered the happiness of Mari more when I was younger – a wife ought to consider the perplexities & cares her husband has to contend with in business & the trouble & anxiety he has in providing for the support of a family."

Still, Louisa sometimes found her spouse of 29 years less than romantic, a lament that she undoubtedly shares with countless women through the years. "February 14, 1860 – Valentine's day – but as yet no Valentines have been rec'd in my family, neither have I heard any allusion to the day until I spoke of it myself."

Days Dark and Dreary

"The poet says, 'Some days must be dark & dreary,'" Louisa wrote in late 1857, "and this has been one of my dark days! O! I am such a lover of peace that it seems to me strife & discord would wear me out... God knows I love my children & would do

1890

Utilized as a cotton warehouse by John H. Glover from 1844 to 1855, Dix Fletcher purchased the building and the nearby Breakfast House in 1855, joined them, and named the business the Fletcher House hotel. The fourth floor of the structure suffered substantial damage when Union troops torched public buildings in Marietta in late 1864. After the war, the establishment (less the fourth floor, which was removed) became the Kennesaw House. Today this building houses the Marietta Museum of History.

1920

For nearly a century, cotton was king in Marietta. Bringing a harvest to town was an important social event, as the attire of these farmers (circa 1903) attests.

anything in my power for their good & happiness – today, Mari has thought proper to lay some restrictions upon Meta [Eliza] & she feels it very keenly – calls us cruel & unkind – I hope she will sometime see her error."

Cox notes that the antics of their daughters sometimes vexed Louisa and Dix. "From the fourth floor of the Fletcher House, a clear view existed of the Georgia Military Institute. Georgia and Eliza would wave sheets from the fourth floor window to attract the attention of the cadets in the barracks. The young men would wave sheets back in reply. This primitive communication continued until Louisa caught the girls, thus ending their privileges in the Fletcher House."

The cadets undoubtedly missed their interaction with Georgia and Eliza, but there were more serious matters to attend. The widening schism between North and South suggested that war was imminent, a prospect that troubled Louisa. "The winter is over & gone, & indeed has flown rapidly by although we've had but little to vary this monotony of life," she wrote on March 3, 1861.

The one thing relieving the tedium of winter, to her way of thinking, was the "political strife between the North & South that has been the dominant topic of newspaper strife & conversation – this being the last day of [President James] Buchanan's rule & tomorrow the first of Lincoln's we shall probably have some change either for better or worse – for one thing I earnestly pray – for peace & not war – seven states have seceded & formed themselves into a Southern Confederacy."

During the turbulent period before the war the Fletchers had an experience that enmeshed them in one of the Civil War's most memorable events. While daughter

Eliza was a student at Antioch College in Yellow Springs, Ohio, she met Marion A. Ross. He later became one of "Andrews' Raiders," a contingent of Union troops led by a civilian, James J. Andrews, that in April 1862 seized the locomotive *The General* and fled north towards Chattanooga.

In a remarkable coincidence, the night before the raid most of the group, including Ross, stayed overnight at the Fletcher House. A sergeant in the 2nd Ohio Infantry, Ross made the connection between his old schoolmate Eliza Fletcher and her father's hotel. After his capture, he wrote Eliza and asked her to plead his case with the Confederate authorities to commute his sentence.

Ross's plea for succor from that quarter was in vain. While Eliza's parents were of Northern birth, it seems that her sympathies were decidedly Southern. As Connie Cox tells it, Eliza informed Ross that she would not aid any Yankee who had come to Georgia to steal a Southern train and burn Southern bridges. One can't help but wonder how she felt in June 1862, when Ross and seven of his companions were hanged in Atlanta.

Much Precious Blood

Cox notes that Dix and Louisa Fletcher were ardent Unionists – that is, they opposed secession and continued to support the North. Thus secession and the war that divided the country were the cause of great anguish: "So much of the New Year has passed & no record yet made in my journal & yet what thrilling events are taking place," she wrote on January 18, 1863. "Many things I care not to record for my country's sake – the war is still raging, fierce & bloody - & I see no prospect of peace – we are boarding a family of Refugees from Nashville, which place is in the hands of the federals."

Her prevailing sentiment was disdain for warfare. "I have not felt inclined to record the events of the war – war is horrible to me in all its details," she wrote shortly after the appalling casualty lists for Gettysburg were published. "I have no sympathy in it – it is still progressing between the North & South – how it will end, or when, God only knows – but I think much precious blood is being shed to no purpose."

Despite their Unionist sympathies, there is no record that the Fletchers aided the federal cause during the war. The same cannot be said of their son-in-law, Henry Cole, who spied for the North. Some of his activities deeply troubled the Fletchers, although whether it was his spying or other transgressions Louisa doesn't specify. "It is a source of deep regret to me that Mari and our son in law are not on perfectly good terms & I am confident it is equally so to Cara [Georgia] but let what will come – I trust our hearts will never be divided – I cannot see the justice of some of Mr. Cole's acts but if he is kind to his wife & children I can forgive all else."

In July 1864, the Fletchers found themselves under the Stars and Stripes once more after Union troops under the command of William T. Sherman occupied Marietta. In her entry on the 25th of that month, Louisa detailed a particularly unpleasant incident. "A month of anxiety & trouble has passed since I last wrote," she begins. "We are once more under the Federal flag but under Military rule – Marietta was taken possession of by the Federals on the 3rd & 4th of this month, during which time we have been subject to many annoyances & some losses – stragglers from the army move about & commit many depredations upon peaceable unoffending citizens which is very much to be regretted as it of course gives them an unfavorable impression of the Federals although some of them have been very kind & gentlemanly."

During this trying period, the Fletchers found their ties to the North particularly beneficial. "Many families have been provided with a guard whose presence secures them from the aggressions of lawless soldiers," Louisa continues. "We were most opportunely relieved by the arrival of the nephew [Dr. Daniel Wilder, a medical officer in the Union army] on the morning of the 4th. Mari went to town in order to get protection & there fortunately met with his nephew who was in search of him & with a brother officer arrived just in time to save a good many articles which were about to be carried off by those thieving soldiers – among other things a valuable family horse to which we are all extremely attached."

Dix Fletcher and Dr. Wilder also prevented the pillagers from confiscating supplies, Louisa writes. "They had entered our house & supplied themselves with sacks of flour, potatoes & meat & were just on the eve of departing with their booty when Mari and Drs. Wilder & L rode up to the gate & I, in my distress ran to meet them informing them what they were about to do, when those officers ordered them at once to dismount & take their plunder back to the house, though some of them rode off with what they had taken as soon as the officers came in sight – our kind nephew & friend remained to dinner & would not go away without leaving his orderly to protect me while his Uncle went to town to procure a guard."

When Union troops later torched public buildings in Marietta, Sherman reportedly spared the Fletcher House because Dix was both a staunch Unionist and a Mason. Nevertheless, cinders from the conflagration spread to and heavily damaged the hotel's fourth floor – the same from which Georgia and Eliza had once flirtatiously signaled cadets.

Alas! My Country!

The destruction and immense human loss wrought by the war saddened Louisa. "I have just passed my 57th birthday & am now once more settled in my home at Woodlawn [the Fletcher's residence outside Marietta], but Alas! My country, my country – I could weep over its fallen greatness! What a state to live in – barely existing from day to day! When will our sorrows have an end!"

Abraham Lincoln's death also shook her. "A most startling tragedy occurred in Washington on the night of the 15th," she wrote on April 23, 1865. "President Lincoln was shot in the Theatre by J. Wilkes Booth a son of the great Tragedian – at the same time William H. Seward, Secretary of State, was assassinated at his residence while sick in bed by one John Smith from Md."

Yet the war's conclusion also brought an end to one of the family's most trying chapters. Georgia traveled to South Carolina to spend time with Henry Cole, who had been arrested and imprisoned in Charleston on charges of spying for the North. Her departure upset Louisa, who was left with the care of the Cole's children. When Cole was finally released in January 1865, partly through the efforts of their old friend Bishop Stephen Elliott, Louisa wrote ecstatically, "Much has transpired since I last wrote in my journal – one of the most joyful events I ever had the pleasure of recording is the return of Cara with her husband which occurred two weeks ago."

I Have a Malady

After the war, Louisa wrote sparingly, sometimes spacing her entries years apart. In part, this was due to space limitations in her journal, prompting her to fill precious pages with only the most noteworthy events. Thus, on September 11, 1881, she wrote of a milestone event in the lives of Dix and herself. "I have but four pages more to fill in my journal – so many events have occurred this year which I ought to record – the first & most important to me was the anniversary of my 50th marriage day which was celebrated at our dear Cara's – everything was done by relatives & friends to render it a success & it was indeed a happy day."

Because of failing health Louisa moved to Georgia's house [Henry Cole had passed away in 1875], where she lived out the remainder of her life. She wrote about the move on October 31, 1882: "I was removed from Woodlawn on July 11th an invalid – have been with my dear Cara ever since & here I shall probably

Georgia Fletcher Cole played the organ for Marietta's St. James Episcopal church for many years.

remain so long as I live. I have a malady for which there is no cure."

Louisa Fletcher died of cancer on January 22, 1884, at the age of 75. Although she never escaped the confines that prevented a 19th-century woman from fully pursuing her own interests, she was survived by a large, well-regarded family and a reunited country that had arisen from the ashes of war.

THESE DEAD SHALL NOT HAVE DIED IN VAIN

The bravery and sacrifice of the men who fought at the Battle of Chickamauga reminds Americans today that North and South had something essential in common.

Daniel M. Roper

I didn't know a soul in New York City. I didn't know anyone within 250 miles of the place. I'd never even been there for that matter. But on September 11, 2001, it felt as if I had been hit in the gut as I watched the horrific attack on New York's World Trade Center. Even though I didn't have any ties to the Big Apple it still felt like the attack was against my city and my people.

Like all Americans, I grieved for the victims in New York, Washington, D.C., and Somerset County, Pennsylvania. We all felt a similar sense of loss judging by what I saw and heard over the next few days. American flags lined both Broad Street in Rome, Georgia, and the highway into Rossville, Georgia, as though it were the Fourth of July. Department stores and grocery chains throughout the state expressed their condolences in full-page newspaper ads. Churches of all denominations held prayer services. Scenes like these and a hundred variations were repeated in Shreveport, Topeka, and Detroit, bringing tears to even the most stoic eye. People all over America reaffirming that Americans, so often internally divided over political, economic, and social issues, are one people when facing an enemy.

Through September 11, we learned that in many important ways we are just like the people of that sprawling, congested, mysterious metropolis where people talk with grating accents, restaurants don't serve grits or ice tea, and the detestable Yankees and Mets baseball teams are adored. We found new heroes in their police officers and fire fighters. And we took a measure of comfort in our rediscovered unity.

Three days after the September 11, 2001 terrorist attacks I was reminded that there was a time when our differences threatened to divide us forever. The reminder came on a visit to Chickamauga Battlefield in northwest Georgia to take photographs for a magazine article. Chickamauga is a place where America's most bitter dispute exacted a terrible cost during the third year of the Civil War.

I pulled into the parking area at Chickamauga's Snodgrass Hill at noon on September 14, 2001, admiring the tranquil beauty of this now peaceful locale, and began to contemplate the blood shed here so long ago. On a September afternoon 138 years earlier thousands of Americans were killed and wounded on this low ridge in the last desperate attacks of the great battle. The toll was staggering.

Chickamauga earned the unhappy distinction of being one of the bloodiest events in American history. In fact, with 35,000 casualties, it is second only to the Battle of

The victorious Confederates held the battlefield for several months (until after the Union victory at the Battles of Lookout Mountain and Missionary Ridge in November 1863). However, the Confederates did not have photographers like Matthew Brady and George Barnard to visit and photograph the area. Union photographers did not have access to the battleground until late 1863. The caption for this 1864 photograph identifies the terrain only as the "Chickamauga battlefield" but the terrain appears to be part of Horseshoe Ridge near Snodgrass Hill.

Gettysburg. The six thousand Americans killed or mortally wounded at Chickamauga was roughly similar to the number who perished in the September 11 terrorist attacks according to estimates available at the time of my visit to the battlefield.

Numbers like these do not adequately convey the human cost. At Chickamauga the dead included Abraham Lincoln's brother-in-law (ironically an officer in the Confederate Army), a noted poet from Cincinnati, a devoted husband whose command included a regiment of Scandinavian immigrants that lost more than 50% of its men in the battle, and a Confederate soldier who a year before had risked his life to take water to wounded Federals during the Battle of Fredericksburg.

New heroes emerged out of Chickamauga's death and despair just as they did in New York City, Washington, and Pennsylvania. Steady men like Union General George H. Thomas who became "The Rock of Chickamauga" by standing firm against repeated Confederate assaults on Snodgrass Hill. Valiant men like Lieutenant William Turner whose adroit handling of a battery of artillery saved a Confederate infantry division from annihilation. Dependable men like Colonel Moses Walker who assumed command of his old brigade, steadying the wavering Federal line on Snodgrass Hill at a moment of great crisis, despite the fact that he

Colonel Hans C. Heg's brigade fought valiantly at the Viniard Farm on the battle's first day. While feverishly working to steady his men, Heg fell mortally wounded. The previous evening he had written his wife, "Do not feel uneasy for me. I am well and in good spirits and trusting to my usual good luck."

General John B. Hood's Confederates participated in the massive charge that decimated the right and center of the Union line on the second day of the battle. After Hood received a severe wound, Confederate momentum in his sector of the battlefield waned considerably.

Two of General James Longstreet's divisions were transferred by train from Virginia to Georgia to bolster beleaguered Braxton Bragg's command. Many of the soldiers arrived at nearby Catoosa Station during the battle. Longstreet did not arrive until after nightfall on the battle's first day. Bragg promptly gave Longstreet command of the Confederate army's Left Wing. The Georgian commanded the troops which exploited the breach in the Union lines nearly destroying the Union Army of the Cumberland. After the battle, Longstreet sharply criticized Braxton Bragg for not pursuing the routed Federal army.

was under military arrest and under no duty to be near the front lines.

Just two months after the Battle of Chickamauga, Abraham Lincoln dedicated the Soldier's National Cemetery at Gettysburg, Pennsylvania. The words he spoke that day honored the Federal dead at Gettysburg, but apply equally to those – both North and South – who fell at Chickamauga: "We here highly resolve that these dead shall not have died in vain, that this nation, under God, shall have a new birth of freedom, and that government of the people, by the people, for the people, shall not perish from the earth."

Lincoln would be supremely pleased to learn that 138 years later his country remained strong and united in the face of new and savage enemies. He would be equally satisfied to know that, as he had predicted, Americans would never forget the brave soldiers who died for their country at places like Gettysburg and Chickamauga. How fitting then that a nation so terribly divided during Lincoln's time will, as one people, always remember those Americans who lost their lives on September 11.

Brigadier General James Lytle's brigade tried to stem the Confederate onslaught as soldiers in gray penetrated deep within the Federal right and center late on the morning of September 20, 1863. Lytle, a well known Cincinnati poet, was mortally wounded at a place now known as Lytle Hill. Many Confederate officers and soldiers made a point to visit the place during and after the battle to pay their respects to the enemy officer who had fought with such fervor against them yet who, in a sentiment unusual in war but commonplace in the American Civil War, seemed to be one of them.

Unlike Robert E. Lee, native Virginian George H. Thomas remained with the Union after his home state seceded in 1861. At Chickamauga, Thomas performed well in command of the Union left flank during the first day-and-a-half of the battle. When the Union right and center dissolved at noon on the second day, Thomas took command of the remaining Union forces on the battlefield and with grim determination successfully defended Snodgrass Hill, saving the Union force from wholesale destruction. His day's work earned him grateful plaudits from President Lincoln and a nickname: The Rock of Chickamauga.

After a brilliant campaign that pushed the Confederates out of Middle Tennessee and put the strategically important city of Chattanooga in Federal hands, General William S. Rosecrans performed poorly at Chickamauga, fleeing the battlefield and leaving command in the capable hands of General George H. Thomas. A month later, Rosecrans would be replaced by Ulysses S. Grant.

BELOW LEFT: Lee & Gordon's Mills on Chickamauga Creek, circa 1864. The dam served as an impromptu, albeit dangerous, causeway across Chickamauga Creek. "As we began the advance our regiment was the extreme left of our line," reminisced Alabama cavalryman John Wyeth years later, "and when we struck the Chickamauga we waded the stream just below the Lee & Gordon mill-dam. Hoping to get over dry, a number of us started to run across the dam; but an officer shouted: 'Get off! They're going to rake you with grapeshot,' and we leaped into the water like so many bullfrogs."

THE GRAVES
AT FARMER'S BRIDGE

In 1864, a small force of Confederate soldiers defied overwhelming odds to repel a much larger Federal force and stubbornly hold an important bridge on the road to Rome, Georgia. During the ensuing battle, ten Confederates fell in combat, and were hastily buried and forgotten. Their graves were recently relocated and identified for posterity.

DANIEL M. ROPER

When the blue-uniformed horsemen suddenly trotted around the curve in the dusty country lane, the Southern soldier pulling advance guard at that spot drew in a sharp breath and felt his stomach churn with fear. Motioning frantically to his comrades, he slid quickly into a rifle pit and raised his musket to his shoulder. Destiny was at his doorstep...

There was no time to question why the Confederacy had less than 100 men to guard a key bridge on the road to Rome, Georgia, with its important cannon factory, mills and warehouses. No time to even calculate their odds against 3,000 Union cavalrymen – an entire division supported by artillery.

As he sighted down his rifle on the lead Yankee, the soldier wondered if he would survive the next few minutes. He put the disconcerting thought from his mind - as he knew he must – and hoped that his family, should he die, would know where he had fallen and that he had done his duty.

By the end of the day, 10 of the Confederates lay dead at Farmer's Bridge. Some 134 years later, a dedicated researcher learned of their existence and rediscovered their graves so that posterity could honor them.

Spring Thaw

When the Union Army in northwest Georgia broke winter camp in the spring of 1864 and resumed its offensive maneuvers, General William T. Sherman sent one-third of his troops – Major General James B. McPherson's Army of the Tennessee – on a flanking march south toward the country hamlet of Villanow. Sherman, reluctant to attack the strong line of Confederate fortifications on Rocky Face Ridge near Dalton, hoped that McPherson's soldiers would find the Rebel rear unprotected, seize the railroad at Resaca, and sever the Confederate supply line. He knew if this strategy succeeded, the Confederate Army would be cut-off, forced to retreat into the mountains, and face destruction.

The arrival of McPherson's troops in Villanow also threatened Rome, a major Confederate manufacturing and transportation center. The people of Rome had good reason to fear the approach of the enemy. Rome was a place of importance, and had already been the target of one Federal thrust.

Located about a quarter-mile upstream from the site of Farmer's Bridge, this old iron bridge spans Armuchee Creek. It was at this place that a detachment of Union cavalry forded Armuchee Creek in an effort to flank the Confederate soldiers posted at Farmer's Cemetery.

The presence of McPherson's troops in Villanow alarmed General Joseph E. Johnston, who commanded the Confederate Army of Tennessee. On May 7, Johnston notified the officer commanding a cavalry division posted near Rome of the disturbing developments: "The enemy are reported as having a division today at La Fayette, and a larger force prepared to join it and march by our left upon Rome or the railroad in our rear. . . A division of the enemy are reported to have been within eight miles of La Fayette last evening, and are expected to be joined by a still-larger infantry and a large cavalry force today. It will be necessary to keep this force under your close observation, and to keep strict watch on the fords between you and Rome."[1]

Farmer's Bridge

When McPherson's Army of the Tennessee occupied Villanow in preparation for its move on Resaca, the job of guarding its right flank fell to Brigadier General Kenner Garrard. A veteran officer who had served throughout the campaigns in Tennessee, Garrard had a division of cavalry at his disposal. In order to thoroughly cover his area of responsibility, Garrard sent patrols west towards Summerville and south towards Rome on the roads through Subligna, the Pocket, and Sugar Valley.

At that time, only one bridge over Armuchee Creek existed. This crossing structure stood eight miles north of Rome on the Summerville Road near the widow

At Farmer's Bridge, Robert H.G. Minty commanded the Union cavalry force consisting of the 4th U.S. and 7th Pennsylvania cavalry regiments and a section of the Chicago Board of Trade Light Artillery. Almost a year later to the day, the 4th Michigan, while under Minty's orders, would capture Confederate President Jefferson Davis at Irwinville, Georgia.

Farmer's place. Each of the routes taken by Garrard's troopers converged just north of this point. Farmer's Bridge was the bottleneck through which all traffic heading to Rome from the north must pass.

To guard against Union probes from Villanow, the commander of the Confederate cavalry division headquartered in Rome posted cavalry pickets along the roads leading north. On the 13th of May, the rattle of musketry and the boom of artillery fire from that direction added to the Rome garrison's growing sense of urgency. "There has been hard fighting all day at Resaca," Acting Assistant Inspector General West Steever reported. "We have not had the particulars of the battle today, but from the reports of the artillery heard here, the firing must have been very heavy."[2]

Partisan Rangers

At that crucial point in time, the responsibility of defending Farmer's Bridge fell to the 12th Alabama Battalion, Partisan Rangers. Organized in September 1862, the 12th Alabama had many new recruits who had little battlefield experience. The battalion consisted of seven companies although, of that number, only one at a time could be spared to guard the Armuchee Creek crossing.

Captain William Lokey's Company G drew guard duty on the 15th of May. To defend the position, Lokey had no more than 50 soldiers according to one estimate. Despite their weakness in numbers, the Southerners held a strong defensive position. A line of rifle pits on the south bank of the creek was anchored on the left by a steep little hill topped by a small cemetery. A hill crowned by the widow Farmer's house anchored the right flank.

Riflemen posted on these hills had a commanding field of fire over the bottomlands north of the creek. Moreover, to get at the Southerners, any attacking force would have to either squeeze across the bridge or ford the creek. All in all, Lokey's Partisan Rangers occupied a strong position that could be held against a larger force –

These nine anonymous grave stones (and a tenth that lay to the side) in Farmer's Cemetery likely bear the remains of the Alabamians killed in action during the skirmish on May 15, 1864.

as long, that is, as the enemy did not arrive with artillery or overwhelming numbers.

Minty's Sabre Brigade

Unfortunately for Lokey and his Alabamians, a division of Union cavalry accompanied by artillery was indeed on its way. On May 15, Kenner Garrard, endeavoring to find an Oostanaula River crossing somewhere north of Rome, galloped south with three brigades of cavalry and a battery of horse artillery.

Garrard possessed detailed information about Confederate troop dispositions north of Rome. He had received a message on the 13th that William T. Martin's division of Confederate cavalry was posted on the Summerville Road some three miles north of Rome.

"A picket of fifty men," the report explained, "stand at Farmer's Bridge, across Armuchee Creek, eight miles from Rome, where it is said rifle-pits have been thrown up. Thirty or forty men patrol John's Valley from Martin's Ferry (nearly west from Calhoun); fifteen men patrol to Floyd's Spring from Farmer's Bridge, and forty or fifty from Farmer's Bridge to Dirt Town.[3]

Garrard, whose orders directed him to cross the Oostanaula River (assuming that he found a suitable bridge or ford) and to disrupt Confederate communications between Rome and Kingston, had a veteran cavalry division at his disposal. The 1st Brigade, under the command of Colonel Robert H.G. Minty and consist-

At a November 8, 1998 ceremony, the ten Alabama soldiers who died defending Farmer's Bridge were finally recognized and honored.

ing of the 4th Michigan, 4th United States and 7th Pennsylvania cavalry regiments and a section of the Chicago Board of Trade Light Artillery battery, would bear the brunt of the day's fighting.

A native of Ireland, Minty had served in the British army before immigrating to Michigan in 1853. He began the war as a major in the 2nd Michigan Cavalry Regiment and steadily advanced in rank. In November of 1862, he was given command of a cavalry brigade that he subsequently led in battle at Murfreesboro, Chickamauga, and Knoxville. By 1864, the sobriquet Minty's Sabre Brigade had been bestowed upon his battle-tested men.

Skirmish at Farmer's Bridge

At 5 A.M. on the 15th of May, Garrard's division, with Minty's Sabres leading the way, broke camp at Dry Creek in Haywood Valley and headed south. Three hours later, advance scouts encountered Lokey's pickets near Farmer's Bridge. The Union cavalrymen drove the gray soldiers back towards the bridge and then impulsively kept right on going.

"The advance vedettes and a few of my scouts charged over the bridge," a chagrined Minty reported, "but the advance guard having halted to allow the column time to close up, they were not supported, and consequently were driven back with one killed and four horses wounded."[4]

The sudden Federal attack, which occurred on a Sunday morning, may have

A contingent of Civil War re-enactors posing as the Cherokee Artillery were on hand to complete the November 8, 1998 ceremony honoring the fallen soldiers at Farmer's Bridge.

caught Company G of the 12th Alabama unprepared. When the first shots were fired by the pickets, the rest of Company G had to saddle up and hurry to the rifle pits along the creek. The Yankee cavalry nearly beat them there. As one of the Alabamians later put it, "[t}he Minie-balls were flying before we could get in line."[5] After quickly assessing the situation, Captain Lokey sent a courier to Rome for reinforcements.

When Minty arrived at the scene, he found "the enemy strongly posted at Farmer's Bridge."[6] Instead of immediately attacking the Partisan Rangers in their well-protected position across Armuchee Creek, Minty sent scouts both upstream and downstream to search for undefended routes across the creek. Receiving reports that "bad fords" existed in both directions, he detailed troops to swing around the Confederate flank by way of these crossings.

Minty sent two companies of the 4th Michigan to the downstream ford and six others and the 4th United States to the ford upstream (probably at or near the present-day location of the iron bridge on the Little Texas Valley Road). When these two bodies of men were in position on the defenders' flanks, Minty planned to lead an assault aimed straight at the Confederate center.

In the excitement of the moment, Captain Lokey may have underestimated the size of the attacking force. With less than 100 men to guard the bridge, it is likely that he would have ordered an immediate retreat had he realized that his foe had at hand three regiments supported by artillery and two brigades in reserve. A com-

Forgotten and unmarked no more, the simple graves at Farmer's Cemetery are now marked for posterity, and a monument details the events of the May 15, 1864 skirmish at this site.

pany simply could not hold back a force that size. Perhaps the repulse of the charge by the 4th Michigan scouts early in the skirmish deceived Lokey as to the enemy's numbers and his own chances. If so, it proved to be a fatal miscalculation on his part.

Some two hours after the opening shots were fired, Minty was finally ready to resume the attack. With a battalion of the 4th Michigan leading the way and the 7th Pennsylvania following, Minty charged the bridge, quickly overwhelming the little contingent of Confederates and dislodging them from their position.

During the fighting, Captain Lokey received a mortal wound. In the confusion, someone ordered the Southerners "to fall back at once." Company G commenced a rather hasty withdrawal toward Rome. "The retreat," Miles A. Cornelius later wrote, "was a race for seven miles until we reached our lines." In the midst of his urgent escape, Cornelius lost his gun and hat.[7]

After pursuing the Alabamians about five miles, Minty's Sabre Brigade encountered a considerable Confederate force occupying a strong position and brandishing four pieces of artillery at Big Dry Creek. Upon learning that Confederate troops also threatened his flanks, Minty ordered a retreat himself - first to a position north of the junction of the Summerville and the Dalton roads and shortly thereafter back at Farmer's Bridge.

Briefly, the hunter became the hunted. The Federal rear guard fell back slowly, skirmishing all the way to the bridge. "The rebels followed me up closely," Minty reported. "They were received dismounted, and handsomely repulsed."[8]

Finally, after a full day of fighting, Minty's brigade and the rest of Garrard's division withdrew to Floyd Springs for the night, leaving the bridge temporarily in Confederate hands once again.

After the battle, the gravely-wounded Captain Lokey was taken unconscious to the widow Farmer's house. As he clung to life, his mother, father and brother traveled from Alabama under a flag of truce to be at his side. The dying officer, however, may not have been aware of their presence. "He never spoke after he was wounded," Miles Cornelius later wrote to Lokey's nephew.[9]

The clash at Farmer's Bridge, a minor skirmish on the periphery of the Atlanta Campaign, is little more than a footnote in history today. Captain Lokey and nine other Alabamians lost their lives trying to halt an advance that would not be stopped. Just three days after the skirmish, Rome fell to a Union infantry division. Perhaps Lokey had died in vain, but Cornelius did not forget him. "No braver soldier," the old veteran would eulogize in a letter written in 1921, "ever gave his life for the lost cause."[10]

Dead On The Field Of Honor

"Thomas Barnard."

"Dead on the field of honor, sir!"

"Cullen Porter."

"Dead on the field of honor, sir!"

"Benjamin F. Porter."

"Dead on the field of honor, sir!"

And so the roll-call went. In a dreary mist under a leaden sky on a somber autumn afternoon, a U.S. Civil War re-enactor stepped forward at the call of each name and removed the Confederate flag draped over each of the new granite headstones.

The November 8, 1998, ceremony was a long time in coming. More than 134 years had passed since the Partisan Rangers had fallen at Farmer's Bridge. But only recently had their identities – and even the location of their graves' – been discovered.

Following the battle, one of the widow Farmer's servants had carried each of the bodies across the road to the cemetery on the little hill overlooking Armuchee Creek. He buried them there in graves that were apparently forgotten in the confusion resulting from the fall of Rome and the Confederate retreat to Atlanta.

Neither the Confederate nor United States governments – nor anyone else for that matter – ever marked the graves as the final resting places of Confederate dead. As the decades passed, knowledge of the graves was lost as, one by one, those who had been alive at the time slowly passed away.

Rediscovery of the Graves

Had it not been for the work of Gilbert R. Smith, who became interested in the skirmish at Farmer's Bridge in the early 1990s, the graves and the men might have been forgotten forever. Smith, then historian of the Nathan Bedford Forrest Camp of the Sons of Confederate Veterans, read accounts of the battle in the *Official Records of the War of the Rebellion* and wondered what became of the Confederate casualties.

One day, while visiting the cemetery on the hill, Smith found a little plot of nine graves marked by small, flat stones inscribed with "grave" and adorned only by a cross (fragments of a tenth stone lay to the side). Smith at once suspected that these belonged to the Alabamians, but was unsure until a friend, William K. Snowden, did some research on his own. Snowden, a retired Marine Corps officer, reviewed the Official Records and other sources and eventually ascertained the identities – but not the location – of the 12th Alabama Battalion soldiers who fell at Farmer's Bridge. Then, Snowden checked all of the cemeteries where reason dictated that the remains might have been buried. When he did not find any of the ten in church cemeteries in their home communities nor in the Confederate cemeteries in Rome and Marietta, the weight of evidence compelled the conclusion that the little plot in the Farmer's Cemetery was the final resting place of the fallen Confederates.

A letter in the Special Collections Room at Rome's Sara Hightower Regional Library finally confirmed this suspected conclusion. There, Gilbert Smith found the letter which had been written in 1921 by Company G's Miles Cornelius to Captain Lokey's nephew. Although Cornelius did not know whether William Lokey had been buried at Farmer's Cemetery, he did state in the letter that "the body of Lieutenant Porter was buried in the cemetary [sic] near the Bridge by an old colored servant of Mrs. Farmer."[11] Given the state of affairs at that time, it is therefore highly likely that all of the casualties were disposed of similarly.

Final Tributes

Satisfied that the graves and casualties had been accurately identified, Smith organized the 1998 ceremony honoring the Confederate soldiers killed at Farmer's Bridge. Under suitably gray skies and accompanied by period music and songs performed by the 8th Georgia Regiment Band and the New Armuchee Baptist Church choir, Smith unveiled new headstones inscribed with the names of the slain men, and a monument detailing the now almost forgotten battle at the site on May 15, 1864.

Near the end of the ceremony, the Cherokee Artillery fired a cannon in salute to the ten cavalrymen who had done their duty for their country. The concussive impact of each discharge blew crisp, gold leaves off a nearby hickory tree, sending them spinning into the mist where they, like those soldiers of long ago, fell to the earth to become one with it once again.

Endnotes

1. U.S. War Department, *The War Of The Rebellion: A Compilation Of The Official Records Of The Union and Confederate Armies* (Washington, D.C., GPO, 1880-1901) (hereafter OR); Series I, Vol. 38, Part IV, p. 674.
2. Ibid. Note 1 at p. 706.
3. Ibid. Note 1 at p. 171.
4. OR, Series I, Vol. 38, part I, p. 816.

5. May 5, 1921 letter from M.A. Cornelius to Samuel A. Lokey. A typed transcript of the letter is in the John Harris papers, Special Collections Room, Sara Hightower Regional Library in Rome, GA.
6. OR, Series I, Vol. 38, Part I, p. 811.
7. Ibid. Note 5.
8. Ibid. Note 4.
9. Ibid. Note 5.
10. Ibid.
11. Ibid.

THE DAY THE WAR CAME TO ROME

In the spring of 1864, Confederate troops proved their mettle when they encountered a Federal force moving on the strongly-fortified town of Rome. The two armies maneuvered carefully and each sought an advantage, but in the end events elsewhere dictated the outcome of this battle and the fate of Rome.

DANIEL M. ROPER

The sun beat down on the weary, dust-covered soldiers as they marched into Rome, Georgia, on the afternoon of May 17, 1864. The Tar Heels and Texans of General Matthew D. Ector's brigade had just finished a 40-mile forced march from Blue Mountain, Alabama. They wore the homespun, butternut-colored uniforms of the western army and were on their way to reinforce Joseph E. Johnston's beleaguered Army of Tennessee at nearby Adairsville.

No civilians were on hand to welcome the tired Rebel soldiers to Rome. No children cheering and clapping. No young ladies waving flags and handkerchiefs. It was the fourth year of the terrible war and far too late for enthusiasm of that nature. In fact, most of Rome's citizens had long since evacuated to safer places, because Rome lay perilously near the path of the Federal troops advancing on Atlanta.

Brigadier General Mathew D. Ector's brigade of North Carolina and Texas infantry arrived just in time to save Rome from an advancing enemy force, but only temporarily.

If possible, most of the citizenry had sold their land and whatever property they couldn't carry with them. The little town now belonged to the Confederate army – at least for the moment.

It is not an exaggeration to say the fate of the Confederacy hung in the balance,

The guns of Fort Stovall were situated on the summit of Myrtle Hill in Rome. This vantage point overlooked the city and delayed the Union army from crossing the rivers in this vicinity.

for the South could not long survive if Atlanta fell. And Rome, with its imposing hilltop forts and sprawling entrenchments, anchored the left flank of the Confederate line of defense that stood between the Yankees and Atlanta.

The Gray General

An eerie silence enveloped Ector's exhausted infantrymen as they marched across the Etowah River bridge and filed down Rome's forlorn main street past abandoned and forsaken buildings. The Noble cannon factory, warehouses full of vital munitions and supplies, fine homes, and blood-soaked hospitals all stood in stark silence.

The Choice House Hotel – once Rome's most affluent establishment where patriotic Southerners had toasted the Confederacy amidst luxurious accommodations – had been converted into a military hospital where disease, agony and death reigned supreme. In the midst of these hotel accommodations-gone-to-hell, a well-dressed officer stroked his beard and contemplated the situation.

Our pickets report a Union infantry division and artillery two-and-one-half miles north of town, Major General Samuel G. French thought to himself. *My orders are to report today to General Johnston in Adairsville. But with the fortifications on the hills surrounding this town, this place can be held. The warehouses are full of supplies; we are still evacuating the wounded; the bridges and munitions must be burned lest they fall into enemy hands; and if the Yankees take Rome, they'll turn Johnston's flank!*

Turning to his courier, French barked an order: "Report to General Ector and

U.S. ARMY MILITARY HISTORY INSTITUTE

Major General Samuel D. French commanded the Confederate forces around Rome on the eve of the enemy assault.

tell him his men are not to board the Kingston train. They are to move north, across the river into the earthworks. They are all I have to stop the Yankees from taking this town."[1]

The Blue General

The dour Union general with the unlikely name of Jefferson Davis stood atop a wooded hill and surveyed the terrain before him. Immediately in front, two hills rose abruptly from the farmland.

To the side of one hill flowed the swift, deep waters of the Oostanaula River. On the far side of the other coursed the even larger Coosa River. Just across both rivers lurked immense hilltop forts guarding the river roads and effectively barring passage by either flank.

The only way into Rome was the main road that snaked through a pass between the two hills in front of Davis, but the rebels had removed every tree and every bit of foliage from the hill slopes in order to create unobstructed fields of fire. On the crest of both hills, towering over the road and fields, were the unmistakable signs of fortifications: bare, red, freshly-turned earth, log barriers, and the dark, silent muzzles of cannon.

"This," judged Davis, "is the strongest fortified place that I have seen in Dixie."[2]

The Historian

"The Confederates built three main forts here," observed Gilbert Smith, a white-bearded, white-maned historian who devoted his retirement years to the study of the Civil War in Rome. "Each was named for a Rome soldier killed in battle: Fort Norton overlooking the Oostanaula River, Fort Attaway guarding the Summerville Road, and Fort Stovall beside the Coosa River on what is today known as Myrtle Hill."

Near the crest of each hill, the Confederates dug step trenches – ditches eight

Myrtle Hill Cemetery is the final resting place of some 400 Confederate soldiers who died in Rome's four military hospitals. On May 18, 1864, Union artillery shells fired at Fort Stovall on this hill destroyed some of the cemetery's monuments and headstones.

feet deep and ten feet wide with a step at the bottom and a head-log at the rim to provide maximum protection for the defender. It was a daunting task indeed for soldiers faced with the prospect of attacking an enemy ensconced in such protective enclosures.

"While the attackers would be on open ground with no cover from enemy fire, the defenders were protected from head to toe by solid earth and wood," Smith (now deceased) explained. "They (the defenders) had to expose only a fraction of their bodies for a scant moment as they stood, aimed their weapons between the trench and the head log, and fired."

Even more disheartening and dangerous to the Union soldiers were the cannon that were placed within protected earthworks known as embrasures. "In addition to the field artillery," Smith continued, "the Confederates brought in five 64-pounder rifled cannon from Savannah or Mobile. Those were monster guns – sea coastal guns."

The only question in this whole defensive scenario was whether or not there would actually be Confederate soldiers occupying those trenches and manning the cannons when the Yankee troops arrived en masse.

The Crisis

For more than a year, the people of Rome had feared and dreaded this day. "It is now known that Rome is seriously threatened by invasion," warned *The Tri-*

Weekly Courier newspaper in May 1863 after legendary Confederate General Nathan Bedford Forrest thwarted a Federal cavalry raid bent on Rome's destruction. "The citizens of Floyd and our surrounding counties should form a military organization for repelling the thieving, house-burning and vandal foe that may venture upon our soil."

The groundwork for local defense had first been laid a year before when a committee of Romans appointed three men in each militia district to recruit a home defense unit. The results were laudable. By mid-1863, units like the Floyd Legion, Fort Infantry, and Rome Works Artillery boasted more than 400 volunteers even though most able-bodied men of suitable age had gone off to war several years earlier.

Rome's newspapers also proposed fortifications for the city. "The abolitionists could never drag their heavy long-range guns this far into the country," *The Tri-Weekly Courier* asserted, "but we could bring guns here by rail which would

Rome historian Gilbert Smith (now deceased) spearheaded efforts to have Fort Norton placed on the National Register of Historic Places.

command every pass within three miles of town, and hold them at bay."

Shortly thereafter, the Confederate government authorized the work, and the newspaper rejoiced. "Our beautiful city is to be fortified at once. An experienced and skillful engineer is on the spot ready to direct the good work [and he] calls on the citizens to furnish hands to accomplish the task."

These preparations inspired confidence that Rome was ready for the enemy. "The Dutch Doodles may expect a warm reception should they conclude to visit us," proclaimed *The Weekly Courier*. Though their doom drew nigh, those residents remaining in the city felt there was a chance Rome might be saved.

The Town

Before the war, Rome had been a prosperous town regarded as "the capitol of Cherokee Georgia" (a reference to its central location in the region from which the Cherokee Indians were removed in 1838). After the outbreak of hostilities between North and South in 1861, the town's importance increased, but in ways the people could not have imagined.

The Day the War Came to Rome

"Rome was a very lively place, and soldiers were seen on the streets day and night," observed H.H.Wimpee, a 13-year-old newspaper vendor at the time. "After the battle of Manassas was fought Rome went wild with excitement. The companies from Rome lost heavily in that engagement, both killed and wounded. Then the hospitals were established and the sick and wounded soldiers were brought here from other places."[3]

Given its Western & Atlantic Railroad branch line and numerous large buildings, it was perhaps inevitable that Rome would become an important Confederate medical outpost. But this distinction did not meet with universal approbation. "It is to be deeply regretted that the Government deemed it to its interest to occupy almost the entire city as a Hospital," *The Weekly Courier* lamented in February 1863. "Nine-tenths of the important business houses are now occupied, and laid off into four distinct hospitals [that are] all crowded to overflowing with inmates."

If the citizenry did not whole-heartedly welcome the military presence in Rome, neither did the soldiers find the town entirely satisfactory. "I shall never take a fancy to Georgia," griped Texan B.F. Batchelor. "She has the hottest days, the reddest hills and the most flies of any state under the sun."

What irritated Batchelor even more than the climate, however, were the exorbitant prices the local population charged for food. "The prices charged [are] almost enough to make one's hair stand on end," the bitter Texan complained to his wife in August 1863. "Georgia…is the wooden nut-meg land of the South and is peopled with genuine money loving Yankees. The key to their good will is money, and with it you can almost buy their hopes of Heaven."[4]

Rome artist Hoyt Brown recently sketched dismounted Texas cavalry defending Fort Attaway during the Union attack.

Brigadier General Jefferson C. Davis's 2nd Division, 14th Army Corps, moved on Rome, which Davis called "the strongest fortified place that I have seen in Dixie."

Ironically, Batchelor never returned to his native Texas and loving wife. He would be killed in battle just ten miles west of Rome five months later, and was buried in the place he so adamantly disliked.

The local population of Rome – and indeed the entire South by this time – fully shared in the despair over the economy and hugely-inflated prices of which Batchelor complained. Everything was in short supply or totally unavailable.

"The prices of clothing began to go up skywards," H.H. Wimpee recalled. "Everything was hard to get even if you had the money to pay for it. Times were so hard that the county and town had to establish a commissary for the soldiers' wives and children, who had nothing to eat."

The hard times were not alleviated by the onset of spring in 1864, either, but war news overshadowed everything else. All eyes were on the front lines just 50 miles north of Rome.

"Battle after battle was fought," observed Wimpee, "and then began the retreat of the Army of Tennessee under Gen. Joe Johnston. Sherman's army swung around towards Rome; our cavalry held them in check out at Dry Creek and skirmished with them until night. The people that could get away left Rome; others that had no conveyances had to stay and take the consequences."

For two years, Rome had prepared for this day. Now the Yankee invaders had finally arrived. The city was about to taste devastation.

The Peril

Jefferson Davis had gone out on a limb and knew it full well. The orders given to him by William Sherman the day before required Davis to cross the Oostanaula River above Rome at the mouth of Armuchee Creek. His mission was to place his Second Infantry Division between Rome and the main body of the Confederate army at Adairsville. But despite the fact there was no bridge and the water was too deep to ford, Davis declined to give up. Instead, he impulsively pushed on south toward Rome, hoping that he might surprise the town's garrison and capture the bridges intact.

Now, Davis had his division in a very delicate situation. In front loomed Rome's fortified heights manned by a force of undetermined strength. To the left lay the Oostanaula River separating Davis from any support or reinforcements from Sherman in the event of crisis. And to the right lay... well, nothing. Davis *was* the right.

The Attack

For most of the morning, Davis' Second division had moved steadily south through the countryside towards Rome, his skirmishers pushing back a thin screen of Confederate pickets.

For some reason, news of this Federal advance did not reach Sam French, the ranking Confederate officer in Rome, until mid-day. French, who was simply trying to get his division to General Johnston in Adairsville as quickly as possible, made a snap decision to defend Rome, and sent Ector's brigade a mile north into Fort Attaway's entrenchments.

Thanks to French's quick thinking, 2,000 gray infantrymen occupied the earthworks when Davis and his Union army troops arrived, instead of the skeleton force of 150 cavalry that had been there just a short time earlier. Then, in the same time it took Davis to deploy his division for battle, several thousand Confederate reinforcements – mostly battle-hardened Texas and Alabama cavalrymen – arrived on the scene.

Noting that the Union army advancing on them was somewhat disorganized and lacking in visible artillery support, the Confederates launched a bold and unexpected attack. General Lawrence S. Ross's dismounted Texans charged the Union center, driving back the surprised Federals nearly a mile.

Eventually, Ross concluded that he could go no further. "Finding the enemy's force so far superior to my own in numbers, and being almost enveloped by the wings of his line, which had not fallen back as the center was driven," Ross reported, "I deemed it prudent to withdraw my command from its advanced position."[5]

Upon their return, the cavalrymen received a surprising welcome. Ector's infantrymen, who were impressed by the horse-soldiers' pluck, applauded the Texans. "[We moved] back to the breastworks in perfect order amid the most extravagant plaudits of the infantry who being witnesses said they did not believe cavalry could fight like [we did]," a trooper proudly recalled.[6]

Surprising Slaughter

Alarmed by the Confederate onslaught which struck his 2nd Brigade, Jefferson Davis ordered forward his 3rd Brigade in support. These men, under the command of Colonel Dan McCook, promptly moved to a ridge east of the Summerville Road (possibly the knoll where Oak Hill, Martha Berry's residence, stands today). Not content to stop there, the foot-soldiers continued forward, advancing up yet another hill. Near the top of this ridge they found the Southerners waiting. The blue and gray riflemen opened fire on each other, laying down a hail of lead in a bloody pitched battle for control of the high ground.

From Fort Attaway, Texan Martin King had a birds-eye-view of the Yankee advance. "The valley was in farms on either side of the road and timber and low flat land where we could not see them [the Yankees]. The battle line came sweeping up from this place through the hills and formed a solid column right across the valley."

A desperate struggle for the possession of the heights ensued. "The Yankees were determined to break through our line," King grimly noted. "On they came with a shout and fixed bayonets, but the boys poured such volleys into their line that it wavered, reeled and fled back to the woods."

Still the Federal soldiers would not give up. "Here," King noted with a hint of admiration, "they reformed and returned with determination to sweep the valley but she would not be swept. Their line forced itself within 20 feet of ours, and it seemed they would mix it with hand-to-hand fighting, but at this juncture, our boys drew their six-shooters and then the Yankees began to tumble into piles. Their line came to a dead halt and stood still for at least ten seconds when it reeled and fled in great confusion."[7]

Having suffered some 400 casualties and with reports of a Confederate force of undetermined strength threatening to his right, Davis decided to call it a day. Despite his losses, he felt good about his day's work.

Davis' Second Division had marched 18 miles, engaged in battle, and now occupied a strong defensive position within a short distance of Fort Attaway and Rome. "My lines as now established," Davis boasted to Sherman, "completely invested the enemy's works on the west banks of the river; my left being so near the Oostanaula and my right so near the Coosa, as to prevent my flank from being turned from either direction."[8]

The Withdrawal

During the night of May 17, Davis' men feverishly built breastworks in expectation that the battle would resume the following morning. By this point, however, events elsewhere had taken control of the situation and sealed Rome's fate in the process.

Having withdrawn his army to Cassville, General Joseph E. Johnston realized that Rome could no longer be held. Orders were issued and, at midnight, Sam French quietly withdrew Ector's and Ross's brigades from Fort Attaway and evacuated Rome. Only a small force of skirmishers remained behind to guard the town.

The sudden evacuation took the people of Rome by surprise. "Going down town [I] found all the cavalry and artillery in the street and headed for the Etowah Bridge showing strong indications of an evacuation [and] which at 10 o'clock we find in full retreat," Reuben Norton jotted in his diary. "It was very unexpected and unaccountable [given] the force and strong position we had."[9]

The Confederate soldier pictured on the right, Thomas Asbury of Rome, served in the 8th Regiment, Georgia Volunteer Infantry, and the 1st Regiment, Georgia Volunteer Cavalry. The soldier who posed with him is unidentified.

At 9 a.m. the following morning, in a dense fog, Davis' skirmishers groped their way up DeSoto Hill and, to their immense relief, found Fort Attaway unoccupied. Davis promptly placed two artillery batteries in the earthworks and ordered his skirmishers forward to measure the level of further Confederate resistance. Brisk artillery fire from Forts Norton and Stovall checked the Union advance and quickly convinced Davis that he needed to find an easier way into Rome.

Davis decided to send the 85th Illinois Regiment across the Oostanaula River well above Fort Norton to threaten Rome from a different direction. The men of the 85th got to work building rafts out of fence rails. Upon finishing, they stripped, loaded the rafts with their rifles, ammunition, and clothing, and swam across the Oostanaula pushing the rafts before them.

Rome was strategically important to both armies in the War Between the States. It was an important commercial center, both in shipping and in the production of supplies such as munitions, cannon, and medical supplies. It also was on the route of Sherman's destructive advance on Atlanta.

"Once on the other side," recalled a bluecoat, "a skirmish line was quickly formed under the direction of Colonel Dilworth and other officers of the Eighty-fifth, which drove the enemy from the city and raised the banner of freedom over rebellious Rome."[10]

Powerless to stop the oncoming Federal regiment and realizing that "the jig was up," the tiny Confederate garrison that had remained behind "defending" Rome withdrew, yielding the city to "the thieving, house-burning and vandal foe."

The Desecration

For the rest of the day, Confederate artillery in Fort Stovall on Myrtle Hill continued to duel with Federal artillery near Fort Attaway. The exchange of fire reportedly resulted in a few casualties, but some of the Union shells fell on sacred ground.

"One thing I deplored," wrote a Texan who witnessed the bombardment. "A grave yard (Myrtle Hill) lay right in front of us and their shots knocked the nice monuments into thousands of pieces."[11]

Finally, even these last Confederate artillerymen withdrew to the southeast. During the ensuing six months of Union occupation, Rome would become an important Federal supply and medical depot. Eventually, however, William Sherman decided to abandon the town in preparation for his "March to the Sea." While carrying out Sherman's orders to destroy public property, Union soldiers burned most of Rome on the night of November 10, 1864.

Endnotes

1. Davis, Major George W. 1897. *War Of The Rebellion: Official Records Of The Union And Confederate Armies* (U.S. Government Printing Office, Washington, D.C.), Series I, Vol. 38, Park IV pp. 717-18.
2. Ibid at page 235.
3. Wimpee, H.H. "A Boy's Recollections Of The Civil War At Rome, Georgia," included in a notebook on file in the Special Collections Room, Sara Hightower Regional Library in Rome, Georgia, entitled "Confederate Memories From The Files Of Rome, Georgia, UDC Chapter."
4. Rugeley, H.J.H, annotated by, 1961. *Batchelor-Turner Letters, 1861-1864: Written by Two Of Terry's Texas Rangers.* (Stick Company, Austin Texan).
5. Ibid note 1, Series I, Vol. 38, Park III, p. 963.
6. Kerr, Homer L., ed., 1976. *Fighting With Ross' Texas Cavalry Brigade C.S.A.: The Diary of George L. Griscom, Adjutant, 9th Texas Cavalry Regiment.* (Hill Junior College Press, Hillsboro, Tx), p. 187.
7. Keen Newton A., 1986. *Living And Fighting With The Texas 6th Cavalry* (Butternut Press, Inc., Gaithersburg, Maryland), p. 55.
8. Ibid note 1, Series I, Vol. 38, Part I, p. 629.
9. May 17, 1864 entry in the diary of Reuben S. Norton. A microfilmed copy of the Norton diary is on file in the Special Collections Room, Sara Hightower Regional Library, Rome, Georgia.
10. Aten, Henry J., 1901. *History Of The Eighty-Fifth Regiment, Illinois Volunteer Infantry* (Regimental Association, Hiawatha, Kansas), p. 172.
11. Ibid note 7, pg. 56.

TRACED WITH FIRE, WRITTEN IN BLOOD

During the Civil War, the people of northwest Georgia endured cataclysmic battles, deprivation, death, and six months of enemy occupation. But even darker and more perilous times would follow the invaders' departure.

DANIEL M. ROPER

The early morning sun cleared a tree-covered ridge and light gleamed in the farmer's eyes. He stood straight, shielding his eyes against the brightness, and looked with satisfaction at the field of dark green, waist-high corn. Behind him, from the direction of the house, came the ordinary sounds of the morning - his wife, Jane, feeding clucking chickens, youngest son Tommie drawing water from the well, and youngest daughter Maggie scolding a mule that had once again wandered into her flower garden.

The farmer's thoughts turned briefly to his eldest sons. He hoped that today, perhaps, the mail would bring a letter from Joseph who was fighting Yankees somewhere near Atlanta. Then, with a stab of still-fresh pain, he thought of James, who left the valley in the autumn of 1861, marching away smartly with the "Freemen of Floyd," only to return three months later in a pine coffin, victim of a deadly measles outbreak at an army camp near Savannah.

Just as the farmer turned his attention back to his corn, he heard the unmistakable sound of mounted troops. He glanced up and saw cavalry advancing slowly up the valley road - so stealthily that he had not noticed the troopers until he heard the creak of saddle leather, the whinny of a horse, and a command uttered by an officer.

An unnatural stillness crept over the farm. The farmer's wife called out in quiet urgency and he saw that she and the children were heading to the house. When he turned to take a final look at the troopers, a gentle breeze stirred the dust, briefly whipping the flag on a staff carried by one of the horse soldiers. It was, as he had suspected, the Stars and Stripes. The farmer laid down his hoe and walked resignedly toward the house.

Inside, his wife picked up the treasured bundle of letters from Joseph and James. She clutched them to her chest and a weary sigh escaped her mouth. After three long years of war, the enemy had come to Texas Valley.

The Cruel Invader

By July 1864, Federal troops had already been in nearby Rome, Georgia, for two months, but none had ventured out as far as Texas Valley. Places like the Joseph Espy farm were simply too remote to invite attention until all of the countryside near Rome had been picked over. With each passing day, tension mounted as the Espys and their neighbors awaited the enemy's inevitable arrival.

Joseph Espy had acquired his Texas Valley land in 1850. By the eve of the Civil War a decade later, Joseph (age 58, according to the 1860 Census) and Jane (53) had a prosperous farm where the family grew wheat and corn and raised cattle and swine. At that point, the household included their children, Joseph G. (22), James H. (18), F. Margaret (23), and David Thomas (10). Daughter Mary had already married and lived nearby.

Judging from the family's Civil War-era correspondence now on file at the University of North Carolina, the Espys were hard working, sober minded, devout, and affectionate. The death of young James in February 1862 devastated the family. His older brother Joseph joined the Confederate army later that year and was likewise sickly, spending many weeks confined in army hospitals in places like Kingston, Forsyth, and Greensboro, Georgia. Consequently, his parents and siblings lived in constant dread that he might suffer the same fate as his younger brother.

On the occasions when Joseph was fit for duty during late 1863 and early 1864, he was often stationed just a day or two's ride from home. His regiment, the 65th

COURTESY GEORGIA DEPARTMENT OF ARCHIVES & HISTORY

The caption to this photograph specifies the location as Texas Valley, circa 1890 and reads: "Old Espy home with family standing in front. It was one of the first homes in the area and was still standing as of October 1977." Census records and other historical documents indicate that the Joseph Espys were the only Espy family residing in Texas Valley in 1890. Therefore, this photograph most likely depicts Joseph Espy (center, with beard), wife Olivia, their children, possibly Joseph's sister Margaret, and other family members. The Espy farm stood near the site of Old Antioch Baptist Church Cemetery but the house and church were moved in the 1980s to make way for Oglethorpe Power Company's Rocky Mountain hydroelectric project.

While husband Robert was far from home serving in the Confederate army as a surgeon, Martha Battey remained in Rome to tend to their home and children. The burning of the city by Federal troops, raids by guerilla fighters, and the murder of neighbor Nicholas Omberg in the autumn of 1864 threatened to unnerve the young mother, but she persevered. She and her husband survived the war and enjoyed long and prosperous lives in Rome.

Georgia Infantry, was part of the Army of Tennessee and participated in the Battles of Lookout Mountain and Missionary Ridge in November 1863 and the Confederate withdrawal towards Atlanta in the spring of 1864. When the armies clashed, Texas Valley was close enough to the front lines for the Espys to hear the not-so-far-off sounds of battle. Thus, the family often knew precisely when Joseph might be under fire, and they fretted about his welfare and the obvious progress of the enemy advance.

The last time that the Espys and their Texas Valley neighbors had known real peace-of-mind had been the previous spring when Nathan Bedford Forrest's Confederates routed Abel Streight's Federal cavalry raiders near Rome. The presence of Confederate troops in the area had discouraged outlaws, prompting Margaret ("Maggie") Espy to write, "The bushwackers are about all sceered out of this country."

The respite was temporary. When the Confederate Army headed north towards Chickamauga a few months later, outlawry returned. In mid September, Maggie wrote of horse thieves and of her hope that the home guard would stop them from "strolling about" the valley.

The situation deteriorated markedly following Union victories in battles around Chattanooga later that autumn. The Confederate army retreated to Dalton leaving open the vast territory between Rome and the Federal army's winter camps near Ringgold.

Over the ensuing months, Union cavalry raids struck deep into northwest Georgia. Letters penned by the Espy family indicate that neighboring Chattooga County was a frequent target.

"The news has come here that there was a raid of Yankee cavalry to Dirt Town [today called Tidings] a few days ago and captured some of the home guards and all their arms and camp equipage," wrote Maggie in January 1864. A few months later, she reported sadly: "There is said to have been a Yankee raid at Summerville yesterday was a week ago and also at Tryon Factory. They are said to have shot one of Larkin Davis's sons and he died on Saturday morning. We so frequently hear of the Yankees being at Summerville we never know when to think it is true."

The people in the valley dreaded the arrival of the invading army, but that event was surprisingly long in coming. The large Federal forces that moved on Rome in May 1864 bypassed Texas Valley, advancing so rapidly that none had an opportunity to detour into the valley. The Espys and their neighbors therefore carried on unmolested for some time while Rome felt the lash of the enemy's whip.

The valley people endured this period totally isolated from friendly forces and organized civil government, always apprehensive that danger and calamity could strike at any moment. Joseph, who by then was stationed near Marietta, understandably feared for his family's welfare.

Sister Maggie hastened to reassure her brother, writing in late June, "We have so far been blessed with [the enemy's] absence which I feel assured will be very welcome news to you. We understood that a report has gone out that we are all torn up but that is a mistake so far as concerns this neighborhood up to the present time."

This surprisingly peaceful interlude in the midst of the terrible war continued for more than two full months. "The enemy has not yet been in here which is a blessing we ought ever to be thankful for - it is one undoubtedly bestowed by Divine Providence," Maggie noted gratefully in late July. "I expect the people in this section is fairing much better than you think for our settlement has so far been blessed by the absence of the cruel invaders and if this great favor continues to us we will have all we need to desire to live on."

The false peace ended shortly thereafter. The first enemy troops arrived at the Espy farm in early August. "They come in the valley across the mountains near [Simpson] Fouché's plantation in the night and stayed til day light," Maggie reported matter-of-factly. "They took nearly all the horses in the valley that they found."

Incidents like this continued for the rest of the summer and well into the autumn months. Later in August, Maggie wrote, "There was one raid through the valley last week but only 4 of the invaders come here. They plundered about the house but took nothing of any value."

A neighbor whose husband was a Confederate officer was not as lucky. "Mrs. Griffin is here tonight so I have a message for [Lieutenant Griffin] from her," Maggie advised. "In the first place, herself and the children are well and she says tell him she cannot tell how bad she hates the Yankees...They only left her one piece of meat, took all of her tobacco and killed one hog (the sow)."

In September 1864, a newly organized federal cavalry unit comprised mostly of Confederate deserters and Unionists scouted Texas Valley and reported that they "could find no enemy nor hear of any more than twenty, supposed to be the Texans that range in that neighborhood." These Texans must have been a welcome sight to loyal Southerners because the Federal cavalry patrolling the valley was part of the greatly detested 1st Alabama Cavalry Regiment (USA). The 1st Alabama, hissed H.H. Wimpee, a 13-year-old Rome newspaper vendor at the time, "consisted of deserters from the Confederate army, and the scum of the earth. They scouted around over Floyd County, plundered the people's homes, and destroyed what they could not use."

Raiders stripped the countryside of livestock and food stores needed for the upcoming winter. Families in the nearby Armuchee Creek valley suffered similar depredations judging from the post-war reminiscences of Naomi Shropshire Bale.

"Desolation," Ms. Bale recollected, "was writ on all the Valley. For three weeks a hundred in our family literally 'lived from hand to mouth,' picking up scraps of potatoes left in the fields, small scattered turnips, and meat from the cattle which the negroes secured and brought in where cows and hogs had been shot. The new corn left was sufficiently soft to be grated on improvised graters, constructed from the mutilated tin-ware. . . Oh! these were strenuous, perilous times."

Union troops continued to patrol Texas Valley until well after the autumn harvest. On November 7, Sherman ordered one patrol to scavenge northwestern Floyd County where they would "find forage plenty in Texas Valley." Sherman hoped that the presence of Federal troops would also "produce a certain effect," further discouraging residents loyal to the South.

Shortly thereafter, Sherman decided to vacate north Georgia. He burned public (and many private) buildings in Rome, Cassville, Marietta, Atlanta, and other towns, and then embarked upon his infamous "March to the Sea."

News of the conflagrations in the northwestern Georgia towns spread quickly. "We hear today," Maggie Espy wrote two days later, "that a portion of Rome is burned up and the Yanks have evacuated the place." Ironically, this misfortune actually seemed to give Maggie reason for hope. "If this be true," she explained, "we will perhaps have some rest from their vile invasion. They have treated us roughly but not so bad but what we can live if they will let us alone."

Unfortunately, it would be quite some time before a respite of that nature would occur. There were still many hard times and much lawlessness ahead.

No Rest Night or Day

After Sherman departed, roving bands of marauders and highwaymen rampaged through Rome and Floyd County, freely pillaging homes and terrorizing area residents. An anonymous correspondent for the *Sumter Republican* newspaper described the sorry state of affairs around Rome:

"Unfortunately, the country is infested with bands of robbers, claiming to be 'independent scouts' which are committing a great many depredations upon the persons and property of the citizens," the writer penned. "A band of these fellows entered [Rome] on the night of [November 15] and robbed

The graves of Joseph, Olivia, Maggie and other Espy family members stand in the Old Antioch Baptist Church cemetery surrounded by Texas Valley's beautiful lakes and mountains.

several houses, having no reference to age, sex or condition, and went off loaded with money, clothing, blankets, sugar and coffee, and such other articles of value as they wanted."

H.H. Wimpee, the teenage newspaper boy, also endured these dark days of guerrilla warfare. "The people of Rome began to return home [after the Federal army left], but our troubles were not over," he wrote after the war. "The scouting bands of guerrillas and robbers began to infest the country, and Rome was visited by such a gang. Mr. Burwell, Mr. Omberg and J.J. Cohen were hung up to make them give up their valuables. We were certainly in a bad fix. If you had a cow it was driven off at night; you could not have a chicken. If you stepped out from your home your house was plundered, and if you complained you were threatened to have your house burned over your head. Conditions were such you could not tell who was your friend."

The lawless conditions made life especially difficult for Rome's women. "I don't undress for fear they [guerrillas] will come," Martha Battey despaired in a letter to husband Robert, a Confederate army surgeon. "I have no money for them to get, and hope they will spare me. Such a life to lead! No rest night or day! I had expected that when the Yankees left I would get to sleep some at night, but it is worse

Today Texas Valley is a scenic locale of pastures, farms and forests surrounded by beautiful mountains. The farm pictured here lies just a few miles east of the old Joseph Espy farm, much of which today lies immersed under the waters of the Rocky Mountain hydroelectric project.

than ever. You don't know anything about it."

The chaos resulted in bloodshed and the death of one of Rome's leading citizens. "They killed Mr. N. J. Omberg last night," Mrs. Battey reported, referring to Rome merchant Nicholas Omberg. "He was out in the yard, he and Mr. [Terrence] McGuire, and they heard somebody cry out, and ran to old Mrs. Quinn, and found they were hanging Mr. [William] Quinn. They met Mr. Omberg and he asked them who they were. They replied, 'Friends.' Mr. Omberg put down his gun and they walked up to him and took all his greenbacks, then shot him. He lived until today. They robbed Mrs. Lumpkin of everything she had, and Peter Omberg, too."

The sudden, deadly violence left the young mother shaken. "I look for them all night," she despaired.

Write the Words in Blood

Another band of cutthroats plagued the countryside north of Rome. These marauders, led by guerrilla John P. Gatewood, arrived one day at the Wesley Shropshire plantation near Dirt Town. Shropshire, a staunch Union man before the war, had served for a time as Floyd County sheriff but later moved his family to a sprawling plantation on Little Armuchee Creek in southern Chattooga County. The Shropshire place stood near the main road between Rome and Summerville and consequently hosted more than its share of "visitors" during the final years of the war.

Many years after the war, Naomi Bale (Shropshire's daughter) still shuddered at the memory of the first appearance of guerrilla fighters in Dirt Town.

"On the 15th of September 1864, we met 'Scouts,'" she wrote. "Indeed, yes, write the words with blood, drape it with the pall of death, trace it with fire, and then one cannot conceive of the full definition of the word. A horde of these marauders made their camp in our neighborhood, committing the most outrageous atrocities on old men, and feeble men. A gang of perhaps a dozen came to my home, pillaged the house taking everything they fancied. Finally, three of them laid hands on my father swearing he should be hung unless he gave them money, gold or silver. A rope was thrown over his head and with an oath [they] started to put their threat into execution."

Frightened as she must have been, young Naomi came to her father's aid. "I threw up my hands and begged for my father's life with all the earnestness of my soul, assuring them he had no specie [money]," she recounted. "The ringleader looked me steadily in the face and said 'I believe you are telling the truth.' I answered, 'On my honor as a lady, and as sure as there is a God, I am.'"

Her ploy worked. "The rope," she continued, "was taken from my father's neck, the miscreant remarking, 'Old man, you owe your life to your daughter; but for her, we would have hung you as high as Haman [referring to the villain in the Book of Esther who was hung at the gallows]."

Just a month later, the Shropshire plantation suffered depredations at the hands the Federal army. "What the 'Scouts' left was all appropriated by the Federals," Naomi chronicled wearily. "Again our home was pillaged from attic to foundation, large army wagons were loaded to the brim with corn, fodder, wheat, cows driven off or shot, hogs the same, smoke-house stripped, pantry swept of every movable article, and that [which] couldn't be moved was broken. The negroes were huddled together in their houses, scared as sheep among wolves.

"After [the U.S. army] left, we were at the mercy of 'wagon dogs,'" Naomi continued. "Three of these prowlers shut my step-sister Em White and myself in a room, swearing they would search us. Em collapsed in a large rocking-chair. One of the prowlers stood with his back against the door while another prowled bureau drawers, wardrobes, turned up beds, etc. I engag[ed] the third in a conversation holding in my hand a heavy wrought iron poker, with which I occasionally 'punched' the fire, but really to give the fellow a whack should he lay hands on me. That 'dog' never made a movement to touch me, although he said he had 'stripped many a damned good-looking woman as I and searched them!'"

The outlaws then turned their attention to Naomi's stepsister. "The prowler having satisfied himself there was no hidden money or valuables in our room, [he] jerked Em from the rocker and began as though he would strip her," recalled Naomi with obvious dismay. Fortunately, the plucky Southern belle's protests worked. "Again, I begged and he let her go. They left very much disconcerted at their failure in securing valuables."

As it turned out, the frustrations of the "wagon dogs" were fully justified. Em and Naomi indeed had valuables hidden about them. "Hoop-skirts were in vogue then," she explained. "So were full skirts. I had several thousand dollars in Confederate money in a bustle around my waist, and my small amount of jewelry with a few keep-sakes in huge pockets under my hoop. Em had her jewelry, silver forks and spoons etc. in pockets under her hoop."

Finally, farms and plantations picked over and then over again, the marauders departed and families like the Espys, Batteys and Shropshires faced the final, bitter winter of the war.

"Northwestern Georgia and Cherokee Alabama have suffered immensely by the depredations of the depraved invaders," Maggie Espy admitted. Yet even then, she refused to concede defeat. "I think their vile invasions are only doing harm to their cause as it only serves to unite the true hearted in striving for just rights," the resolute young woman concluded.

With the surrender of the Confederate armies and the collapse of the government in the spring of 1865, the long, devastating war finally ended. Joseph Espy and Robert Battey both survived the carnage and made their way back to Rome. They returned to find devastated homes, a desolate countryside, and families that had endured warfare of a different kind – the desperate days of the guerrilla depredations in northwest Georgia.

COURAGE WORTHY OF AN HONORABLE CAUSE

During Sherman's bloody campaign for Atlanta, a quiet farm in the rolling foothills near Dallas, Georgia, became a devil's playground of death, destruction, and despair – a place now known as the Hell Hole.

MARION BLACKWELL, JR.

As I walked near the trenches from which Confederate troops had once poured withering fire into the ranks of attacking Yankees, I suddenly confronted a grubby, ragtag company of Rebel soldiers armed with muzzle-loading rifles, equipped with wooden canteens, and outfitted in an endless variety of mismatched hats, torn and dirty shirts and trousers, and scruffy boots.

These men were Company B of the 32nd Alabama Infantry Regiment, re-enactors on maneuvers through hallowed ground. Every detail of their equipment and accouterments was authentic, as were their attitudes and demeanors. One lounging rifleman told me, "We ain't re-enactors, we're skirmishers."

Visitors to Pickett's Mill Battlefield Historic Site may encounter "ghosts in gray" like these re-enactors from the 32nd Alabama Infantry Regiment.

A hundred yards up the road I found the men of Company A with their regimental photographer using an ancient camera mounted on a tripod to make genuine ferrotype photographs. He hastily carried each photo plate to his portable developing studio and carefully placed it in a tray of chemicals. The developed pictures looked very similar to those produced by noted Civil War photographer George Barnard near this place 145 years ago this spring.

Then a bugle sounded, others answered its call, and three companies of the 32nd Alabama sprang into formation, loaded their rifles, and marched off in the direction of Benjamin Pickett's mill.

Until the summer of 1864, Pickett's Mill in Paulding County was a peaceful place. Built by his father, Malachi Pickett, on land that had been in the family since 1830, the mill was used for grinding wheat and corn into flour and meal for local farmers. Water traveled down a long flume from a dam on Pickett's Mill Creek and poured onto the slots of the over-shot mill wheel. A drive shaft connected to this wheel turned the large mill stones that crushed the wheat and corn.

The war would call Benjamin Pickett from his mill. Little is known of the poignant details of how Benjamin Pickett said his goodbyes to his family before riding off to the Battle of Chickamauga. The Pickett home was up the hill a short distance from the mill. He probably would have shaken hands and said goodbye to J.C. Harris, his partner at the mill, before turning and going uphill for the final time with his family. No doubt he, his 26-year-old wife Martha, and their four

young children shared long embraces, many kisses, and countless tears before he rode off for good.

There would have been more tears if they could have known that Lieutenant Benjamin Pickett of the 1st Georgia Cavalry would die at Chickamauga, and that his mill and home would later be destroyed as an intense battle raged through these Paulding County fields and woods.

The site of this battle is now known as Pickett's Mill Battlefield State Historic Site. The Visitor Center includes a museum, theatre, and maps, all of which enable visitors to understand the complex engagement. Several miles of well-marked trails wind through the rugged terrain and cross Pickett's Mill Creek, offering beautiful hiking opportunities even if one is not interested in the military history of the area.

The Battle of Pickett's Mill was pivotal in General William T. Sherman's Atlanta Campaign. Union forces had systematically pushed General Joseph E. Johnston's smaller Confederate army all the way back from Chattanooga to Kennesaw Mountain. The well-fortified mountain effectively blocked Sherman's approach to Marietta, and then Atlanta. In an effort to avoid having to make a frontal assault on Kennesaw, Sherman attempted a flanking movement around Johnston's left. Union troops moved as rapidly as possible toward the town of Dallas, but poor roads, bad weather, and rugged terrain slowed their pace, enabling the Confederates to extend their lines to face them.

If Sherman's armies could get around the Confederate lines at this point, it

Visitors to Pickett's Mill Battlefield Historic Site will enjoy seeing the log cabin, which occasionally hosts demonstrations of 19th century living.

would enable the Yankees to attack Marietta from the west, without having to assault the heavily fortified Rebels on Kennesaw Mountain.

On May 27, 1864, the armies clashed just north of Dallas. Union forces under General Joseph Hooker fought Confederate troops at New Hope Church, while Federals under General Oliver O. Howard fought Southerners under General Patrick Cleburne at Pickett's Mill.

As Howard's Union forces advanced into a deep ravine they found themselves slowed by a thick undergrowth of briars, bushes, vines, and trees so dense that the soldiers could see only a few feet ahead. Units became disoriented, separated, and lost, and the Union soldiers were exhausted by the tough going in the Georgia heat and humidity.

The Confederates awaiting the Union troops on the higher ground near Pickett's Mill soon began pouring rifle and cannon fire down among the confused enemy ranks. Federal attempts to gain a better position were only partially successful and the bloody ravine soon earned the nickname of Hell Hole, a fiendish place filled with lost, wounded, maimed, and dead boys in blue.

In his report following the battle, Confederate General Patrick Cleburne praised both his own men and their foe: "The enemy advanced in numerous and constantly reinforced lines. His men displayed a courage worthy of an honorable cause, pressing in steady throngs within a few paces of our men…[Confederate General] Granbury's men…were awaiting them, and throughout awaited them with calm determination, and as they appeared upon the slope, slaughtered them with deliberate aim."

The conduct of the men in his command prompted Union General Thomas J. Wood to report, "Never have troops marched to a deadly assault, under most adverse circumstances, with more firmness, with more soldierly bearing, and with more distinguished gallantry." While that may have been true, the bloody repulse of the Union attack so frustrated Sherman that he declined to include the battle in his official report or even later in his memoirs.

As darkness fell on the evening of May 27, 1864, the Battle of Pickett's Mill seemed to be over except for sporadic firing. General Granbury's troops charged into the gloomy woods to clear them of any remaining Yanks, after which Cleburne reported, "The Texans, their bayonets fixed, plunged into the darkness with a terrific yell, and with one bound upon the enemy, but they met with no resistance. Surprised and panic stricken, many (Yankees) fled, escaping in the darkness; others surrendered…"

When the final tally was made, Federal troops killed and wounded totaled about 1,600, while Confederate losses were about 500. This bloody clash, as well as casualties suffered at New Hope Church and Dallas, convinced Sherman that he could not flank Johnston's left. Union forces then withdrew from the Dallas-New Hope-Pickett's Mill area and marched back to their entrenchments facing Kennesaw Mountain, where preparations began for what would prove to be a disastrous assault on the heavily fortified Confederate position on that mountain.

Benjamin Pickett's home and mill were destroyed during the course of the battle, but his family fled and survived. Also destroyed were the home and mill of the

Bob Redmond's illustration of Pickett's Mill before its destruction during the Civil War.

BOB REDMOND

Leverett family and the Zach Brand farm house. All of these structures were demolished not by weapons, but by soldiers who dismantled the structures piece by piece to construct fortifications.

In 1984 Georgia State University completed an extensive archeological study of several sites within the park, primarily around the Zach Brand house. This survey produced numerous pottery shards, buttons, nails, and remnants of household goods, as well as bayonets, Minie balls, and fragments of cannonballs and rifles. Surveyors also discovered evidence that the site was occupied by Stone Age and Native Americans for thousands of years before white settlers moved in. Some of these artifacts are displayed in the Visitor Center.

Visitors to Pickett's Mill Battlefield State Historic Site will enjoy the modern, informative Visitor Center, a pioneer-era log cabin from the 1840s recently moved to the park from its original location, picnic areas, and well-preserved trenches and artillery emplacements. If you're fortunate, you might even encounter the veteran re-enactors of the 32nd Alabama Infantry Regiment who, almost ghostlike in butternut and grey, again stand watch over the Hell Hole at Pickett's Mill Battlefield.

Important information: Pickett's Mill Battlefield Historic Site is located at 4432 Mt. Tabor Church Road, Dallas, GA 30157. For more information telephone (770) 443-7850 or visit http://gastateparks.org/info/picketts/

THE CHATTAHOOCHEE RIVER LINE

An imposing network of fortifications barred the Union Army's way to Atlanta from the north, leaving just one question: Would the enemy dare to assault these earthworks?

By Marion Blackwell, Jr.

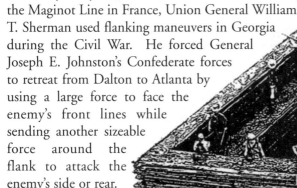

Long before France built the fortified, theoretically invincible Maginot Line along its border with Germany, an early, impressive version of that famous defensive bulwark was built in Cobb County, Georgia, on the hills overlooking the Chattahoochee River. Both fortifications were put to the test and ultimately doomed to the same fate – they were outflanked by mobile enemies.

Seventy-five years before the Germans unleashed lightning warfare and bypassed the Maginot Line in France, Union General William T. Sherman used flanking maneuvers in Georgia during the Civil War. He forced General Joseph E. Johnston's Confederate forces to retreat from Dalton to Atlanta by using a large force to face the enemy's front lines while sending another sizeable force around the flank to attack the enemy's side or rear.

Sherman had the luxury of using this tactic since his army outnumbered Johnston's nearly two to one. Johnston, when faced with the threat to his vulnerable flank or rear, countered by withdrawing and re-entrenching further back. It was either that or face attack on his flanks by a well-armed, more numerous foe.

This pattern of flanking and withdrawing, which historian Bill Scaife refers to as a minuet, continued until the Confederate forces pulled back to the Chattahoochee River just north of Atlanta. In preparation for a determined stand at this vital point, the Confederates built the Chattahoochee River Line – fortifications the likes of which Sherman had never encountered. Built almost entirely by a labor force of more than 1,000 African-American slaves in July 1864, the River Line was a series of connected earthworks meant to prevent Sherman from taking Atlanta.

This George Barnard photograph shows Confederate fortifications northwest of Atlanta, between Peachtree Street and the Western & Atlantic Railroad. While these earthworks were south of the Chattahoochee River line, they portray the lengths to which Confederate engineers went to protect the city.

The River Line included a large artillery stronghold at the northern end of the fortifications in Vinings (at a point near today's Polo Lane) close to the Chattahoochee River. The line of forts crossed Atlanta Road (south of today's I-285), continued south through Oakdale (on the ridge now traversed by Oakdale Road) and continued to another strong point near Nickajack Creek (close to what is now Veterans Memorial Highway).

Brigadier General Francis Asbury Shoup, a brilliant officer on Johnston's staff, designed and supervised construction of the Chattahoochee River Line. Johnston approved Shoup's plan for a string of impregnable fortifications on the hills, and the job was done before the Southern army retreated from Kennesaw to Marietta and then Smyrna.

A graduate of West Point, Shoup was educated in the design and use of military fortifications. Before the war, he was posted at St. Augustine, Florida, and undoubtedly explored and studied the imposing battlements of Castillo de San Marcus. This colonial-era Spanish fort utilized bastions – small, arrowhead-shaped bulwarks protruding from the main fort. Gunners in these bastions could fire into the sides and backs of an enemy approaching the fort's main wall. Likewise, defenders on the main wall could fire at those attacking the bastions.

The Chattahoochee River Line, sometimes called Johnston's River Line, consisted of 36 of these arrowhead-shaped forts connected by a strong wall of log palisades and trenches. Over the years, most of these forts, commonly called "Shoupades," have been destroyed as Vinings and Oakdale developed, but a few still remain today.

The most accessible Shoupade – and the one most likely to be preserved – is that near the southern end of the River Line at Veterans Memorial Highway; another is close to Oakdale Road, partly in an apartment complex and partly in the front yard of a residence; a third lies near Atlanta Road in the "Olde Ivy" development; yet another is found on Fort Drive, off Oakdale Road, and features a Shoupade and an artillery fort recently saved from development through hard and dedicated work by local preservation groups and activists. A few more Shoupades are found in the yards of homeowners and on church grounds.

Sherman had no desire to assault the imposing Chattahoochee River Line. Just a few days before, he had suffered a stinging, bloody defeat when his troops attacked well-entrenched Confederate defenders on the slopes of Kennesaw Mountain. Persuaded that there was little to gain and much to lose in attacking strongly fortified lines, Sherman again resorted to flanking, and about a month later approached Atlanta from relatively undefended points well to the south of Shoup's fortifications.

So, did the Chattahoochee River Line perform the task for which it was designed and laboriously constructed? This question is often debated among students of the Civil War. Some feel that Johnston intended to stop Sherman here, while others argue that the line was only meant to delay the bluecoats until the Confederates could withdraw across the river.

Shoup's plan was based on the hope that Sherman would not proceed against Atlanta with such an impregnable and well-manned fort in his rear. Also, the River Line would command Sherman's supply line, the Western & Atlantic Railroad, threatening his source of armaments, supplies, and personnel. Confederate Generals William J. Hardee and Patrick Cleburne, and Georgia Militia commander General G.W. Smith, praised Shoup's genius in designing and building the line so quickly, but Generals Johnston and John Hood failed to appreciate the complexities and utility of the innovative earthworks.

Following their withdrawal from Marietta and Smyrna, Confederate soldiers briefly occupied the River Line. When Federal forces in hot pursuit encountered the works, bristling with cannons and Shoupades, they prudently decided not to waste lives by throwing men against such an impregnable obstacle.

When General Johnston learned that he had been out-flanked and that Sherman's troops had crossed the Chattahoochee above and below his stronghold, he ordered his troops to abandon the works and withdraw into the fortifications around Atlanta. The River Line did achieve one of its two possible objectives – it protected Johnston's force and gave it time to safely cross the Chattahoochee River and reassemble in Atlanta. The Federal army had, however, greatly diminished the effectiveness of the Chattahoochee River Line the same way the German Army would negate the strength of the Maginot line in 1940 – by sidestepping it.

THE MYSTERY OF
SWEETWATER CREEK

The ruins of this pre-Civil War community and factory have lain dormant for almost 140 years, ever since the day the factory was burned and the workers loaded into railroad boxcars and shipped to prisons in the North. Most of these individuals were never heard from again. Today, an interesting state park highlights this historic site, answering many questions about the ghost town and its former residents.

GARY ELAM

Hiking the Red Trail along the bank of Sweetwater Creek, through the edge of the beautiful, dense woods, I find it hard to believe that this once was Factory Road, the main street of a town of over 200 people. Except for the well-maintained trail, one would be hard-pressed today not to think he or she were simply walking in a north Georgia forest. This peaceful setting, however, hides a dark secret.

Today, Red Trail is an easy walk where one can enjoy mountain laurel, native azaleas, and an assortment of wildflowers under a shady canopy of pine, oak, poplar, and beech trees. A sharp-eyed person can detect the remains of the old millrace, built to divert creek water to a mill. About a half mile from the parking lot, the remains of the old mill itself suddenly come into view, a building that, in 1860, was five stories high – taller than any building in Atlanta.

The factory processed raw cotton into yarn and cloth, obtaining power for its machinery from an undershot waterwheel that weighed approximately 25 tons. Today, the surviving mill walls are the nucleus

of the Sweetwater Creek State Conservation Park – 2,549 peaceful acres about ten miles west of Interstate 285 on the south side of Interstate 20. The skeletal remains of the old factory still show some of the dark charring from the fire set by contingents of Gen. William T. Sherman's troops in 1864.

In addition to some nine miles of blazed trails through the woods, park visitors can enjoy a 215-acre lake (the George Sparks Reservoir), which holds catfish that are mighty good eating, and carp that are amazingly good fighters. The well-stocked bait shop can provide anglers with all manner of fishing supplies, snacks, and other paraphernalia. You can even rent a canoe there if you want.

The large shady lawn area along the edge of the lake is not only a great place for fishing, but also a good spot for young children to pester the ever-present waterfowl, while their parents shoot snapshots. There are boat ramps (electric motors only), a couple of playgrounds, rest rooms, and a dozen picnic shelters scattered around the park.

Inside the visitor center at the park, a staff of congenial, helpful rangers are on-site from 8:00 a.m. until 5:00 p.m., every day of the year – even Christmas Day! Here history buffs and Civil War enthusiasts can peruse old photographs, purchase books and souvenirs, and see a scale model of the old mill up close.

The "modern" story of Sweetwater Creek begins in 1832, six years before Federal troops evicted the Cherokees, Native Americans who had lived in the area for several thousand years. The only remaining tribute to the Cherokees in this vicinity today is the name Jack's Hill, where old Chief Jack supposedly is buried.

It was in 1832 that the State of Georgia began dividing this area into 40-acre land lots, and distributing these lots to the general public via lotteries. Phillip J. Crask must have been ecstatic when he won Lot 929 just eleven miles east of Villa Rica, because gold had just been discovered at that site! Disappointment, however, must have soon followed ecstasy, because by 1837, Crask had paid no taxes, and his land was sold on the courthouse steps to John Boyle for the grand total of $12.50.

Boyle fared considerably better in the real estate market than had Crask. After holding the property for only eight years, he sold it in 1845 for $500.00, an achievement which represented a handsome profit on his investment.

The new owners were former Georgia governor Charles J. McDonald of Cobb County and his business partner, Colonel James Rogers of Milledgeville. The two men no doubt recognized immediately that the topography of Sweetwater Creek was perfect for a water-powered factory. The water in the splashing creek drops 23 feet at the site, and the many slabs of gray creekstones offered plentiful building materials for lining a millrace and forming a foundation for the mill.

The site offered other assets as well. Timber was plentiful, and red bricks could be fired right on the mill property from abundant clay.

As the mill's two-foot-thick brick walls began to rise on the creek bank in 1846, an upstream dam was built across the creek at the entrance to the millrace. A series of gates along the millrace were used to control the flow of water and keep the large wheel turning at the right speed. The millrace funneled water into the mill through the arch on the west (trail) side of the building. The water turned the wheel, then exited through the east side arch and returned to the creek. The tremendous amount of energy generated by the wheel was distributed to machines throughout the building via a complex system of gears, shafts, and leather belts.

The old mill's windows are a study in design today. They flare to the inside

in order to disperse as much natural light as possible throughout the building – a lighting system that eliminated the need for oil lamps which were constant fire hazards.

As the mill and millrace took shape, so also did Factory Town. Its main street, Sweetwater Factory Road, was more than likely its only street. Interestingly, the Brevard Fault Zone runs directly under and along the creek, and has pushed up the nearby cliffs that parallel the creek, making any side roads virtually impossible in the area.

Sweetwater Factory Road ran from the mill north to Ferguson's Crossing, a distance of about half a mile. If one were heading south along this route in the 1860s, Ferguson's Crossing was the last bridge across Sweetwater Creek before it plunged into the Chattahoochee River several miles downstream. For the factory, this ancient road was a link to the railhead in Atlanta. Unfortunately, a few years later, it also became a convenient point of access for invading Union troops.

On December 21, 1849, the Sweetwater Manufacturing Company began production of cotton yarn and cloth. The mill had 60 to 70 workers, and thereby supported a town of more than 200 people. The mill managers built houses high along the wooded bluff above the factory, and rented them to mill families. Other mill workers lived in nearby areas and walked or rode horses or mules to the factory.

A classic "mill town" company store was built at the base of the tree-studded hillside. It supplied the basic needs of the community. The first two floors of the store building were shared by retail space, storage, and the Sweetwater Factory Post Office, which opened in August 1850. The storekeeper and his family lived on the top floor. The only remnant of the old store today is a leaf-filled depression beside the Red Trail.

Following its construction, the mill was soon a busy place, taking in four huge bales of

cotton at a time for processing. The cotton bales were delivered from Atlanta and Marietta by mule wagons. They were brought into the mill on an upper floor, and gradually processed until the fluffy cotton worked its way down to 6,000 spindles and 90 looms where yarn and other products were created. By the late 1850s, the mill was producing 750 pounds of yarn each day.

Charles McDonald had been concerned for a number of years about the growing threat of a war between the South and the North. In 1857, after James Rogers apparently had left the partnership, McDonald reorganized the company as the New Manchester Manufacturing Company. He brought in new machinery that tripled the factory's output, then wisely sold his personal interest in the company for $50,000, a fortune in those days.

The name of the mill town then became New Manchester, and was so shown on the maps of Campbell County (later, Douglas County). At the onset of the War Between the States, the Confederate government contracted with the mill to provide muslin and osnaburg (a strong unbleached cotton fabric, loosely woven, lighter than canvas, but heavier than linen). Osnaburg was used to make clothing, sacking, and tents.

As one might expect, it was this government contract that ultimately proved to be the undoing of the mill as well as most of the mill employees. From the day it became a supplier for the Confederate government, the New Manchester operation became a legitimate military target. During his ruinous "March to the Sea," Sherman ordered the destruction of New Manchester, along with its "sister mill"

in nearby Roswell, Georgia.

On July 2, 1864, Union cavalry from Kentucky and Illinois arrived in the vicinity, and one week later the factories were put to the torch. Amazingly, the mill workers were charged with treason, and became prisoners-of-war. In one of the most controversial actions of the Civil War, the New Manchester POWs – mostly poor women and children – along with "operatives" from the Roswell mill, were herded to Marietta, loaded into railroad boxcars on the Western & Atlantic Railroad, and shipped under deplorable circumstances to Louisville, Kentucky. Here they were detained until they signed an oath of allegiance to the United States; they were then scattered to other detention areas throughout Ohio and Indiana for the duration of the war, most of them never to be heard from again by relatives and friends back in Georgia.

When the war ended, the Roswell mills were rebuilt, but the new Manchester facility was abandoned. For this reason, a City of Roswell exists today in Fulton County, and a ghost town now exists along Sweetwater Creek.

To get to Sweetwater Creek State Conservation Park, take I-20 west from Atlanta. Take Exit #44 (Thornton Road), turn left and go one-quarter mile; turn right on Blairs Bridge Road and follow it to Mt. Vernon Road, then turn left into the park. For more information, telephone (770) 389-7275 or (800) 864-7275, Monday through Friday, 8 a.m. to 5 p.m. As always, www.gastateparks.org will also work for you. Park hours are 7 a.m. to 10 p.m. Annual education programs include History Month Lectures in February, a Native American Festival in June, and a New Manchester Commemoration in September.

ONE LEGGED RUFUS KELLY DEFENDS THE LITTLE TOWN OF GORDON — ALONE

Just one thing stood between the blue hordes under William T. Sherman and the town of Gordon - a one-legged Confederate veteran determined to face the enemy.

HUGH T. HARRINGTON AND ALEXANDRA FILIPOWSKA

In early 1861, James Rufus Kelly of tiny Gordon, Georgia, did what thousands of other young men were doing. He went off to war. Southerners set forth a variety of reasons for enlisting in the Confederate army during the Civil War. Many mentioned "securing their rights," while others desired simply to protect their homes and families from the threat of enemy invasion. In a uniquely personal way, Rufus Kelly got the chance to actually confront the enemy on home soil.

Kelly enlisted in the Ramah Guards, an infantry unit comprised primarily of young men from Wilkinson County, Georgia. The Guards, named for the community's Old Ramah Church, mustered in as Company B, 14th Regiment, Georgia Volunteer Infantry. The 14th Georgia participated in many of the deci-sive battles in the east including Seven Pines, Chancellorsville, and Gettysburg.

A staid Kelley posed for this portrait many years after the Civil War.

Rufus saw many of his comrades fall over the years of bitter strife. He remained in the front lines until he received a serious leg wound on May 23, 1864 at Jericho Ford, Virginia. A piece of shrapnel tore into his flesh and the injury resulted in amputation. A surgeon removed his right leg four inches above the knee.

Four months later, Rufus received his discharge and hobbled back home to Gordon. Not yet 20 years old, he was crippled for life and the war was over for him. Or so he thought.

On the March

Two months after his discharge, Kelly found himself right back in the thick of things. In November 1864, General William T. Sherman led his Union army out of Atlanta en route to Savannah. Sherman's left wing, some 30,000 strong, marched east and then south towards Milledgeville, the state capital at the time.

The Confederate force defending Milledgeville was meager. It was a rag-tag assembly of store clerks, Georgia Military Institute cadets, and pardoned prisoners from the State Penitentiary uniformed in striped prison apparel. The unit totaled a laughable 700 soldiers. The commander, General Henry C. Wayne, was a West Point graduate and an experienced officer. He recognized the limited fighting ability of his small contingent of soldiers. Clearly, they were in no position to make a stand against

When Henry C. Wayne prudently withdrew his contingent of Confederate troops from Gordon, an indignant Rufus Kelley remained behind to face the enemy alone.

Sherman's masses. Wayne prudently withdrew his force and marched twenty miles south towards Gordon.

November 21st proved to be another in a long line of cold, bleak days for the Georgia Militia. The Confederacy was on the ropes and there was little good news to warm the hearts of Wayne's refugee army. They huddled around fires in Gordon while the right wing of Sherman's army, another 30,000 veteran soldiers, made a feint towards Macon and advanced toward Gordon from the west.

General Wayne knew that he must retreat yet again. This time he intended to lead his troops east, following the railroad across the Oconee River. There they could take up a stronger defensive position on the river's east bank.

As he sat on the porch of Gordon's Solomon Hotel contemplating the dim prospects for his makeshift army, General Wayne was surprised to see a young man on horseback ride into town. The rider wore civilian clothes, carried a rifle, and had a pair of crutches strapped to his horse.

The one-legged horseman approached the general, snapped a salute, and introduced himself as Rufus Kelly. When Kelly offered to ride west and keep an eye out for the approaching Union army, General Wayne told him to go ahead. Kelly saluted and left immediately.

It was supposed to be a special day for Rufus Kelly. It was his 20th birthday, but there wasn't going to be a celebration. Instead, the events about to unfold would give him legendary status in Wilkinson County for many years to come.

Much of what is known today about Kelly's actions comes from T.D. Tinsley, an eyewitness who penned a 1927 *Confederate Veteran Magazine* article about the day's events. According to Tinsley, Kelly galloped back into Gordon just a few hours after his departure. He reported to General Wayne that thousands of Union soldiers were approaching from the west. Wayne thanked him for the information and Kelly left town to continue his observations.

Demoralizing Retreat

Wayne issued orders for his motley army to board the train and for the engineer to travel east as soon as the engine got up steam. When the soldiers finished loading and the train was ready to depart, General Wayne climbed aboard the last car and took a seat. Glancing out the window, his eyes took in the startling sight of Rufus Kelly riding into town, his horse pounding down the dusty road.

Wayne went to the rear platform and received Kelly's report that the Yankees had arrived at the edge of town and would attack any minute.

Kelly was, in turn, astonished to find the Confederate soldiers preparing to depart. His emotions got the best of him

William F. Chancellor served with Rufus C. Kelley in the 14th Georgia Infantry Regiment. The uniform and equipment suggest that this photograph was taken early in the war. In 1863, Chancellor served in a firing squad that executed a deserter from the Ramah Guards.

and he blurted out, "General, what does this mean? Don't we make a stand?"

General Wayne replied, "No, it would be ridiculous to attempt to stop Sherman's army with this force. We're going to the Oconee River Bridge where we may be able to hold them."

This news was more than Rufus could withstand. He exploded in anger, "You're a white-livered cur with not a drop of red blood in your veins!" Then he turned to the soldiers and continued his denunciations, "You damned band of tuck-tails, if you have no manhood left in you, I will defend the women and children of Gordon!"

From his vantage point on the train's rear platform, T.D. Tinsley witnessed Kelly turn his horse, face the oncoming enemy, and cock his rifle. As the train slowly gath-

COURTESY HUGH HARRINGTON

This headstone in the Liberty Methodist Church cemetery notes Kelley's service in the Confederate army.

ered speed, Rufus stood resolutely at the station, shooting and loading as fast as he could at the advancing mass of blue-coated soldiers. The sound of his steady firing gradually faded into the distance as the train chugged its way towards the Oconee.

As defeat by the Yankees became evident, Kelly realized that the situation was hopeless. After staring death in the face, the one-legged soldier at length decided that the time had come to beat a hasty retreat. He galloped away, turning occasionally to fire at his pursuers.

Making His Escape

When Kelly neared a thicket of woods, he turned the horse off the road in hopes of escaping detection. This sudden maneuver proved too much. Kelly lost his balance and fell to the ground. His horse, along with his crutches, continued on, disappearing from view into the timber.

Within moments, Kelly was surrounded and taken prisoner by a body of Federal cavalry. They interrogated him about the terrain, but he refused to provide useful information to the enemy. The federals then tried to persuade Kelly to cooperate by reminding him that he was in civilian clothing and would be shot, within a few days, for spying. When that didn't work, they loaded him onto a wagon and carted him off with the rest of the prisoners of war.

Since Kelly had only one leg, his guards understandably did not consider him much of an escape risk. But they had misjudged their man. Several days later, the unit camped beside a swamp near Sandersville, Georgia. That night, Kelly rolled out of the wagon and alternately crawled and hopped into the swamp using a branch for a crutch.

When he had carried himself as far as he was able, he faced yet another peril. He was in a swamp, soaking wet, during one of the coldest Novembers on record. Rufus Kelly was in danger of freezing to death.

One Legged Rufus Kelly Defends the Little Town of Gordon–Alone

With renewed vigor, Kelly continued moving. Eventually, several hours later, he saw the flickering light of a campfire in the distance. He knew that it could possibly be Union soldiers or deserters from either army, but he had no other choice at that point. The longer he remained in the swamp, the greater his chances of dying from exposure. He had to seek shelter from the people at the fire even if it meant being recaptured.

The men around the campfire were startled when a one-legged man covered in mud and shivering uncontrollably staggered out of the swamp. To his good fortune, Rufus had stumbled upon refugees hiding from Sherman's army.

Kelly recuperated at their camp for several days. Then, when the Yankees moved on, the refugees abandoned their hiding place and returned home. Kelly made his way to the family farm near Gordon.

Rufus Kelly had fought his last battle, evaded recapture, and never again would go to war.

Post-War Years

After the war, Rufus Kelly taught school in a one-room building close to Gordon. He eventually received a $100 per year pension from the State of Georgia for his service to the Confederacy and was eligible to receive an artificial limb, which he declined to accept. He later married and raised a family.

From time to time an enterprising newspaper reporter or magazine writer tracked down Kelly for a story and at least one poem was written about his defense of Gordon. When the brave, aged defender passed away on September 19, 1928, he was the sole surviving member of Company B, 14th Georgia Infantry. He rests in the Liberty Methodist Church cemetery in Twiggs County.

THE SAGA OF SAVANNAH'S CIVIL WAR IRONCLADS

During the Civil War, the shipbuilders of Savannah constructed four powerful iron-clads that struck fear into the hearts of the crews on Union blockaders. The only question was whether these Confederate warships would venture out of port to give battle.

JIM MILES

Just six days after the surrender of the United States garrison at Fort Sumter in April 1861, President Abraham Lincoln issued a proclamation authorizing the blockade of Southern ports. In response, the Confederate States quickly moved to augment coastal forts with a fleet of armored warships. Savannah was one of many Southern cities transformed into a naval shipbuilding center, and by the end of 1864 the ironclads *Georgia, Atlanta,* and *Savannah* had been launched and commissioned there, and a fourth, the *Milledgeville*, was nearly complete.

Construction of the Savannah ironclads was slowed by a lack of iron plating and engine parts, problems that plagued the entire Confederate Navy. Most of the armor consisted of flattened railroad rails bolted to a thick interior framework of oak and pine, and the overworked Confederate rail system couldn't spare many rails.

Propulsion machinery for the ironclads was manufactured in Columbus, Georgia, and was generally of good quality, but proved inadequate to move such heavy vessels. The completed ironclads were so slow, unstable, and so difficult to maneuver that they were useless as rams and ocean raiders. Even excursions across a calm river were adventurous, making the behemoths useful primarily as floating batteries used in support of Fort Jackson and Savannah's newly constructed earthworks. Although abject failures at their intended purpose of raising the Union blockade, the presence of the ironclads was nonetheless a serious deterrence to Union forays up the Savannah River.

Even if the ironclads had been fit for extensive travel, they would have been hampered by a chronic lack of fuel. Only 45 coal cars were available to support the needs of the naval vessels at Columbus, Savannah, and Charleston. Eventually, these three ports were defended by a total of nine ironclads and numerous smaller vessels, and fuel was always in short supply.

The Savannah ironclads leaked badly because they were made of green timber caulked with cotton. Pumps operated continuously to keep the ships afloat, and with time the situation worsened as ravenous worms weakened the wooden hulls. A sailor stationed aboard the *Georgia* called her a "box (for she is not a vessel)," and added that conditions were "horrible. She is not fit command for a sergeant of marines."

Likewise, the *Savannah*, a floating sieve, was a miserable place to live and work.

Designed to be impervious to heavy enemy shells, the armor denied men working below deck both light and ventilation, and working conditions in the stifling Savannah summer heat were all but intolerable. The interior of the ironclad was so suffocating that the crew had to live on a tender.

Deserters from the *Savannah* who reached the Federal garrison at Fort Pulaski claimed her crew was very unhappy with conditions aboard. One sailor wrote, "I would defy anyone in the world to tell me whether it is day or night if he is confined below without any means of marking time…I would venture to say that if a person were blindfolded and carried below and turned loose he would imagine himself in a swamp, for the water is trickling in all the time and everything is so damp."

Ladies Gunboat and Mud Tub

Savannah's first attempt to build an ironclad produced the *Georgia*, often called the "Ladies Gunboat" because women in cities across the state, including Savannah, Augusta, Macon, Milledgeville, and Rome, raised $75,000 of her $115,000 cost. Work on the *Georgia* increased to a feverish pace when Fort Pulaski fell to a Union bombardment in April 1862, an incident that Savannahians believed was a prelude to an attack on the city from the sea. That threat never materialized, but the ship was hurriedly completed in six weeks and launched in May 1862.

Her workmen started with an old barge and built a thick wooden gundeck, or casemate, with a steep slope of 45 degrees to deflect enemy shot. Iron four inches

In 1862, noted artist Alfred R. Waud sketched a Confederate "flag of truce" fleet in the Savannah River going down to the Leary & Hermann Livingstone to take off exchanged "rebel" prisoners.

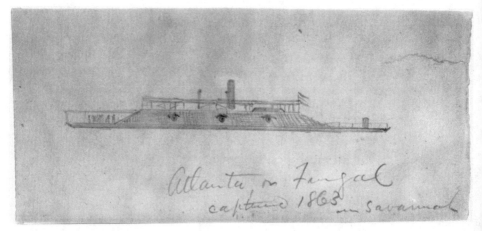

The SS *Fingal* was a steamship converted into an ironclad and renamed CSS *Atlanta*. Waud sketched it in 1863.

thick weighing 500 tons covered the gun deck, mostly a double layer of railroad T-iron fitted together. The *Georgia* was a trial and error experiment by workers who had scant shipbuilding experience. Because they left no plans, drawings, or records of the ironclad's construction, estimates of her dimensions range from 260 feet in length and 60 feet in width, to 160 feet by 50 feet. A recent underwater survey of her wreckage at the bottom of the Savannah River near Fort Jackson shows 120 by 44 feet to be a more accurate measurement. Her casemate was probably 12 feet high, with her armored sides ending at the waterline.

The *Georgia* was armed initially with three 32-pounder rifled cannon, two nine-inch smoothbores, and other guns that fired from ten armored gunports, one on each end and four in each broadside. Lieutenant Washington Swathmey commanded her compliment of 13 officers and 109 sailors.

As a ram, or even as a moveable vessel, the *Georgia* was an utter failure. In a class of ships famous for their lack of propulsive power, the *Georgia* ranked dead last. Her inadequate engines could not generate enough propulsion to overcome tidal currents. The current of the Savannah River flowed at four knots an hour; the *Georgia* could make but two knots.

The *Georgia* soon became a pathetic joke, variously described as a "marine abortion," "a splendid failure," and a "nondescript marine monster." Mariners called it "a swamp in an iron box" and a "mud tub." She was towed to a specially prepared log pen near Elba Island and opposite Fort Jackson, ready to fire a broadside to guard the shipping channel of the Savannah River. The much maligned ship was thus reduced to the status of floating artillery battery.

Despite her flaws, however, *Georgia's* mere existence terrified Union naval officers. According to one naval commander, all of his officers "imagine they see iron-clads and rams." This prospect, he noted, made one officer "look 10 years older," another "will go crazy next," and a third "is broken down."

Branded as Cowards

While the *Georgia* was taking shape, construction began on a second ironclad, the *Atlanta*. Her first incarnation was as the steamship *Fingal*, one of the first vessels secured by the Confederacy to run the blockade.

Purchased in Scotland in September 1861, *Fingal* was immediately loaded with a priceless cargo of 10,000 rifles, one million cartridges, cannon, pistols, swords, and medical supplies. Her uneventful maiden cruise took *Fingal* first to Bermuda and then into Savannah on November 12 of that year. The coal shortage delayed a return trip to England for a month. By the time *Fingal* was finally fueled and packed with cotton intended for hungry English textile mills, a Federal blockading fleet appeared and sealed tight the sea routes out of Savannah.

Unable to escape as a blockade runner, Confederate officials elected to convert *Fingal* into an ironclad of the *Virginia* [also known as the *Merrimac*] class. She was cut down to the deck, which was widened and strengthened with three feet of wood and iron plate. A casemate, sloping 30 degrees to deflect shot, covered the gundeck. The armor consisted of two layers of two-inch thick, seven-inch long flattened railroad iron secured by large bolts to three-inch thick oak timbers and 15-inch pine timbers.

Fingal received two seven-inch guns and two six-inch rifled cannon mounted on pivots that could be swiveled to fire out of the eight shuttered gunports, one each at bow and stern, and three on either side. An iron sheathed ram was added to the bow, along with a spar for a torpedo that would detonate on contact with another vessel. This formidable looking warship was 204 feet long and 41 feet wide. As a result of her reinforced hull and armor, she drew 16 feet of water, twice what she had drawn as an ordinary steamer.

After six months of labor, the ship, rechristened the *Atlanta*, was completed in July 1862. With her iron hull and efficient English machinery, she was the most mechanically reliable Confederate ironclad built to that date, but she still leaked. Moreover, the armor plating reduced her speed from 12 miles-per-hour to six miles-per-hour. A midshipman called the officers' quarters "the most uncomfortable I have ever seen" and he complained that his only personal possessions were two hooks from which he slung his hammock.

The *Atlanta*'s initial cruise panicked Fort Pulaski's Federal garrison. A New York Herald correspondent wrote that without Union monitors to counter the threat posed by *Atlanta*, the blockading ships "have before them an excellent opportunity of learning what it is to be blown out of the water."

These fears proved premature, however, for the *Atlanta* endured four additional months of shakedown cruises in vain attempts to correct steering and leakage problems. By January 1863, the ironclad had been commissioned, but missed several opportunities to accomplish a *Virginia*-like victory against the all wooden blockading fleet. When the *Atlanta* crept down the Savannah River to attack the Federal fleet that month, its path was barricaded by obstructions – stone filled wooden cribs placed by the Confederates to prevent a Union fleet from coming up the river to attack Savannah – so she couldn't close on the Union ships.

The *Atlanta* could only clear the river obstacles at high tide. Her next attempt to attack the Union fleet in February was thwarted by winds that prevented the tidal surge. In late January 1864, Federal Admiral Samuel F. DuPont, in command of the South Atlantic Blockading Squadron, learned from sources inside Savannah that the *Atlanta* was about to attack his blockaders, so he ordered the monitors *Montauk* and *Passaic* towed to Savannah.

The *Atlanta*'s captain, Josiah Tattnall, was subjected to intense criticism from several quarters – the public, the South's vocal newspapers, and other military commanders. All blamed him for failing to lift the Federal blockade, relieve pressure on besieged Charleston, and recapture nearby Port Royal, South Carolina, which had been occupied by Union troops early in the war. A Southern sailor expressed his fear that the Navy would be "branded as cowards by the unthinking portion of the citizens of Savannah."

In March, Tattnall sailed to Wassaw Sound and prepared to strike the enemy base at Port Royal. Unfortunately, two Confederate draftees deserted to Fort Pulaski and revealed his plan, prompting the Union commander to order three monitors to take station off Savannah. Tattnall, believing his crudely cobbled ship could not defeat the monitors, and fearing that the Federals would attack Savannah during his absence, canceled the foray until the monitors returned to Charleston.

When several mighty monitors repeatedly attacked Fort McAllister on the Ogeechee River south of Savannah during the winter of 1863, the understandably concerned citizens urged the *Atlanta* to aid those gallant defenders. The ironclad was unable to operate in the Ogeechee's shallow waters, however.

Tattnall was soon relieved of command for his perceived shortcomings in favor of Richard L. Page, who was thought to be a more aggressive officer. Page spent a month attempting to repair the *Atlanta*'s steering, but found himself removed in favor of William A. Webb, who had a reputation for reckless aggressiveness.

When an attack by a flotilla of monitors threatened Charleston in April 1863, Confederate General P.G.T. Beauregard requested that the *Atlanta* make a diversionary attack to relieve the pressure. The general was informed by Savannah authorities that such action was not possible. Later, Beauregard angrily summarized, "None of these Confederate vessels or ironclads were seaworthy, and, beyond river or harbor defense, none of them rendered effective service."

The Confederate Navy Department also faced criticism from the public fueled by newspaper accounts that fostered the myth that the *Atlanta* was the most powerful ship afloat. The Federals shared this opinion, but the ironclad was still a primitive, makeshift gun platform.

Ram Fever

Although a third Confederate ironclad, the *Savannah*, was nearly complete,

Alfred R. Waud sketched the Confederate gunboat *Beauregard* patrolling the Savannah River. Given the river's depth and the obstacles placed in the channel to prevent Federal ships from coming upstream, the bigger ironclad vessels were limited in their ability to navigate the river.

Webb dismissed a suggestion that he wait for her and execute a combined attack on the blockading fleet. The boastful Webb proclaimed that "the whole abolitionist fleet has no terror for me," and he was ready to take on several monitors with just the *Atlanta*.

A week after assuming command, Webb steamed off to attack. An engine failed and he was forced to delay his planned triumphal cruise for yet another month. Hearing rumors of Webb's activity DuPont confided, "We have a ram fever on again." So DuPont promptly dispatched two monitors, the *Weehawken* and *Nahunt*, to Savannah. Both ships were protected by ten inches of turret armor and armed with one 11-inch and one 15-inch smoothbore cannon. They would face the *Atlanta*'s four inches of iron and inferior guns.

According to Webb, his grandiose plan was to "raise the blockade between here and Charleston, attack Port Royal, and then blockade Fort Pulaski." Afterward, he might turn south to Florida waters. The *Atlanta* was provisioned with ammunition and food for an extended voyage, and before dawn on June 16, 1864, her bunkers were filled with coal. The ironclad cast off and proceeded down the Wilmington River to Wassaw Sound with hopes of surprising the patrolling monitors at dawn. Webb intended to sink one monitor with his spar torpedo, then concentrate solid shot at the base of the second monitor's turret to jam it.

At four a.m. the night watch aboard the *Weehawken* shouted an alarm – the *Atlanta* was coming. Captain John Rodgers ordered his crew to stations, and they cleared for action as the monitor steamed directly for the *Atlanta*. John Downes in the *Nahunt* followed.

Sighting the monitors, Webb immediately turned the *Atlanta* out of the channel to engage the Union ships. According to later accounts, Webb's pilots assured

William Waud sketched Thunderbolt Battery, one of many Confederate defensive works guarding the approach to Savannah from the sea.

him there was sufficient water, but the *Atlanta* ran aground on a sandbar. After five minutes of frenzied activity, she was able to back off, but the ponderous battleship could not be steered adequately. She ran hard aground a second time, her gunports poorly positioned to fire on the approaching enemy ships.

At 600 yards the *Atlanta* sent a shot that splashed between the two oncoming monitors. The *Weehawken* held her fire and deliberately stalked to 300 yards, then fired her 15-inch gun. The huge solid shot, propelled by 30 pounds of powder, smashed into the *Atlanta*'s side and dislodged large iron and wooden splinters from the bulkhead, wounding 16 men and rendering 40 more senseless from concussion. The impact knocked the *Atlanta*'s shot out of their racks, adding to the damage. An 11-inch projectile followed, crashing into the lightly armored knuckles, springing a seam and starting a serious leak. The third shot struck a shutter as it was opening to fire, wounding half the gun crew. A final shot ravaged the pilot house, incapacitating both pilots and a helmsman, and stunning a second.

Webb saw no alternative but ignoble surrender. After 15 minutes of battle, *Atlanta* had fired only seven poorly aimed shots that failed to strike a target, and the *Nahunt* was rapidly moving in to join the *Weehawken*. The massive shells fired by these monitors were certain to penetrate the *Atlanta*'s thin armor and wreak destruction on her crew. Webb raised a white flag and addressed his crew: 'I have surrendered our vessel because circumstances over which I had no control have compelled me to do so. You all know that if we had not run aground, the result would have been different, and now that a regard for your lives has influenced me in this surrender, I would advise you to submit quietly to the fate which has overtaken us."

Webb surrendered 165 officers and crewmen, most of them converted infantry, who were imprisoned at Fort LaFayette in New York Harbor. When they were later exchanged, 40 chose to remain and fight for the North.

The *Atlanta* would find her way to sea once again, although not in a manner Webb might have anticipated. The ironclad was taken to the Philadelphia Navy Yard for repairs. In February 1864, she sailed to Fortress Monroe, Virginia, and became part of the United States Navy's James River blockading squadron. The *Atlanta* helped isolate Richmond during the war's final year and was scrapped in 1866.

Loss of the *Atlanta* stunned the people of the South. For months they had read glowing accounts of her invincibility by the Confederate press and expressions of fear in Northern papers. Rumors abounded that her surrender was the result of incompetence, treason, and even mutiny among the crew.

For his easy victory, Captain Rodgers of the *Weehawken* received both a promotion and the thanks of Congress. This resounding victory prompted the production of additional monitors to completely seal Southern ports.

Little But Rust

Work began on the *Savannah* in 1862. Upon her completion in mid-1863, William H. Hunter took command. She was 174 feet long, 45 feet wide, and was armed with five rifled guns. Her engines and boilers were constructed at the Columbus Naval Iron Works. The *Savannah* was considered a powerful vessel but the Union blockade had grown ever stronger. With the unhappy evidence of the *Atlanta's* fighting ability fresh in mind, Confederate naval officials refused to send the *Savannah* out to fight.

A year-and-a-half passed without any Federal attempt to capture Savannah from the sea, but in December 1864, the city's fall to Union General William T. Sherman seemed certain. Plans were drafted to prevent the *Savannah* from falling into Union hands. Preparations were already underway to destroy Confederate Navy property, and a requisition had been made to equip her crew with packs and canteens. These sailors were about to rejoin the infantry.

On December 10, Confederate Secretary of the Navy Stephen Mallory sent these instructions: "Should Savannah fall, do not permit our vessels...to fall into the hands of the enemy. Destroy everything necessary to prevent this." On the 19th, General Beauregard traveled to Savannah from Charleston to meet with Commander T.W. Brent, who was in charge of the fleet in Savannah. They determined that the *Georgia* would be sunk, while the *Savannah* would cover the Confederate army's evacuation out of Savannah, delay Sherman's pursuit, and then fight through the blockade and steam for friendly Charleston.

Confederate General William Hardee, defending the city, requested the *Savannah* and *Georgia* be sent up the Savannah River to protect vital bridges. This plan was not implemented because the *Savannah* drew too much water, and towing vessels were not available for the *Georgia*, which had lain useless for two years at Elba Island and near Fort Jackson. Until this point, these vessels had done little but rust.

When the withdrawal of Confederate troops from Savannah began two days later, the *Savannah* cruised up the river to Hutchinson Island and joined Confederate land batteries in shelling the left of the Federal line to divert attention from the evacuation.

That night, the *Georgia's* guns were spiked and she was scuttled at her moorings. When sailors opened her seacocks, she sank like the rock she was, so quickly that many men were forced to scramble for safety without their possessions. The *Georgia* had never even fired her guns in anger.

The ironclad *Milledgeville*, recently launched but not completed, was burned to the waterline and sank mid-river. She would have been the most powerful ironclad built in Savannah, armed with four heavy guns and armored with six inches of iron rather than the standard four. Despite the weight of her iron, she was not top heavy, thought to be quite seaworthy, and her propulsion system operated on English boilers.

A fifth ironclad under construction was burned on the stocks, along with the building and supplies in the Navy Yard, ship building facilities, steamers, and an unfinished torpedo boat.

Roll of Futility

When the sun rose over a smoke-shrouded Savannah on December 21, 1864, only the *Savannah* remained afloat. Mallory, stung by mounting criticism of the Navy's poor performance, asked Brent to fight the ironclad to the last: "Under any circumstances, it is better that these vessels should fall in the conflict of battle…than that they should be tamely surrendered to the enemy or destroyed by their own officers," he urged. "If fall they must, let them show neither the weakness of submission nor of self-destruction, but inflict a blow that will relieve defeat from discredit."

Mallory's plea notwithstanding, a sailor aboard the *Savannah* recorded, "If we are attacked we will follow the course of the other ironclads and either blow up or get captured." Brent tried to escape Savannah into Wassaw Sound, but Confederate torpedoes anchored in the river proved difficult to remove quickly and effectively blocked the ship's escape route. This was just as well for the crew, because Admiral John A. Dahlgren, who had designed the devastating guns mounted on the Union monitors, learned of the planned escape and ordered his own ironclads to patrol every channel.

At sunrise on December 21, Union troops gleefully occupied Fort Jackson and climbed the ramparts to raise the United States flag. Looking across the river, they were startled by the sight of the CSS *Savannah* lying at anchor near Screven's Bluff. A battery of field artillery was unlimbered and opened fire on the ironclad. In reply, the *Savannah* defiantly ran up the Confederate flag and returned fire, briefly driving the enemy from their guns.

The Federals responded by harmlessly bouncing numerous shots off the *Savannah*'s thick hide. One shell entered a smokestack, but failed to detonate. Otherwise, the *Savannah* might have indeed gone down in a blaze of glory. The exchange of gunfire lasted throughout the day, hindering the Federal pursuit of the Confederate troops that had withdrawn from Savannah.

After dark, Brent ran the *Savannah* to the South Carolina side of the Savannah River. His men left the ship and joined the Confederate troops marching to Hardeeville, South Carolina, where the erstwhile sailors boarded a train for Charleston. Before leaving the Savannah, her crew set a slow match to the magazine, and at 11:30 p.m. on December 21, 1864, the ironclad died in a magnificent explosion seen and felt over a wide area.

"It lit the heavens for miles," wrote one soldier. "We could see to pick up a pin where we were (several miles distant) and the noise as awful." Ships anchored in Tybee Roads felt the tremors, and windows rattled on Hilton Head. The Savannah Squadron of the Confederates States of America had ceased to exist.

In the end, it must be acknowledged that Savannah's ironclads did not accomplish a great deal, but that was typical of the Confederate Navy's fleet of iron-sheathed vessels. Of the 22 completed, four were captured and the remainder were blown up or scuttled by their crews. Thirty other unfinished ironclads were destroyed by Confederate forces so that they would not fall into enemy hands.

GENERAL SHERMAN'S GEORGIA SWEETHEART

While blazing his path through Georgia in 1864, Union General William T. Sherman came across the dwelling place of an old flame. He was startled and dismayed, but would his lingering affection for this southern belle protect her magnificent plantation home from destruction?

DANIEL M. ROPER

Trees and shrubbery conceal the attractive, but by no means grandiose, ante bellum mansion from view. Travelers on busy U.S. Highway 27 zoom by and seldom notice the house. Even those who live nearby are largely unaware that a Confederate general once resided there. Fewer still are the ranks of those familiar with the remarkable story of a youthful William T. Sherman's courtship of the general's sister and how the sway she held over the future Union commander stayed his hand during the height of the Atlanta Campaign in 1864.

I came across this intriguing story while researching the history of the house – called Greenwood – and its first residents, the Pleasant Stovall family. To be honest, I was skeptical, for while truth may be stranger than fiction, this tale, it seemed, was simply too good to be true.

His Road Led to Rome

Pleasant Stovall was a successful 53-year-old cotton merchant when he moved from Augusta to Rome, Georgia, in 1846. He had acquired hundreds of acres of Oostanaula River bottomland north of town and established his

ABOVE: After she rejected Sherman's advances, Cecelia Stovall married Charles T. Shelman of Cartersville. She was fated to hear from her old suitor one more time when Sherman, in the midst of his military campaign to take Atlanta in 1864, unexpectedly showed up at the Shelman house. OPPOSITE PAGE: It was William T. Sherman's "cold, cruel eyes" that prompted a youthful Cecelia Stovall to reject him as a suitor.

Greenwood plantation there. Pleasant had a bit of wanderlust, however, and by 1850 had moved on, eventually settling in Athens, Georgia.

During his lifetime, Pleasant married three times (outliving his first two wives) and sired 13 children. When he moved to Athens, two of his sons, Marcellus and George, remained in Rome, where they made marks of their own; George as the owner of the *Southern Recorder* newspaper and Marcellus as a planter who succeeded his father as the owner of Greenwood.

Eyes Cold and Cruel

As a youth, Marcellus Stovall had developed an acute aversion to the cold. While a student at a Massachusetts boarding school he learned that icy weather aggravated his rheumatism. So he had returned to his home and family in Georgia and, at just 17 years old, joined the Richmond Blues, an Augusta militia unit. He served in Florida during the Second Seminole War, and his demonstration of promise and ability led to an appointment to the United States Military Academy at West Point in 1836.

When Marcellus's younger sister, Louisa Cecelia Stovall, visited her brother at the academy, she caught the eye of his roommate, a young man from Ohio named William Tecumseh Sherman. According to some accounts, a smitten Sherman proposed to the dark-haired, dark-eyed southern belle, but she declined, explaining, "Your eyes are so cold and cruel. I pity the man who ever becomes your antagonist. Ah, how you would crush an enemy!"

In response to this rejection, the spurned suitor gallantly replied, "Even though you were my enemy, my dear, I would love you and protect you."

Several other West Pointers wooed Cecelia Stovall, including Joseph Hooker and Richard Garnett, but she eventually married a Georgia planter, Charles T. Shelman. They would establish Etowah Heights, a magnificent plantation overlooking the Etowah River near Cartersville, and had ten children.

After graduating from the Academy, William Sherman married Ellen Ewing, the daughter of his adoptive parents, and embarked on a military, financial, and teaching career that took him to posts all across America, from Augusta (coincidentally

COURTESY JANICE PATTERSON

Lingering fondness for the lady he was once smitten with persuaded Sherman to spare Etowah Heights from the torch in 1864, but flames ultimately claimed the structure in 1911.

Cecelia's hometown) to San Francisco to Louisiana. The outbreak of the Civil War found him in St. Louis, and in May, 1861, he received a commission in the Union army. Just two months later, he would be one of the few federal officers to perform well at the Battle of Manassas, a bloody affair in which George T. Stovall, a younger brother of his old love, was killed in action.

Once Friend, Now Foe

Sherman's roommate from his West Point days, Marcellus Stovall, had not remained at the academy long. He discovered that New York winters were nearly as cold as in Massachusetts, and his arthritis soon flared up. The young cadet wished to return to Georgia badly enough that "it looked like he was on a campaign to get kicked out of the academy," noted his biographer, Dr. C.L. Bragg, in a recent interview. "Marcellus managed to get arrested for desertion, confined to quarters for a month, faced trial, and was dismissed from the academy."

Surprisingly, Stovall's abortive stay at West Point proved beneficial in his civilian life. "It counted in his favor instead of against him," said Bragg. "He was active in the militia after returning to Augusta, became a successful businessman, and then followed his father to Rome in 1846." Stovall parlayed his brief military education into a succession of commissions in the state militia, including major of the 210th Battalion in 1840, colonel of the 10th Battalion in 1843, and captain of the Rome Guards in 1852.

On the eve of the Civil War, Stovall was busy organizing the Cherokee Artillery in Rome. His military experience resulted in a series of promotions that culminated with the rank of brigadier general. "He was a good leader who was well thought

158

of by his men," Bragg observed. "He excelled at the Battles of Murfreesboro and Jackson and performed well at Chickamauga."

Like Sherman at Manassas, Stovall did well in a battle in which most of his contemporaries fared poorly. At Missionary Ridge, a decisive Union victory, Stovall's brigade stood its ground and then retreated in orderly fashion while most of the other Southern troops, especially those in the center, broke or retreated in disarray.

There were several occasions, including Missionary Ridge, when Stovall and Sherman were involved in the same battles, although the former roommates never directly engaged each other. "As best as I can determine," Bragg said, "the closest they physically came to each other was at the Battle of Jackson, Mississippi, in 1863. A lot of Yankees were killed in front of the Confederate lines. Sherman asked for a truce to gather up the dead and his request, actually penned by a subordinate, came through the lines at Stovall's Brigade and remains in Marcellus Stovall's papers in Augusta."

To Ever Shield and Protect You

Sherman became commander of the Military Division of the Mississippi in 1864 and from that post directed the Federal advance on Atlanta. Marcellus Stovall's brigade participated in numerous skirmishes and battles as the beleaguered Confederate forces tried to halt the invader, but Sherman pressed forward mercilessly until he unwittingly arrived at Cecelia Stovall Shelman's doorstep in June.

By the time the Yankees arrived, the Shelman family had long since evacuated to a safer locale. They left behind a trusted servant to look after Etowah Heights and, according to the version recorded by George Magruder Battey in his *History of Rome and Floyd County*, the following transpired:

"An old negro mammy sat on the front steps moaning her life away. 'Oh, Ginrul, whut yo' gwine do? I sholy is glad Missus Cecelia ain't here to see it wid her own eyes!'

"'Miss Cecelia?' queried Gen. Sherman, as the little hob-goblins began to prance around his memory chest. 'Who lives here, auntie?'

"'Missus Shellman, – Cecelia Stovall Shellman, sur, an' she's gone away now, bless her politeness!'

"'My God!' exclaimed the warrior. 'Can it be possible?'

"Momentarily he bowed his head, a lump formed in his throat, he swallowed hard and his eyes became moist. On learning from the old woman that Mrs. Shellman had sought safety in flight, Gen. Sherman ordered his plundering soldiers to restore everything they had taken, and he placed a guard to protect the premises. Then he said, 'Auntie, you get word to your mistress that she will be perfectly safe in returning here, and when you see her, do you hand her this card from me.'

"On his card Gen. Sherman had written, 'You once said I would crush an enemy, and you pitied my foe. Do you recall my reply? Although many years have passed, my answer is the same now as then, 'I would ever shield and protect you.' That I have done. Forgive me all else. I am only a soldier."

As a young cadet at the U.S. Military Academy, Marcellus Stovall's roommate was William T. Sherman. During the Civil War years later, the two commanded opposing forces that met on battlefields from Mississippi to Georgia.

Reality or Embellishment?

Is this remarkable tale factual? Dr. Bragg, author of *Distinction in Every Service: Brigadier General Marcellus A. Stovall, C.S.A.*, thinks so, even though no one has been able to locate Sherman's note to Cecelia. "There are many different versions of what happened," Bragg observed, "but I'm convinced the core of the story is true. The Stovall papers at Augusta State University include a letter from a niece who saw the note and one of Marcellus's grandsons also said that he had seen it as a child."

In similar fashion, the late Lucy Cunyus, a respected Bartow County historian, once told Michele Rodgers, Director of the Bartow History Center in Cartersville, that she had seen the note.

While Sherman was moved to spare Cecelia Shelman's house, some of his troops had ransacked Marcellus's Greenwood plantation and freed his slaves. "So, after the war, Marcellus relocated to Augusta where he spent the remainder of his eventful life engaged in the fertilizer business and various civic duties," Bragg commented.

William Sherman died in New York City in 1891; Marcellus Stovall died in Augusta in 1895; and Cecelia Shelman died in Cartersville in 1904. Ironically, the house that Sherman had spared from the torch in 1864 suffered a fiery fate on New Year's Day of 1911, when it burned to the ground. The property stands vacant today.

Thus, Greenwood in Rome is one of the last tangible links to the once-prominent Stovall family's presence in northwest Georgia, a link to the story of a general's affection that survived decades of separation and a bitter war. Today, Greenwood is a residence for Berry College staff, but even Berry officials know little about the Confederate brigadier general who once lived there or the amazing story of the spell his sister cast over William T. Sherman.

THE TRAGIC BATTLE OF COLUMBUS

It was a totally unnecessary battle, the war having ended five days earlier, but these combatants simply did not receive the news in time.

MICHAEL WILLIAMS

In 1865, the South had been devastated by the Civil War and the end was obvious to all but the most resolute. The city of Columbus, Georgia, boasted a population of 15,000, including 3,000 slaves. It also maintained a force of some 2,000 Confederate soldiers who drilled each week in readiness for action should they be needed. Most of these men were either far too old or too young for active duty. Their ages ranged from 12 to 80,[1] but they soon would be cast into a tragic bloody engagement that was both unnecessary and the last major battle of this terrible war.

By this time, the Columbus area had long been depleted of able-bodied men between the ages of 16 and 40. They all had answered the call to duty in the previous four years, and many of them had long since departed this earth, slain in the bloody conflict that gripped our nation.

The local army units in Columbus were commanded by Colonel Leon Von Zinken, a German immigrant who had commanded the 20th Louisiana Infantry at the Battle of Chickamauga. Von Zinken was under the command of General Howell Cobb, who was headquartered in Macon, Georgia.

On April 14, 1865, Von Zinken received a communication from Montgomery,

This early photograph taken while the C.S.S. *Jackson* was still afloat on the Chattahoochee, was obviously accomplished prior to 1865. Visible on deck are the crew.

CONFEDERATE NAVAL MUSEUM, COLUMBUS

Alabama. He was informed that Union General James Wilson, leading a force of 12,000 cavalry, had captured that city without a fight. The communication went on to explain that Wilson was now turning his attention to Columbus, which he considered to be the hub of Georgia industry.

Unfortunately, neither Wilson nor the people of Columbus were aware that the war had essentially ended five days earlier when Gen. Lee had surrendered to Gen. Grant at Appomattox Courthouse in Virginia. Communications being what they were in 1865, especially during a devastating war, the news simply had not yet reached the Deep South. Moreover, the Confederate government had not yet capitulated, so here and there armed resistance in the South continued for a time after Appomattox.

A Thriving City

Columbus is a port city on the broad Chattahoochee River directly across from present-day Phenix City, Alabama. During the Civil War, Phenix City was known as Girard. It was a sparsely-populated rural area comprised basically of simple farms.

In contrast, Columbus was a thriving industrial town whose factories produced swords, bayonets, cotton products, iron, munitions, and much more. There was also a naval shipyard where two ironclad ships, the CSS *Chattahoochee* and the CSS *Jackson* were moored.

Faintly visible is the oval outline of the ironclad outer hull of the C.S.S. *Jackson* where it sank at its mooring after being set afire by Union troops in 1865. When this photo was taken in 1965, recovery efforts for the vessel were on-going. It may be viewed today at the Confederate Naval Museum in Columbus.

CONFEDERATE NAVAL MUSEUM, COLUMBUS

Two bridges connecting Columbus with Girard spanned the Chattahoochee. They were the Fourteenth Street Bridge (the Upper Bridge), and the Crawford Bridge (the Lower Bridge). Broad Street in Columbus was the city's hub of commerce, along which could be found dozens of shops, stores, factories, doctors' offices, churches and attorney's offices.

Several Confederate forts dotted the nearby countryside surrounding Girard and Columbus. They were primarily constructed of earthworks and, because of a severe shortage of manpower, were often unmanned entirely in 1865.

Not all of the citizens of this area were loyal to the Confederate cause. One local industrialist, Randolph Mott, flew "Old Glory" from his front porch and defied anyone to tamper with it. His house was situated on the Columbus side of the river next to the Fourteenth Street Bridge. Although Mott was a slave owner, he was opposed to Southern secession.[2]

Preparing To Be Attacked

On the morning of April 15, 1865, Von Zinken issued a proclamation to the citizens of Columbus to prepare for the impending attack from Gen. Wilson's force. Those who were unable to assist in the defense of the city were instructed to leave at once.[3]

Those who were able-bodied were instructed to report for duty. Though they were few and far between, those very young and very old who answered the call can only be greatly admired today. This was a time when young boys did not have a childhood, and when aged men could not rock peacefully on their front porches. To the contrary, it was a desperate time.

Many citizens began burying their gold, silver, jewelry and other valuables they felt the "looting Yankee invaders" might steal. The memory of the theft and destruction after the fall of Atlanta was still fresh on everyone's mind. Today, no doubt, untold riches remain buried in the vicinity of many former homes throughout the South where the owners perished without revealing the location of these buried war-time valuables.

Gen. Cobb arrived in Columbus later that afternoon to help coordinate the city's defense. He brought with him as many soldiers as he could muster from Macon.

The Rebels dug trenches and lined the bridges with cotton bales soaked in oil so that they could be quickly burned in case of defeat. The forts were all manned and a line of defense nearly two miles long was formed on the Alabama side of the river.

The Confederate defenders, as well as Wilson's raiders, who were enroute, were totally unaware of another development that had occurred during the night. At that time, on April 14, President Lincoln had been shot at Ford's Theatre by actor John Wilkes Booth. He had died on the morning of the 15th.

Ironically, John Wilkes and his brother, Edwin, both renowned stage actors of that day, had performed a number of times in Columbus. John Wilkes' stage manager, Mathew Canning, lived in Columbus.

A Yankee Assault

On Easter Sunday, April 16, 1865, 3,000 Rebel soldiers waited patiently for the coming invasion. Around 2 p.m., a frantic young horseman rode briskly toward the Confederate line. He had been scouting the enemy advance west of Girard. He reported to his Confederate comrades that the Yankees would be upon them very shortly.

Roughly 30 minutes later, the Union troops came into sight of the Confederate line. Suddenly, there was a burst of gunfire as defenders in two of the Confederate forts located on Crawford Road opened fire.

Two Federal cavalry brigades, commanded by Generals Andrew Alexander and Edward Winslow, ignored the attack and charged the Crawford Bridge. They were met with a hail of gunfire from another fort as well as from a small line of defense at the bridge.

The Union soldiers were less than 100 yards from the bridge when the Confederates, who were greatly outnumbered, retreated to the Georgia side of the Chattahoochee River. As the last Confederate crossed the bridge, he hurled a torch onto the oil-soaked structure. Within seconds, Crawford Bridge became a blazing inferno.

Cut off from easy access to the city, the Union troops were, for the moment, thwarted. Wilson's men retreated to the hilly area surrounding Girard. There, the Union general regrouped his men and planned a new strategy of attack as he eyed the entrenched positions and other fortifications of the Confederates.

A Second Assault

Union General James Wilson was a seasoned commander. He had enjoyed a measure of success in night-fighting, so he reasoned that an attack on Columbus at night would result in less loss and greater success than a daylight assault. At 8:00 p.m., his men readied themselves for another assault, this time striking at the Fourteenth Street Bridge. There, once again, the invaders were met with a barrage of gunfire from small weapons, shells, canisters and musketry.

Fortunately for the Union troops, the inexperienced Confederates wasted much of their ammunition by firing over the heads of the Yankees. Six dismounted companies of the 3rd Iowa Cavalry Regiment charged and captured the rifle pits at the bridge within minutes. The Confederate riflemen were both outnumbered and too inexperienced to hold their positions.

Two companies of cavalry under the command of Captain R.B.M. McGlasson raced through the breach in the line, but were surprised to discover a second line of Confederate defenses. They nevertheless pushed ahead as bullets buzzed like angry hornets by their heads.

In the darkness, many of the Confederates mistook the Union cavalry for fleeing comrades, and allowed them to pass through the Confederate line unmolested. Realizing their mistake, the Confederates turned and began attacking the

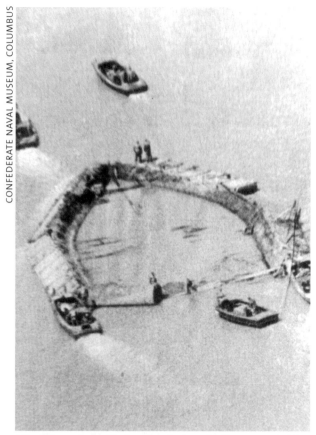

CONFEDERATE NAVAL MUSEUM, COLUMBUS

Union forces on the bridge who now found themselves being fired upon from both sides of the bridge. One can only imagine small boys and very old men embroiled at night in such a confusing melee.

Suddenly, a second wave of Union forces stormed the bridge from the Girard side. Fighting on the bridge soon became hand-to-hand (at least as far as the Confederates were concerned, since most of their weapons were single-shot rifles and muzzle-loaded muskets). The cries of wounded soldiers, the crack of gunfire and the clash of swords and bayonets echoed through the twilight as the Confederates were cut down.

After being raised with flotation devices, the fore portion of the C.S.S. *Jackson* is dragged to a dock in 1965 where it was spirited away for cleaning and preservation prior to being displayed at the museum.

Death Throes

The sounds of battle soon began to ebb as the smaller Confederate force was pushed back across the river to the Columbus side. As the fighting moved from the bridge into downtown Columbus, several local women rushed onto the bridge to see if any of their loved ones were among the dead and wounded. Randolph Mott, watching from his rooftop, saw the deathblow being delivered to the Confederates. He later remarked, "The Confederacy was defeated in my front yard."

The bridge, once a symbol of unity between the two communities was now a battleground for a nation divided. It was spattered with the blood of scores of courageous young boys and aged men. An estimated 40 men lay dead and wounded on the bridge that day.[4] It quickly became crowded with doctors and medics – both Northern and Southern – once enemies, but now united, in an effort to attend the wounded. Old animosities were forgotten in this moment of desperation. The moans of the dying and the wails of the grieving women mourning the losses of loved ones filled the night air.

Meanwhile, in the downtown area, the Confederates realized they were beaten and began to lay down their arms. One thousand Southerners were quickly rounded up and their guns confiscated. The Battle of Columbus had ended in the defeat for the Rebels, echoing the death throes of the old Confederacy.

The final toll that day was nine Confederate dead and 20 wounded. The toll for the Union was 25 dead and 20 wounded. Corpses were scattered along the trenches on the Alabama side of the river and on the bridge.

With the surrender of the combatants, the city of Columbus was at the mercy of the Union troops. The residents waited anxiously to see what Wilson had in mind for the city. Most returned to their homes to wait and pray.

Burning Columbus

When the sun rose the next morning, Wilson handed down his orders. Anything that could be used for the continuance of the war was to be destroyed. As a result, all textile mills, the sword factory, the naval yard, the naval iron works, the cotton warehouses, the muni-

Union General James Wilson led a cavalry force 12,000 strong on a raid through Alabama and Georgia during the closing days of the Civil War.

tions factories – everything – was burned to the ground. Over 50,000 bales of cotton were destroyed that day.

As a large cloud of black smoke ascended and hung over the city, many local businessmen pleaded with Wilson to spare their businesses. Their outcries, however, fell upon deaf ears.

The two Confederate ironclads, the *Chattahoochee* and the *Jackson*, were set ablaze and adrift in the river, left to sink once their wooden vitals had been burned out from within. They soon sank into the murky depths of the Chattahoochee River where they would remain for 100 years.

Despite the claims of some historians today, looting by Union troops was not uncommon. On this day, rioting broke out and both Union troops and freed slaves began breaking into local businesses and homes, taking what they wanted and vandalizing freely. Theft, vandalism, assault and worse were the order of the day. Columbus residents, now disarmed, were powerless to stop the mayhem.

Mott, the Union sympathizer, met with Wilson and even entertained him in his home, no doubt relishing his position as an "untouchable." He reportedly remained tight-lipped about the ultimate demise of the city, but it has been recorded that he later said he felt Wilson's destruction was excessive. While he had his differences with many of the locals, some of them were still his friends. To most of the locals, however, Mott was nothing more than a traitor.[5]

Following the complete destruction of Columbus, Wilson departed the town in a horse-drawn carriage. He left a small garrison behind to maintain order in his absence. His next destination was Macon, Georgia. He planned to conduct his attack of that city in much the same manner as he had destroyed Columbus.

Fortunately for Macon residents, Wilson received word that the war had ended before he began his assault of that town. Macon was thus spared destruction.

Years later, Wilson reportedly expressed remorse for what had occurred in Columbus. He stated somewhat haughtily, "Had I known the war was over, I would have spared them."

The day after the battle, funeral services were held at Linwood Cemetery for the Confederates felled in the battle. They were given military funerals with their coffins draped with Confederate flags. There were no 21-gun salutes because the conquered citizens still were not allowed to have firearms.

Old Wounds Heal Slow

Columbus eventually recovered from the devastation of the Civil War, and regained its place as an industrial center. In 1880, General Wilson returned to the town, arriving by train this time. Interestingly, he apparently expected a hero's welcome, and was disgusted when the citizens of Columbus ignored him. He departed the following morning, angered by what he called "insolence."

In 1910, in an effort to heal old wounds, the city erected monuments to all the soldiers killed that fateful day. On the south end of the present-day historic district

The Confederate Naval Museum in Columbus, Georgia, is a popular destination for Civil War history enthusiasts. Visitors can view recovered ironclad battleships from the old South and learn more about how the war was pursued at sea.

in the town is a monument to the Confederate dead. Appropriately, on the north end is a monument to the Union soldiers killed. It is one of the few such devastated towns in the South that today honors not only its native sons killed in battle, but also those of the army that slew them.

A few blocks away is Linwood Boulevard where Linwood Cemetery is located. Over 1,000 Confederate dead who perished during and after the war are interred there. Their section of the cemetery is designated with a cannon and a Confederate flag.

In 1965, historians retrieved the CSS *Chattahoochee* and the CSS *Jackson* from the dark waters of the Chattahoochee. These two ironclads are now displayed at the Confederate Naval Museum on Victory Drive in Columbus. At the museum, visitors can view many different artifacts of the Confederate Navy, including the *Jackson*, the *Chattahoochee*, cannons, portions of the ironclad *Merrimac*, authentic uniforms, and hundreds of other items.

Endnotes
1. *Georgia Historical Quarterly*, Fall, 1975.
2. ibid
3. *Columbus Ledger Enquirer*, April 19, 1987.
4. ibid
5. ibid

ALEXANDER H. STEPHENS AND THE LAST DAYS OF THE CONFEDERACY

The diminutive statesman was small in stature, but a giant in the political arena of his day, serving as a United States Congressman, Vice-President of the Confederacy and Governor of the State of Georgia.

BRIAN BROWN

In his day, he was called "Little Aleck" by those who knew him – this prominent former Georgia politician, renowned legal scholar and Vice-President of the doomed Confederate States of America. To his credit, Stephens was a reluctant secessionist, holding out to the very last at the crucial Georgia Convention of 1860. His intelligent, reasoned and respected voice helped steer the South through many of its darkest days in the 1860s and '70s.

His was a life of contentment and deep personal satisfaction, excepting of course the frail health that had always plagued him and the stressful requirements of his many duties as Vice-President. Over the course of the Civil War, he would argue many times the merits of reconciliation, but the die had been cast, and there was no reversing the course of history.

By early 1865, his closely watched participation in the Hampton Roads Conference fell under great scrutiny. His suggestions concerning a graceful exit from the war served primarily to further alienate him from his boss and political adversary – President Jefferson Davis.

It must have come as no great surprise to Stephens, on the morning of May 11, 1865,

GEORGIA STATE PARKS AND HISTORIC SITES

Many items displayed in Liberty Hall have been left just as they were the day "Little Aleck" died.

when Union troops came knocking on the door of his beloved Crawfordville home, Liberty Hall. He knew the war had been over for months – possibly years – and it was just a matter of time until the final death knell of the old Confederacy was sounded.

That day began inauspiciously enough and yet it apparently was a beautiful spring day. Stephens relished it, describing it as "a most beautiful and charming morning" in the journal he kept. That, of course, was prior to the intrusion of the Union troops later that morning at his home.

Robert Hull, the son of one of Stephens' associates from nearby Athens, Georgia, was at the residence, as were the usual contingent of black manservants in whom the vice-president placed such high regard. A servant named Tim alerted Mr. Stephens about 10 a.m. to the presence of Yankees in the front yard.

Stephens already knew that Union troops were scattered all over the state, rounding up members of the Confederate leadership. He had been "looking for something of this kind; at least, for some weeks had thought it not improbable."

Stephens' initial contact was with Captain Saint of the Fourth Iowa Cavalry, who informed the vice-president that he (Saint) was under direct orders of General Emory Upton, stationed at Atlanta, to arrest and bring Stephens into custody. After allowing him to pack some belongings into travel trunks, the contingent of troops readied for the journey.

Prior to departing, Captain Saint told Stephens he would be allowed to take two of his servants with him. Stephens chose Henry and Anthony, two brothers from

Governor Alexander H. Stephens's funeral in Atlanta on March 8, 1885 was a momentous event.

Richmond who needed a way back home to be with their mother.

As the detachment left the house for the train station, the servants were observed to be emotional, weeping publicly. Stephens noted in his journal, "My own heart was full…too full for tears."

After a brief stopover in Washington, Georgia, home of the equally noted Robert Toombs and site of the final meeting of President Jefferson Davis and his Confederate cabinet just a week earlier, the train carrying the prisoners steamed toward Atlanta. Stephens did not yet know that President Davis had been captured while fleeing through South Georgia just two days earlier.

On May 12, at 8:30 A.M., the men arrived in the devastated city. There, Stephens was first made aware of Davis' capture at Irwinville, and of the surrender of Clement C. Clay, the Alabama Senator and ardent secessionist. The ruins of Atlanta were particularly distressing to the frail statesman and brought on him a great rush of emotions about the Confederacy and his presumed place in its history.

"How strange it seems to me, that I should thus suffer, I, who did everything in the power of man to prevent them," he noted in his ever-present journal. He lamented his inability to steer the Confederacy to an earlier peaceful resolution to the war.

Throughout the entire ordeal, Stephens described how he was equally impressed by the niceties extended to him by General Upton, and was most taken aback when the General offered him unlimited use of his bank account in Europe. Stephens refused, of course, but was nevertheless left humbled by the gesture.

On the morning of May 14, the train carrying the prisoners departed Atlanta and was en route to Augusta. It made a brief return to Crawfordville in order to allow the vice-president to gather a few additional belongings for the long journey and his ordeal ahead. He had hoped desperately that his brother and confidant, Linton Stephens of nearby Sparta, would be able to see him off, but it was not to be. Linton had taken ill and was too sick to rise from his bed. A large

GEORGIA DEPARTMENT OF ARCHIVES & HISTORY

Alexander H. Stephens and his "faithful attendant" posed for this photograph at Brady's Gallery in Washington D.C. on May 7, 1879.

crowd of local folk, nevertheless, gathered at the train station made Stephens proud as they bid him farewell.

Upon reaching Augusta, all the prisoners consistent with the Confederate executive department, were paraded through town on their way to a tugboat that would carry them downriver to Savannah. Stephens noted in his journal that the proceeding "looked much like a funeral procession." Ironically, that was exactly what it was. It was the funeral procession for the old Confederacy, dead at last, all of its major players in the custody of the Union.

Lieutenant Benjamin Pritchard of the Fourth Michigan Cavalry (which had earned fame as the captors of Jefferson Davis some days earlier), was now in command of the prisoners. Included in the prisoners' ranks was "Fightin' Joe Wheeler," the Augusta-born general who had proven himself one of the stellar cavalry officers for the Confederate Army.

On May 19, the steamer *William P. Clyde* onto which the men had been herded in Savannah, reached Hampton Roads, Virginia, and anchored there, awaiting further instructions. Davis was deported to Fortress Monroe, and Captain Fraily of the USS *Tuscarora* made Stephens aware that he would be transferred to that boat and taken to the prison at Fort Warren in Boston harbor.

DAN ROPER

A.H. Stephens State Park in Crawfordville, Georgia, features a Confederate museum with one of the finest collections of Civil War artifacts in Georgia, including uniforms and documents. Liberty Hall, Stephens' home, has been renovated to its original 1875 condition, and is fully furnished and open for tours.

When the *Tuscarora* finally reached Boston on May 24, close to midnight, Stephens was spent from the journey and ready to meet whatever destiny awaited him. The following morning he was introduced to the elderly commandant of Fort Warren – General John Adams Dix – a hard-line Unionist who was born when John Adams was beginning his presidency. Stephens steeled himself for the worst, but was pleasantly surprised when Dix also did his best to make Stephens feel at home.

In stark contrast to President Jefferson Davis who was considered to be "Public Enemy Number One," Vice-President Stephens received none of the ill treatment that unnecessarily plagued his superior. His first few weeks at the fort were spent in a slightly damp, lower cell, where he was temporarily confined, but he soon was given free reign of the grounds.

Stephens' greatest distress came from the absence of his brother, Linton, and a concession was even made to absolve this discomfort when, in September, his brother arrived and awaited him in Boston until his parole on October 12, 1865.

During Stephens' imprisonment, a number of influential Southern periodicals (the few still in publication) filled their editorial pages with appeals for his swift release. The *Louisville Journal* bestowed the laurel of "most brilliant man in the South" upon him, while the *Macon Telegraph* urged, "He is needed by the entire South."

Stephens had been among the most inconspicuous spokesmen for the Lost Cause, a slight shell of a man from a hamlet in the Georgia piedmont. Nevertheless, his enlightened views and belief in the Confederacy did not die with his arrest and imprisonment. After his quick release, he returned to north Georgia where he again became involved in the politics of the South, helping to rebuild the state of Georgia.

The astute politician felt he could best serve his people as a voice of reason during the uncertainty and chaos of Reconstruction. From 1873 to 1882, he remained a strong stabilizing force in the United States House of Representatives, and spent most of his free time writing history and corresponding with the leaders of that day.

On October 4, 1882, Stephens was elected governor of Georgia, due largely to the machinations of others. His quiet dignity, studious judgment and character were respected by one and all, and his leadership was urgently needed in that desperate time in his state. Though he had expected to retire, he agreed to take on this new mantle of leadership nonetheless.

By this time, however, Stephens' health was tenuous at best, and the statesman apparently had known it. He would survive only five months, dying at the Governor's Mansion in Atlanta on March 4, 1883. Among the pallbearers at his state funeral were five former governors and two illustrious generals – John Brown Gordon and Robert Toombs.

Briefly interred at Oakland Cemetery in Atlanta, Stephens' remains were later re-interred at his beloved Liberty Hall in 1884. An inscription on his memorial at Liberty Hall best describes the ambiguity that was Alexander Stephens: "Here sleep the remains of one who dared to tell the people they were wrong when he believed so, and who never intentionally deceived a friend or betrayed even an enemy."

(A.H. Stephens State Historic Park is operated by the Georgia Department of Natural Resources. It houses one of the finest collections of Civil War artifacts in Georgia, and pays tribute to the life of this noted Georgia politician. For more information, telephone 706-456-2602.)

DID A GEORGIA RESIDENT HELP ASSASSINATE PRESIDENT ABRAHAM LINCOLN?

He was a close friend and business manager of the man who killed the President of the United States. Whether or not Mathew Canning was ever involved in the conspiracy remains a mystery today.

MICHAEL WILLIAMS

In June 1991, Scott Winslow Associates, Inc., of Nashua, New Hampshire, advertised for sale a $100.00 check written by John Wilkes Booth, assassin of President Abraham Lincoln. This rare collector's item fetched $15,000, and just may represent condemning evidence against one of Booth's co-conspirators who has remained in the shadows for more than 140 years.

John Wilkes Booth

The check was drawn on a Washington, D.C. bank account that was opened shortly after Booth made a clandestine trip to Canada in 1864. Historians have long believed this account was used to finance Booth's conspiracy against Lincoln. The check was written on December 16, 1864, approximately five months prior to the assassination.

Of local interest is the fact that the check was written to M.W. Canning, a resident of Columbus, Georgia. Was Canning an accomplice in the assassination? Certainly, this one piece of evidence would not be enough to implicate him, but so little has been written about Canning that he naturally emerges from the pages of history as a mysterious enigma.

175

Today, there in fact is only one known photograph of this man of mystery, compounding the curiosity of historians. He was an actor in the theater, just as was Booth, and his career was also stellar. He worked with the most notable actors of his time, and helped launch the careers of many aspiring thespians of his day.

In a bizarre accident in 1860, Canning, ironically, nearly killed John Wilkes Booth. Had the death actually occurred, history obviously would have been rewritten dramatically.

Early Life

Mathew W. Canning, Jr., was born in Philadelphia, Pennsylvania, in 1830. The son of a stone cutter, he had attended college and was admitted to the Pennsylvania Bar in 1853. Rather than practice law, however, Canning chose to pursue his first love – the theater.

According to Michael Kauffman, author of *American Brutus: John Wilkes Booth and the Lincoln Conspiracies*, Canning arrived in Columbus, Georgia, in early 1859 to begin his career. He leased two theaters, one in Montgomery, Alabama, and Temperance Hall located on present-day First Avenue in Columbus.

Located on the Chattahoochee River, Columbus is a port city. Across the river was Girard, Alabama, now known as Phenix City. Much of Columbus' industry was comprised of mills and various factories as well as the cotton industry. It was a rough and tumble town, but included many individuals who enjoyed patronage of the theater.

Did A Georgia Resident Help Assassinate President Abraham Lincoln?

A local newspaper in Columbus produced both a daily edition and a weekly edition. Interestingly, the founder of the newspaper, Mirabeau Lamar, found fame as the second president of the Republic of Texas. Mathew Canning was about to make his mark on national history as well, but it wasn't the type of history most people would prefer.

Mathew W. Canning, Jr.

The Booth Family

Despite its somewhat small size, Columbus had a total of six theaters at the time of Canning's arrival. Such competition undoubtedly would have been a concern to most entrepreneurs, but Canning apparently was undaunted. His confidence in his ability to succeed was due largely to his relationship with the highly respected Booth family.

At the time, the Booths were considered the first-family of theater in the United States, a dynasty comparable to the 20th century Barrymores. Junius Brutus (J.B.) Booth, or "Mad Booth" as he later came to be known due to his bouts with insanity, was the family patriarch.

Although his once-stellar career was eventually overshadowed by alcoholism and mental illness, J.B. Booth had achieved significant renown in the theater in his younger days. In adulthood, he fathered four sons, three of whom also pursued a career in the theater.

Junius, the eldest, acted occasionally, but more enjoyed management of a theater than performing in it.

Edwin was the star of the family. Handsome, well-mannered and humble, his performances were riveting. He had played for the crowned heads of Europe as well as the President of the United States, and was so widely admired and adored that he could not walk down the street without being recognized. Crowds of admirers would often gather around him to ask for his autograph, and women swooned when in his presence.

It was John Wilkes, however, who was the iconoclast of the family. He was the

177

Ford's Theater

youngest of the three theatrical brothers, and often was described as handsome yet impetuous. Contrary to his more popular older brother, Edwin, John preferred to seek fame rather then acquire it naturally. He also lacked discipline, often missing rehearsals. Many managers ultimately became irritated and refused to work with him because of his immaturity.

John had performed with Edwin on several occasions. While his older brother received glowing reviews, John often was harshly criticized. As a result, he eventually began distancing himself from his legendary surname, billing himself simply as "John Wilkes," dropping the "Booth." In later years, however, he apparently sought to re-identify himself with his famed family, once again billing himself with the family surname.

Temperance Hall, under the capable management of Mathew Canning, produced its first play in early 1859. Canning's star performer was his good friend, Edwin Booth.

Edwin's performances were well-received and profitable for both men. His tour in Columbus lasted throughout most of 1859. At the end of the engagement, he left Columbus and opened at Canning's theater in Montgomery, Alabama.

John Wilkes In Columbus

Before he departed Columbus, Edwin asked a favor of Canning. The elder Booth wanted to help his younger brother John advance his career in the theater. He asked Canning to book John at the two theaters.

Canning had never worked with John, but he reasoned that John's last name would help sell tickets to the performances, so he agreed to book him. It was a decision that would haunt Canning for the rest of his life.

Did A Georgia Resident Help Assassinate President Abraham Lincoln?

John Wilkes Booth arrived in Columbus in October 1860. Canning began advertising the upcoming production of *Romeo and Juliet* in which Booth would have a co-starring role. At the time, Booth was displeased that he was billed as John Wilkes Booth for the reason explained earlier. As a result, later billings listed him only as John Wilkes.

His first appearance at the Temperance was scheduled for October 5, 1860. Booth appeared in the leading role in *Lady of Lyons*. The following day, he and his fellow actors received excellent reviews in the *Columbus Sun*. The exultant Booth was understandably pleased, especially since he had received a number of previous bad reviews while performing in the North.

Unstable Behavior

Canning was pleased as well, and looked forward to a profitable engagement with John Wilkes. However, the theater owner soon noticed something about Booth that caused him great concern. Unlike his brother, Edwin, who was gentle and mild-mannered, John Wilkes was temperamental and immature, and often behaved in a dangerously reckless manner. It was a trait that nearly cost him his life on the evening of October 12, 1860.

According to Kauffman's *American Brutus*, that evening, Booth was scheduled to appear in the lead role in *Hamlet*. One hour before curtain, he was in his dressing room taking – of all things – target practice with a handgun. The situation was complicated by the fact that the weapon was a rusty old pistol that belonged to Canning.

Booth had drawn a target on the wall and was shooting at it. He had fired one shot and reloaded the gun when Canning walked in. The theater owner was surprised to see the young actor discharging a firearm indoors. What if someone had been on the other side of the wall at which Booth was shooting?

According to Kauffman's account of the incident, Canning immediately asked for the gun, but Booth refused to relinquish it. "Look how rusty it is," Booth reportedly said off-hand, as he pulled away from Canning.

Greatly concerned for his actor as well as his business, Canning reached for the gun once again. This time, he was actually able to get a grasp on it. At the same moment, the gun discharged.

Booth immediately shrieked in agony as the round exploded from the barrel and ripped through his thigh. Canning was dumbfounded, but immediately sent someone to summon a doctor.

The physician arrived shortly thereafter and began administering aid to the wounded actor. Meanwhile, less than an hour prior to curtain, Canning stepped out on the stage and announced that the evening's performance would be cancelled. It was just one in a long line of bizarre incidents involving John Wilkes Booth during his lifetime.

After an inspection of Booth's thigh, the doctor reported to Canning that the actor was lucky to be alive. The bullet had lodged in his thigh very close to the femoral artery and the cautious physician refused to remove it for fear of endangering Booth's life.

As a result of Booth's incapacitation, changes in the cast were required, and attendance suffered at the theater. Booth recuperated for a number of weeks and then departed for a performance in Montgomery, leaving Canning somewhat in the lurch.

According to reports, the young actor eventually expressed a measure of gratitude to Canning for his patience and assistance after the accident. He asked the theater owner to continue managing and arranging bookings for him, to which Canning unwisely agreed.

Guilt by Association

In the course of the next four years, Canning arranged many bookings for John Wilkes Booth. At times he reportedly found himself at his wits' end with the actor. Booth continued to miss rehearsals, and his behavior proved not only immature, but dangerously erratic as well.

It was this bizarre behavior that ultimately would cast suspicion on Canning after Lincoln's assassination. On more than one occasion, Booth sent Canning suspicious telegraphs that tended to implicate the theater owner as an accomplice.

Booth also requested that Canning accompany him on outings for target practice once again with a handgun, and Canning amazingly agreed. Transcripts from the files of Provost Marshal John H. Jack indicate that the spot at which the target practice took place was on the escape trail Booth later took on the night he shot Lincoln, a detail which also focused suspicion in Canning's direction.

Worse yet, prior to the assassination, Booth wrote Canning several checks that were drawn on the bank account used to finance his plot. After Lincoln's death, Mathew Canning was arrested on the night of April 15, 1865, by order of Provost Marshal Jack and taken to the Old Federal Prison in Baltimore, Maryland. There, he was held along with Junius Booth and John Clarke, the husband of Booth's sister Asia.

Over the following two weeks, Canning was questioned extensively in an attempt to ascertain his actual relationship with Booth and his whereabouts on the night of Lincoln's assassination. Witnesses had placed Canning at Ford's Theater every night for two weeks prior to the assassination, but on the fateful night of the killing, Canning stated he had been confined to his home. Unfortunately, there was no one who could corroborate this claim.

During Canning's interrogation, more details began to emerge concerning Booth's escape route. Canning realized Booth had taken him out shooting at several locations along that same route. He quickly realized how suspicious it made him appear.

Despite his other less virtuous qualities, John Wilkes Booth was anything but

The Springer Opera House, Columbus, Georgia

unintelligent. According to historians, he was very well acquainted with the conspiracy laws as they existed at the time. He knew that under these laws, his fellow conspirators could not testify against him. He therefore went out of his way to implicate everyone he knew, so that in doing so, their testimony would be inadmissible in court.

Ford's Theater

According to the provost marshal's report, the last time Canning saw Booth alive was in December 1864. By that time, his friendship with the unpredictable Booth was strained. Canning was at Ford's Theater where he was managing the actress Vestvali.

During one particular engagement, the actress was experiencing problems and explained she did not wish to perform that night. Canning reportedly explained to her that President Lincoln would be in attendance, and upon learning this, the actress relented.

According to other details of the provost marshal's report derived from Canning's later testimony, Booth arrived at the theater late that day and gave Canning a check for $100 in payment of a booking fee. As he did so, he casually stated that he was on his way to Virginia to buy some land.

Upon learning of Booth's intended trip, Canning reportedly warned the actor that he might get caught behind Confederate lines, to which Booth cryptically responded, "You never fear for me. I'll be alright."

Booth then reportedly added, "I'll tell you something..." but after a moment's hesitation, the actor changed his mind, and said simply, "No, I won't do it."

According to his later testimony, Canning explained that he didn't think much of Booth's comments, since he was prone to outlandish remarks, and his secessionist sentiments were well-known. They were just more in the long line of erratic behaviors by the strange actor.

Despite his planned trip, Booth did attend the performance that night. At the end of the evening, he was seen following the President and First Lady as they were walking out of the theater.

Edwin Booth, brother of John Wilkes Booth

According to Canning's later testimony, he (Canning) walked out to the street where he saw Mr. and Mrs. Lincoln standing on the sidewalk waiting for a carriage. Booth was only a short distance away staring with great intensity at the President.

When Lincoln climbed into the carriage, Booth reportedly turned to Canning and said, "Come on." The two walked for a number of blocks in silence, and finally Booth said, "I want you to do me a favor." He asked Canning to speak to John Ford, the owner of Ford's Theater, and persuade him to book Sam Chester for an engagement. Booth reportedly explained that Chester was a dear friend who was in need of work. Canning agreed to speak with Ford about the matter.

Condemning Telegram

Later that evening, Canning received a telegram from Booth that stated cryptically, "Don't fail to hush the matter." Canning, by his own testimony, was perplexed by the meaning of the wire, and telegraphed Booth to ask what he had meant. He received no reply.

A few days later, Canning received a note from Booth saying that the telegram was supposed to read, "Do not fail to push the matter." Apparently, the message was in regard to Chester. Canning thought little more of the matter.

During his interrogation following Lincoln's assassination, Canning discovered that Booth had asked Chester to hold the door for him when he fled Ford's Theater after the shooting. Chester wanted nothing to do with the matter, however, and declined. Nevertheless, Canning, at that point, realized the strange telegram from Booth was a deliberate attempt to implicate him [Canning] in Lincoln's murder.

In an interview published in the *Cincinnati Enquirer* on January 19, 1886, Canning provided some very interesting details concerning his interrogation. He pointed out how he had described to his interrogators the incident when he had accidentally shot Booth in the leg. When asked if the bullet had been removed, he replied that it had not been.

Upon further interrogation, Canning revealed that he may well have been either a slow-witted or extremely gullible individual – perfect for manipulation by some-one of the mental capacities of John Wilkes Booth. In the *Enquirer* interview, Canning described how Booth had been tormented by a large boil on his neck. He explained that the doctor had told Booth that the malady was not a boil but a cyst that would have to be cut out, but that he could not complete the procedure him-self because he had no assistant.

Canning went on to describe how Booth had then volunteered him (Canning) as an assistant and told the doctor to proceed. "When the doctor made his first swipe with the scalpel I almost fell to the floor," Canning said. "The black blood gushed out and it appeared as though he had cut his head off. All at once, I fell to the floor, fainting."

Canning said Booth was laid up for about a month after the procedure, but eventually recovered. "But do you know," said Canning to his interrogators, "that the ball I shot into his leg came out the hole in his neck!"

The fact that Canning could appear to believe such a preposterous claim (which Booth had completely fabricated), would lend credence to the assumption that the theater owner, despite his business acumen, was not a terribly bright individual.

Aftermath

On April 26, 1865, Junius Booth and Canning were informed that John Wilkes Booth had been hunted down and killed. Both men reportedly expressed mixed emotions. John Wilkes' problems were ended, but theirs were just beginning.

The following day, the assassin's body was brought to the Federal Prison in Baltimore. The Booths and Canning were asked to positively identify the remains. Canning reportedly pointed to a scar on the actor's neck, as well as to the scar on his leg made by the gunshot wound. Following the identification by these and other witnesses, Booth's body literally was buried beneath the prison. It remained there for four years until it was transferred to the Booth family cemetery in Baltimore.

Since there was little concrete evidence against Canning, he was released from Federal Prison in Baltimore in early May 1865. He was exhausted, yet relieved to be free.

Canning eventually returned to his career of theatrical management. Edwin Booth, however, went into seclusion after his younger brother's death. He was convinced his acting career was finished.

Interestingly, eleven months later, with little money or prospects, Edwin inquired if Canning would arrange some bookings for him. Surprisingly, though some theater goers jeered him with disparaging insults, Edwin ultimately made a triumphant return to the stage. According to Stanley Kimmel's *The Mad Booths of Maryland,* his New York opening set a record on that day as the city's largest box office draw to that date.

Canning returned to Columbus, Georgia, twice during the 1870s as a representative of Edwin Booth. Both times, Edwin appeared at the Springer Opera House, the city's newest theater, where he appeared in the production of *Hamlet.* He was well-received.

During his first visit to Columbus after his release from prison, Canning returned to his old theater – Temperance Hall – to see what remained there. To his disappointment, he discovered it had fallen into disuse. One of the last battles of the U.S. Civil War had been waged only a block away, so there had been considerable destruction in the vicinity.

Mathew Canning continued in theater management until the late 1880s. He eventually retired to Long Branch, New Jersey, where he died in August 1890. His actual involvement (if any) with the assassination of Abraham Lincoln remains a mystery today.

LAST WILL AND TESTAMENT

Insight into a prominent Confederate congressman's rather unusual conduct during the Civil War may lie in the caustic comments he penned in his Last Will and Testament.

Daniel M. Roper

F*irst, I desire my place known as Glenwood near Rome, Georgia to be held for the use and benefit of my wife for and during her natural life. This is meant to carry with it every thing possessed – furniture, library, stock, carriages, etc.*

On May 18, 1888, Augustus Romaldus Wright penned these words in his Last Will and Testament. The opening instructions dealt with the needs of his wife, Adaline, and hinted that Wright was a man of means, as was indeed the case. His words also served as a prologue to some decidedly caustic denunciations to follow.

Wright was a man of many interests and abilities who held lofty positions while in his prime. He was a prominent lawyer, former superior court judge, ordained minister of both Methodist and Baptist denominations, U.S. Congressman from 1857 to 1859, colonel in the Confederate Army, and member of the Confederate Congress.

Despite his stature and obvious southern pedigree, there were questions about Wright's loyalty to the South before and during the Civil War. These doubts arose from his role in the events leading to secession, followed by his rather unusual activities during the war.

Whether justified or not, Wright's reputation suffered then and remains tarnished even today, nearly 150 years later. I first heard misgivings expressed about Wright a decade ago when I spoke of him to a Rome lawyer whose grandfather had been a Confederate cavalryman. The lawyer rubbed his chin and said, "My father did not like that man. He was not a loyal Southerner."

How did the allegiance of a man of such distinction, who had four sons in the Confederate Army and a son-in-law who died in the service, come to be called into question? There is no doubt that some of the suspicions stemmed from Wright's unpopular opposition to secession before the war, but the real culprit was his quest for reconciliation during the war.

Wright's integrity always served him well, but at times his personality created friction. He was opinionated and stubborn, qualities that encouraged regular crusades that rubbed his foes – and not infrequently his friends – the wrong way. Yet I believe these traits, embodied in the prickly comments Wright offered in his Last Will and Testament, were those of a man incapable of disloyalty.

I desire my wife to be disturbed in no way, wishing to make the remainder of her days as pleasant as possible in a world of great riches and pride, & human woes, arising from what the Apostle James calls, "the oppressions of rich men, whose garments (from their multitude) he declares are moth eaten."

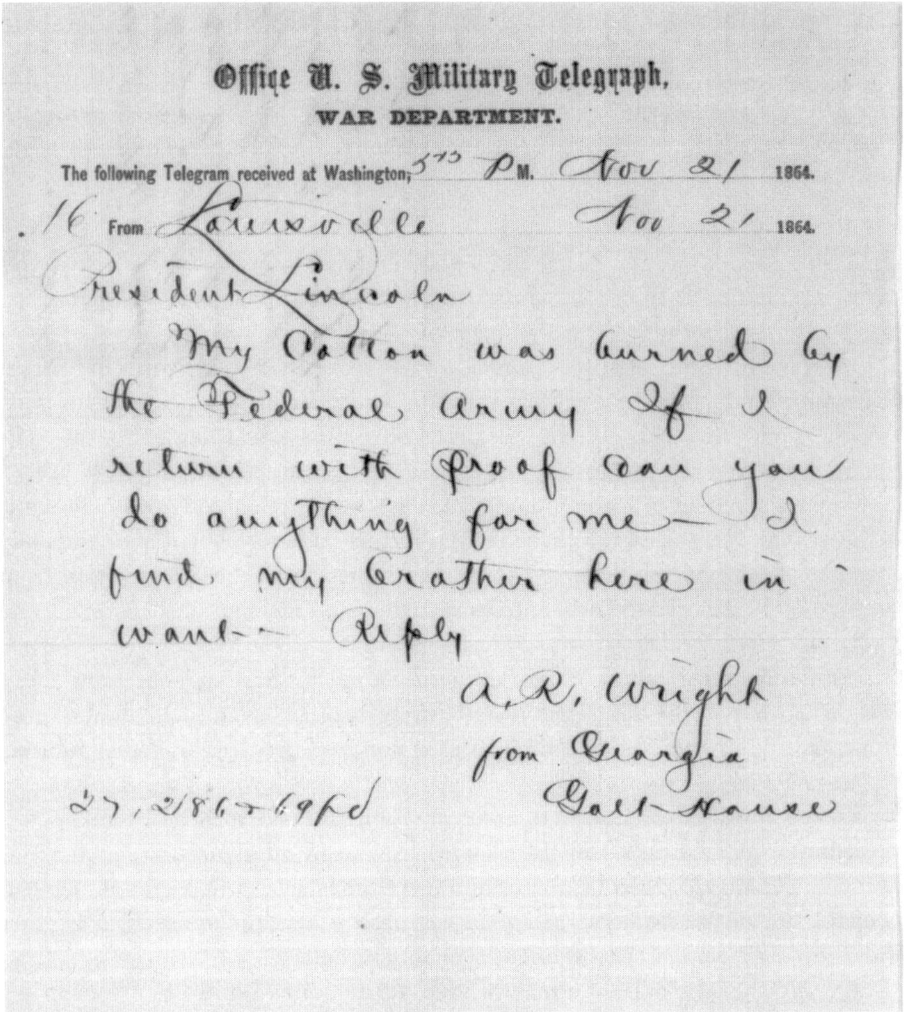

Office U. S. Military Telegraph,
WAR DEPARTMENT.

The following Telegram received at Washington, 5:15 P.M. Nov 21 1864.

16 From Louisville Nov 21 1864.

President Lincoln

My Cotton was burned by the Federal Army If I return with proof can you do anything for me — I find my brother here in want — Reply

A. R. Wright
from Georgia
Galt House

27, 2/86 69 fd

Shortly after meeting with Abraham Lincoln in Washington D.C., Augustus Wright wrote the president from Louisville, Kentucky, to request help.

I desire, however, she may, as much as possible, come out from among them, and join her sympathies to the laboring, working, humble poor. The rich, nearly all of whom are leaders in the churches, are the whitest sepulchers of earth, beautiful without, but within, full of rottenness and dead men's bones.

Wright had always been a consort of rich and influential men, so his mistrust of the rich and influential seems unusual. He was a classmate of Alexander H. Stephens and Robert Toombs at Franklin College in Athens, partnered with some of Rome's leading attorneys, and had several business ventures with Alfred Shorter, a financier and trader who founded the Rome college that bears his name today.

Yet Wright had enemies too, primarily arising from disagreements over political

Augustus R. Wright

issues. Simpson Fouche, an educator and planter who had known Wright for many years, became a bitter foe. Fouche encouraged Francis Shropshire, Wright's son-in-law, to oppose Wright's candidacy in the election for delegates to the 1861 Secession Convention in Milledgeville. Shropshire won the election and cast his vote in favor of disunion.

Wright's ante-secession sentiments were well-known and widely detested. In testimony before Congress after the Civil War, Wright vividly described the unrest in Rome on the eve of secession. "Now public sentiment in the South is very violent," he explained. "You have never been, any of you, at the starting of a revolution. You have no idea how it sweeps the land. I made a speech in the City Hall of Rome, and but for a few personal friends, they would have killed me right there."

Despite the turmoil created by their strong opposition to secession, Alexander Stephens and Augustus Wright were chosen to be two of 10 delegates sent by Georgia to the February 1861 convention of the seceded states to create a new national government, and it was there that Stephens was chosen vice-president. It seems that principled men like Stephens and Wright suffered no grievous harm to their reputations notwithstanding their efforts to preserve the Union.

Once secession became a reality, Wright threw his support to the new Confederacy. He organized a military unit, Wright's Legion, and briefly served as commanding officer of the 38th Georgia Infantry Regiment. He soon resigned, however, in order to serve in the Confederate House of Representatives. His election to that body proved that he still held the confidence of the people in his district, a state of affairs that would not last much longer.

Wright's penchant for taking unpopular stands continued while he served in the Confederate Congress. One instance occurred when he issued a scathing indictment of the struggling new nation's treatment of its prisoners of war. Neither did he wholeheartedly take to the idea of Southern independence. When the fortunes of war turned against the Southern states, Wright offered a resolution encouraging reunification of North and South. There followed bitter, acrimonious denunciations of Wright by his colleagues, the press, and many Southerners, and in 1863

COURTESY FORREST SHROPSHIRE

When Wright sought election as a delegate to Georgia's Secession Convention, he was defeated by his son-in-law, F.C. Shropshire who voted in favor of secession. In 1862, Shropshire became ill and died in Cumberland Gap, Tennessee, while serving on Confederate general Kirby Smith's staff.

he lost his bid for re-election.

Wright returned to Rome, but the advance of the Union Army under General William T. Sherman soon threatened the city. So Wright and his family sought refuge at their plantation on the Coosa River in Alabama. Sherman, who was aware of Wright's pro-Union sentiments, later sought an audience with him in an effort to gain his cooperation in an improbable peace plan.

Sherman was convinced that Georgia had grown weary of war by late 1864 and might be enticed to rejoin the Union. "[If Georgia will] withdraw her quota out of the Confederate army," he wrote Abraham Lincoln, the Federal Army would not desolate the land, and Sherman would "keep our men to the high roads and commons and pay for the corn and meat we need and take." Sherman wanted Wright to travel to Washington, D.C., to discuss this proposition with Lincoln.

Although he must have known he was in an awkward position, Wright went. It is unclear whether his participation in Sherman's scheme was voluntary. Documents in official war records suggest that Wright willingly served as Sherman's emissary. Testifying before Congress in 1871, however, Wright claimed that he had been placed under arrest by Federal troops and taken to Atlanta to see Sherman.

Whatever the circumstances, Wright spent two weeks in Washington talking with Lincoln, "more or less every day." According to Wright, Lincoln said that he "had his proclamation of amnesty written for the whole South, from Mr. Davis down to the humblest citizen…and…the day we laid down our arms it would be published, and the South restored to her high rights in the Union, as far as was in his power." Lincoln also implied that Wright would be appointed military governor of Georgia.

Sherman's plan for peace never bore fruit, and the South soon surrendered. But Wright's role in the affair left a bad taste in the mouths of many Southerners who supported the Confederacy until the bitter end, and raised grave questions about his loyalty.

Wright bequeathed his house, Glenwood, to his wife in his Last Will and Testament. Glenwood stood a few miles north of Rome, where Berry College's Barnwell Chapel stands today. The college saved parts of the house when it was demolished early last century and used them in the construction of Glenwood Cottage, which still stands today.

Was Wright a traitor? There is one piece of evidence that is quite damning. In a September 30, 1864, letter to Sherman, a Union general wrote, "[Augustus Wright] reports Hood's army across the Chattahoochee, a portion at Villa Rica, all moving on Blue Mountain.

Had Wright knowingly provided military information to the enemy? I long struggled with this possibility. Given his record, service to the Confederacy, and perhaps most importantly his four sons serving in the Southern army, it seems unlikely. Perhaps he thought the information was already public knowledge, which was indeed the case.

When I came across Wright's Last Will and Testament on file in the records of the Floyd County Probate Court, I read his caustic comments with some amusement. Then I realized that his harsh words mirror his character and help explain his actions during the Civil War.

I warn [Adaline] *to keep out of debt, for her happiness while on earth. To fall under the extortions of the money power, in its woes, can be compared to nothing but the tortures of the damned. Like the Inquisition, at every turn of the screw, they dislocate a limb, till the subject lies a mangled corpse. Let her love simplicity and walk in truth.*

Wright's rebuke of the wealthy and the powerful, and his loathing of the hypocrisy found in the churches of his day, are the words of an idealist; of a man who valued truth, honor, honesty and character above riches, prestige, and haughtiness. His entire life gave proof of his character, and his Last Will and Testament reflects his idealism. For such a man, treason was unthinkable.

Was there disloyalty to the South in Augustus Wright's work for reunification? He put it this way in his testimony before Congress seven years later: "While there was never a time during the whole war that I did not desire the restitution of the Union, yet I never saw the day that I was willing to lay down arms without terms consistent with our rights and honor, and never did I do an act that I did not believe was for the welfare of the Southern states."

A YANKEE HERO OF GETTYSBURG AND A GEORGIA CONNECTION

In a twist of ironic fate – or of fortune as the case may be – a resident of the state of Maine made a decision that quite likely affected the course of a nation. Instead of moving to Georgia to pursue the love of his life, Joshua L. Chamberlain chose to remain in Maine, and would be ultimately credited with the outcome of the most critical battle of the entire War Between the States.

ANNE BUCKNER BURGAMY AND HUGH T. HARRINGTON

In 1852, a 27-year-old woman named Frances "Fannie" Adams traveled from Maine to Milledgeville, Georgia, to be a music teacher. Even though the Civil War was nine years in the future, her presence in Georgia came close to having a major impact on the battle of Gettysburg and perhaps the outcome of the war itself.

The battle of Gettysburg is considered by many to be the pivotal battle of the entire war. The battle came at a time when the Confederate Army was on the offensive having moved into Pennsylvania to threaten the capital of the United States. Due to manpower, materiel and production capacity shortages this would be, in all likelihood, the Confederacy's last shot at seizing Washington, D.C.

A victory on the battlefield was critical. A successful campaign, especially one on enemy soil, might bring about recognition of the Confederacy from foreign governments as well as the possibility of a negotiated peace after two long years of war. A large-scale defeat would mean a loss of men and equipment that would be almost impossible to replace. Failure would not only put the Confederacy on the defensive again but would alter the military strategy to one of desperate survival and avoidance of the final catastrophe.

When one thinks of Gettysburg, "Pickett's Charge" inevitably comes to mind. That famous assault on the third day of the battle by 12,000 Confederate troops moving right into the mouths of the cannons upon the heights of Cemetery Ridge is said by many to be the actual turning point of the war.

The key to victory at Gettysburg was not Pickett's Charge, though. The key engagement actually took place a day earlier at Little Round Top. If one considers the Union positions in the battle as being shaped like a fishhook, Little Round Top would be at the end of the shank – the far left of the Union line. Cemetery Ridge, the objective of Picket's Charge, would be along the length of the shank. The bend and the hook itself would be East Cemetery Hill and Culp's Hill.

Colonel Joshua L. Chamberlain,
commander of the 20th Maine Regiment

The Milledgeville home of Richard M. Orme and his wife, Abby.

Control of Little Round Top was essential to victory. Artillery placed on Little Round Top would be able to cover a wide area. If the Union held this high ground the Confederate forces would be vulnerable. If the Confederates were able to take Little Round Top their artillery would rain destruction upon the Union forces all along Cemetery Ridge. The Union rear, on the back of the slope of Cemetery Ridge, would also come under fire.

Additionally, as Little Round Top was at the end of the Union left it may have been possible for Confederate forces to go around the Union flank and attack the rear of the Union army. Not only would this be an untenable situation for the Union army, it would also place Confederate forces between the Union army and Washington, D.C. – a disastrous scenario for the Federals.

Despite its strategic importance, on the afternoon of July 2, 1863, Little Round Top was occupied by only a handful of Union signalmen. The imminent danger posed by that situation was suddenly realized, and a brigade was rushed up the hill to secure the position.

At the far left of the line established on the slope that day was the 20th Maine Regiment commanded by Colonel Joshua L. Chamberlain. Chamberlain was 34 years old and an unlikely officer. He had no military training. Rather, he had spent three years at Bangor Theological Seminary.

Upon graduation from Bangor, instead of becoming a minister, Chamberlain had taken the position of professor of rhetoric and modern languages at Bowdoin College. In 1862, he took a leave of absence from Bowdoin, left his wife and children, and joined the army.

A year later, Chamberlain found himself commanding a regiment positioned at the most critical location on the battlefield of Gettysburg. In the next few hours the decisive and heroic actions of this professor, this man of God, would not only secure the Union left but would earn him the Medal of Honor. Joshua Lawrence Chamberlain was about to enter the realm of legend.

Chamberlain was ordered to "hold that ground at all hazards."[1] He instructed his men to take cover behind what rocks were available and to expect a determined attack. Within minutes of his arrival at Little Round Top his regiment came under artillery and rifle fire. The enemy charged, approaching to within yards of his position. They were beaten back but they came again and again. Chamberlain noticed Confederate soldiers moving to his left so he stretched his line to meet them.

According to a later description by Chamberlain, the edge of the fight rolled backward and forward like a wave. With desperate assaults along the entire front of his thin line Chamberlain later wrote that he saw "squads of the enemy brake (sic) through our line in several places, and the fight was literally hand to hand." Ammunition was running low and his men gathered ammunition from fallen soldiers of both sides.

After a couple of hours of repeated attacks Chamberlain's regiment had suffered over 30% casualties. He could see the Confederates forming for yet another assault and "it did not seem possible to withstand another shock like this now coming on." The situation could not have been worse as "...my ammunition was soon exhausted. My men were firing their last shot and getting ready to club with their muskets."

Despite the desperate situation, Chamberlain did not forget his orders to "hold that ground at all hazards." He wrote, "It was imperative to strike before we were struck by this overwhelming force in a hand-to-hand fight, which we could not probably have withstood or survived...I ordered the bayonet."

The order to fix bayonets and charge "ran like fire along the line, from man to man, and rose into a shout, and with which they sprang forward upon the enemy, now not 30 yards away." Waving his sword, Chamberlain led his men into the face of the attackers. Many of the Confederate soldiers surrendered to the howling men from Maine carrying unloaded rifles. Others were killed or wounded. The rest turned and fled.

Little Round Top, the vulnerable and valuable position on the Union line, was secure. The critical moment of this critical battle was over.

This fierce afternoon combat at Little Round Top has been well described in historian Ken Burns' TV documentary *The Civil War*, and in Michael Shaara's book *The Killer Angels*, which was made into the movie *Gettysburg*.

While the men of the 20th Maine fought with extraordinary courage they could not have done so without Chamberlain's leadership. His personal charisma carried his men to the heights of their great achievement. If the 20th Maine had been there but under command of a different officer, the outcome likely would not have been the same. Chamberlain was that sort of leader.

In a strange twist of history, Chamberlain, the man who so powerfully influenced the outcome of the battle of Gettysburg and perhaps the entire war, earlier had almost abandoned Maine to become a Georgian.

In 1852, Chamberlain was deeply in love with his fiancé Fannie Adams, the lady who had relocated to Milledgeville to become a music teacher. He was not pleased when she went to Georgia while he remained behind studying at the Seminary. For a couple of years he vacillated about his future plans, but he never wavered from his desire to marry Fannie Adams, wherever she lived.

Fannie stayed in Milledgeville for three years living at the home of Richard M. Orme and his wife, Abby. Richard Orme was the editor and publisher of *The Southern Recorder*, one of the most influential newspapers in the South. His wife, a distant relation of Fannie, ran a school in Milledgeville.

Following his training at Bangor, Chamberlain had come to the conclusion that he was not interested in a career in the ministry. He had decided that he wanted to be a college professor. The Ormes suggested that he take a position as a professor at the University of Georgia.[2] Had Chamberlain followed the lead of the Ormes, he would have been teaching in Georgia and not available to command the 20th Maine on Little Round Top. The outcome of the battle and the war itself might very well have been quite different.

The window of historical opportunity was briefly open but Chamberlain did not take advantage of it and move to Georgia. In the process, he quite likely changed the course of a nation.

Fannie left Milledgeville in the fall of 1855 and returned to New England where she married Chamberlain – no doubt much to his delight. Neither of them ever visited Georgia again.

Endnotes

1. Battle descriptions and quotations from report of Col. Joshua Lawrence Chamberlain, July 6, 1863.

2. Letter from Frances "Fannie" Adams to J.L. Chamberlain, dated Milledgeville, June 23, 1853.

RETURN TO CHICKAMAUGA

Something about a Georgia battlefield mystified everyone except those who had fought there, and it served as a reminder of the high cost exacted by the Civil War.

MARION BLACKWELL, JR.

Hot dust from the horse's hoofs and the carriage wheels hung in the air. Septembers in Georgia are always hot and dusty. Dust clung to sweat on the lone passenger's face and on his lone hand, but it bothered him not. It covered his black suit and wide-brimmed gray felt hat, but he did not notice. His attention was focused on the land around him: the rutted dirt road, the cultivated fields of corn and cotton, and the dark, foreboding shade of the forests of oak and pine. Twenty years had passed since two great armies clashed here on the banks of Chickamauga Creek, and the once-ravaged land still showed many scars of battle.

"Where to, Colonel?" asked the driver. With soft words and gestures the Colonel directed the carriage through twists and turns, standing in the carriage often, searching for the particular site, and finally instructing, "Stop here. This is it." On the side of the road was an immense corn field with brown stalks eight feet tall and the largest ears of corn he had ever seen. On the far side of the corn field was the forest, its shadows as dark and shrouding as they were on the day he led his men here.

Samuel Augustus Burney of Madison enlisted in the Panola Guards (Company G), Cobb's Legion. This photograph was taken in 1861. In a letter to his wife written November 15 of that year, he described a "most melancholy occurrence" when Cobb's Legion mistakenly fired upon friendly troops, killing a major and wounding several others. "I squatted in a tree top," he detailed. "There were no Yankees there, but our men thought so and fired on [them]. I did not fire as I saw no one but what I knew were our men. So I am not to be blamed for what happened, as I had presence of mind not to fire."

Not really men, but boys. Georgia boys, filled with the excitement of war, from towns like Macon, Columbus, and Decatur – all assembled here to stop the invaders from the north.

It was in the woods behind him where he had formed his regiment in line of battle, with bayonets fixed, and it was here where he had exhorted them, "Do not let them spoil this sacred soil of Georgia!" Where the tall corn now grew was then a meadow of knee-high grass gleaming in the summer sun, decorated with patches

William F. Gay (left) and John Gay of Jasper County stand for a portrait in 1861. The two brothers were 18 and 19 years old, respectively, when they enlisted in the Glover Guards (Company G), 4th Georgia Regiment. John was wounded at Chancellorsville and was present at the surrender at Appomattox. William was twice wounded in action, and near war's end sought to join General Joseph Johnston's force in North Carolina, only to find that they too had surrendered. William then walked all the way home to Newborn, Georgia, and kept his rifle and army jacket. John lived until 1877 and William until 1916.

of blue and yellow flowers, deceptive in its tranquility. And it was here that he had commanded them, "Now here we go, lads. Regiment, forward! For God, for home, for country…give 'em hell!"

But in the shadows of the trees on the far side of the meadow there were other boys, dressed all in blue, some kneeling, some standing, with rifles cocked, waiting, watching the brown and gray line as it advanced across the contested meadow. The boys in blue heard their leader whisper, "Steady, steady, hold your fire. One good volley, then retire."

With sabers and bayonets glossy in the bright sunlight, regimental colors streaming ahead, the Colonel's regiment advanced rapidly across the glade. Their heads held high, their muskets lowered, their Colonel shouting, "Forward, forward!"

Some heard, from the dark woods ahead, the one word – "Fire!"

A brief rattle of muskets was followed immediately by thunderous flame as the hidden blue

For reasons unknown, Reuben Harrison Nations of Whitfield County went "abroad" to enlist. He served in the Farmer Guards (Company I), 12th Louisiana Regiment. He suffered wounds to both legs necessitating amputation below each knee. After the war he returned to Whitfield County.

LEFT: This unidentified Confederate soldier is fully accoutered with wooden sling canteen, rife equipped with Maynard priming system, shoulder belt with cartridge box, and waist belt with cap box. He posed in front of an elaborately painted studio backdrop. The condition of his uniform and gear suggest that he served in the Army of Northern Virginia and that this photo was taken early in the war. RIGHT: The dash and aplomb of the Confederate cavalryman is well-represented by Joseph W. Morrow of Covington. He served in Company F, 2nd Georgia Cavalry, in the commands of both Nathan B. Forrest and "Fighting" Joe Wheeler.

line projected a blizzard of lead and steel to meet the Regiment. A six-gun battery of polished brass artillery spewed fire with canister, and the Regiment melted into the Georgia soil.

Still standing in the carriage, the Colonel relived it all again, as if it were just now happening. He saw his boys stumble, the Regimental colors fall to the ground and not be picked up, and in the space of a gasp he saw his people around him without limbs, without jaws, without heads, without life...enriching this Georgia soil with their native blood. He remembered the sting when a round of canister carried away his own left arm, to be left upon the field forever. It, too, had eventually disappeared into the soil.

But that was twenty years ago. The empty left sleeve of the dusty black suit was pinned up now, and the field of carnage was now a field of corn.

With a loud rustle of dry corn leaves a farmer with hoe in hand walked out from between the tall rows and saw the Colonel gazing at his crop. Mopping his brow, the farmer addressed the Colonel, "Like my corn, do you? All my neighbors wonder why it grows so green and high. Sometimes I wonder why myself."

The Colonel's fingers lightly touched the brim of his gray hat, shielding the anguish in his eyes from the farmer's proud stare.

The Colonel knew why.

ABOVE: In 1861, Gordon County's fierce looking Chitwood brothers (Daniel, John, and Pleasant) enlisted in the Bartow Yankee Killers (Company A), 23rd Georgia Regiment. Pleasant died of chronic diarrhea in Richmond, Virginia in 1862. Daniel and John were captured with most of their regiment at Chancellorsville on May 2, 1863. They were freed in a prisoner exchange three weeks later and served throughout the remainder of the war. BELOW: This is one of just a few photographs of a Confederate military unit. Organized in Augusta where this photograph was taken, the Oglethorpe Infantry (Company D), 1st Volunteer Regiment, Georgia Infantry posed in striped trousers in April 1861. Note the drummer, the chevrons on the sleeves of several corporals and sergeants, and the officer at far right.

This impressive looking veteran is Warren A. Moseley, photographed at a reunion in Macon in 1912. He served in the Baldwin Blues (Company H), 4th Georgia Regiment and was twice wounded in action. His uniform is a bit of a mystery – the collar bears three stars, the insignia of a colonel, but records detail that Moseley's highest rank was captain.

Georgia's last surviving Confederate veteran, William J. Bush, is honored in Fitzgerald, circa 1945. Bush, who was affectionately known as "General" later in life, was actually a private during the war. He served briefly in the Ramah Guards (Company B), 14th Georgia Regiment. After three months, he was discharged, probably due to his age (16). He later served in the Georgia Militia and took part in several skirmishes. He was 107 years old when he passed away November 11, 1952.

ABOVE: William Franklin Edwards, photographed with niece Mary Edwards and I.W. Edwards, displays the flag of the 42nd Georgia Regiment, circa 1905. Edwards served as color sergeant for the regiment, which surrendered with the Confederate garrison of Vicksburg, Mississippi, in July 1863. Vicksburg. Mr. Edwards was the regiment's last color bearer and hid the flag in his coat, carrying it home after the war ended. BELOW: The men in gray pose at the Sandersville library on Confederate Memorial Day in 1916. The drummer is Thomas Harris Sparks who served in the Jackson Guards (Company B), 59th Georgia Regiment. The instrument was made by a man in nearby Warthen, who carved Sparks' name on it. Sparks lost the drum on a battlefield, but years later his son saw a notice in an Atlanta newspaper placed by a New Yorker who wished to return the drum to its owner.

ABOVE: "Uncle" Steve Eberhardt at a gathering of Confederate veterans in Thomasville in 1924. Eberhardt had been a slave who accompanied his master during the war. Afterwards, he settled in Rome, Georgia, and became a fixture at Confederate reunions. His ensemble included flags, feathers, and guinea hens. BELOW: Twenty-five years after his capture by federal troops in South Georgia, Jefferson Davis, the only president of the ill-fated Confederacy, traveled to Macon for the Georgia State Fair in October 1887. The fair featured a Confederate veteran's reunion. Davis is in the carriage drawn by white horses. The prominent building is the Lanier House on Mulberry Street.

The bearded, gray gentlemen of Camp 1670, United Confederate Veterans, strike a pose at Fort Gaines on Confederate Memorial Day, 1915. The banner on the right appears to bear the legend "Fort Gaines Guards," and at least one of the men in the photo (T.M. Brown) served in that unit – Company D, 9th Georgia Regiment.

By 1890, the men who had enlisted in the Confederate forces as youngsters – and sometimes as boys – were middle-aged and graying. When this group of Walton County veterans assembled they displayed a photograph of a comrade who had recently passed away.

ABOVE: Since its organization in 1894, the United Daughters of the Confederacy has worked faithfully in its efforts "to honor the memory of those who served and those who fell in the service of the Confederate States of America." The Margaret Jones Chapter gathered at the R.C. Neely house in Waynesboro, circa 1900. BELOW: A new generation pauses to honor the old: The Adeline Baum Chapter of the Children of the Confederacy gathered in Dublin, Georgia, circa 1925.

As the aging veterans of the Lost Cause began passing away in large number in the late 1800s and early 1900s, citizens in nearly every Georgia county raised funds to erect monuments in their honor. Here an unidentified veteran poses beside Albany's Confederate Monument on Confederate Memorial Day 1903. Notice the garlands of flowers and the portraits of Jefferson Davis and Robert E. Lee.

The citizens of Toccoa gathered for the unveiling of the Confederate monument in Stephens County, circa 1925. This memorial was erected by the local chapter of the United Daughters of the Confederacy.

The citizens of Thomasville assembled in 1916 for the dedication of a monument to John Triplett, a Confederate veteran and founder of the *Thomasville Times*.

James Longstreet's funeral procession included the Queen City Band, Candler Horse Guards, Governor's Horse Guards, and Confederate veterans (including at least two amputees). Longstreet, affectionately known as "Old Pete" and "Lee's War Horse," was the most prominent Confederate field officer from Georgia. He died in Gainesville on January 2, 1904 and is buried in Alta Vista Cemetery.

"Furling the Flag," by Richard Norris Brooke, depicts the dejection at the Confederate surrender at Appomattox Courthouse, Virginia, in April 1865.

THE FIRST SHOTS
OF THE CIVIL WAR

*When a bitter political disagreement between South Carolinians incites a fateful duel,
the contestants choose to meet on a remote Georgia island.*

RAY CHANDLER

As dawn broke on August 16, 1832, two men in a clearing on a small island in the Tugaloo River near Hatton's Ford, Franklin County, Georgia, stood back to back, took ten paces forward, turned and slowly raised their pistols. Two cracks broke the morning silence, and a group of bystanders rushed toward one of the men as he staggered and slumped to the sand.

While the history books tell us the Confederate shells fired on Charleston Harbor's Fort Sumter in April 1861 were the first shots of the Civil War, you could argue that the first shots were the cracks of those two dueling pistols in the Georgia backwoods 29 years earlier. The man hit was named Turner Bynum, Jr., the 25-year-old editor of a Greenville, South Carolina, newspaper, and he would linger in agony for three days before he died.

The man Bynum faced that morning was Benjamin Franklin Perry, the editor of a rival Greenville newspaper, and years later Perry became governor of South Carolina. He would regret to the end of his days killing Bynum, whom he described in his memoirs as "a young man of talents, wrote well, high spirited and of unquestioned courage," but the same red hot politics that would lead to the bombardment of Fort Sumter brought both men to that uninhabited island near Hatton's Ford

Hot Blood

It was the Age of Jackson and the hot political issue of the day was federal tariffs. President Andrew Jackson was waging war on the economic policies of the Whigs, epitomized by what a leading Whig, Kentucky's Henry Clay, called the American System: a strong central banking system to promote capital and stiff tariffs to promote agriculture and home-grown manufacturing.

At first, tariffs appealed to Americans, but by the late 1820s many in the predominately agricultural South came to view high duties on imported manufactured articles as punitive, and they agitated for open markets that would mean cheaper goods. Northern manufacturers, on the other hand, wanted tariffs to continue to dampen foreign access to American markets.

The fracture of sectionalism quickly became apparent. In 1828, as Jackson was winning his first term in office, a still higher tariff was imposed, one so steep its detractors came to call it the Tariff of Abomination. Opposed to stiff tariffs at

heart, Jackson saved most of his fire for the central banking system, so he disappointed those who believed tariffs were the greater evil.

It was also the Age of Calhoun, as in John C. Calhoun, the hot-blooded upcountry South Carolinian who served as Jackson's Vice-President. Here, the anti-tariff crusaders had their St. George. A staunch unionist in outlook and actions early in his political career, Calhoun had supported tariffs until opposition in his home state became overwhelming. He then became more stridently outspoken and sectionalist over the issue. In South Carolina and much of the South at the time, his stance placed him on the side of the angels.

In 1832, South Carolina moved headlong toward crisis. Calhoun led the way by espousing the view that whenever a state thought an act of the federal government infringed on a state's rights under the Constitution the state could declare the act null and void within its boundaries. The issue of nullification arose, drawing a firm line between those holding strong unionist views and their opponents supporting states' rights doctrines, some of whom began calling for secession. The always red-hot politics of South Carolina had reached white heat.

No Jurisdiction

Benjamin Perry was a supporter of tariffs, and a strong unionist to his core. The 27-year-old Perry had been a successful attorney in the Greenville area before becoming editor of the *Greenville Mountaineer* in 1829, a move aimed at giving him a stage from which to trumpet his opinions. He was an eloquent and credible foe of nullification practically in Calhoun's backyard in what is today Clemson.

At the time, there wasn't a pro-nullification newspaper in the South Carolina upcountry. Enter Turner Bynum. The young South Carolina College-educated journalist and writer – he had published a book of poetry – was invited to become editor of the *Southern Sentinel*, an anti-tariff, pro-nullification newspaper established in Greenville to fight a war of words with Benjamin Perry.

Bynum arrived in Greenville in June 1832 and by August 4 was so engaged in the nullification fight that he lambasted Perry personally in a scathing editorial. Perry responded by challenging Bynum to a duel.

Dueling was not an unusual act at the time. In the hot-blooded politics of the day, issuing a challenge to duel was intended to intimidate and humiliate a political opponent, and it was a way to prove a man's readiness to back his words and honor by risking his life. Dueling certainly wasn't new to Perry; on three previous occasions he had challenged Greenville men to duels and had in fact stabbed another in an altercation over politics.

Bynum was equal to Perry's challenge. Their war of words would be settled by pistols at dawn.

The site selected for the contest was an island of about 60 acres near Hatton's Ford on the Tugaloo River, near the Georgia shore. While the two didn't offer any explanation why they chose this site, it is fairly easy to surmise: Under the Treaty of Beaufort, islands in the Tugaloo River belong to Georgia. Although dueling was fairly common in the antebellum South, it was also illegal, so choosing a site in Georgia meant the South Carolinians were not violating the laws of their own state.

Islands in boundary rivers were particularly good places for duels since uncertainties about jurisdiction could be raised as a legal defense. That was especially true of the often-argued and disputed river border between South Carolina and Georgia.

Twelve days after Bynum fired his editorial broadside, the two men, along with their seconds, met their deadly dawn. By eyewitness accounts, Bynum fired first, and his bullet ripped through the lapel of Perry's coat. Perry's bullet followed almost immediately and tore through Bynum's body just above his right hip.

By the numbers, Bynum was unlucky twice over. Relatively few people died as a result of duels, given the inaccuracy of smoothbore dueling pistols at the standard distance of about 50 feet. A historical survey of antebellum dueling reveals that overall only one in 14 duelists died; of those wounded, only one in five.

But Bynum was fated to die a hard death, and five days after the duel was buried in the Old Stone Church cemetery, near modern day Clemson and near Calhoun's home.

Union Man

The Perry-Bynum duel didn't solve anything. The Nullification Crisis moved forward and, in November 1832, a state convention passed an Ordinance of Nullification. Benjamin Perry served as a delegate to the convention and voted against the ordinance.

Whatever his feelings on tariffs and the wisdom of limited federal government, Andrew Jackson was an ardent nationalist. The Union must be preserved and the law must be enforced. He denounced South Carolina's actions, began preparing for military action, and asked Congress to authorize the use of force to collect tariffs. He also sought a reduction in the tariff rates.

On both counts, Jackson got what he wanted. The passage of a compromise tariff in 1833 allowed the South Carolina convention to repeal the nullification ordinance while saving face. The crisis subsided, but it drove Calhoun from the vice-presidency and into more strident fights over states' rights.

After the Nullification Crisis ended, Benjamin Perry resigned as editor of the *Greenville Mountaineer* and entered politics. Elected to the state legislature in 1836, he served through the end of the Civil War. He continued to champion a strong Union, but ironically praised Calhoun's states' rights stance over Northern efforts to curb the spread of slavery into the West.

Though a vociferous foe of secession in the late 1850s, when it became a fact in 1860 he served as a district attorney under South Carolina's Confederate government while also continuing to serve in the legislature. In 1865, he was appointed a district judge. Well known for his unionist views, he was appointed by President Andrew Johnson as South Carolina's provisional governor after the Civil War.

Despite his successes, however, whenever the memory of his duel with Bynum was resurrected, Benjamin Perry grieved over the young man's death and regretted to the end of his days firing what may have been the first fatal shot in the bitter disagreement that led to Civil War.

Sources
The Keowee Courier
The Oconee Journal-Tribune
History of South Carolina by Walter Edgar
The Duel: Aaron Burr, Alexander Hamilton and the future of America by Thomas Fleming

THIRTY-ONE BOYS

By Emma Cottrell

They lie in a quiet Georgia wood,
at the end of a short trail;
not where they died
nor where they fell
a hundred and forty years ago,
but carried here
by wagon and cart
in blazing sun, shadowy moonlight,
pouring rain, chilling wind.

War killed them.
Robbed them of their youth.
Butchered them
with cannon ball, bullets, bayonets.
Some met death on lonely country roads
or fierce, unnamed bloody skirmishes;
still defending, still rallying,
refusing to believe Atlanta had fallen.
Others died in the hospitals at Oxford College,
their mangled bodies cut-apart even more
by doctors desperate to save them.

They lie together,
thirty-one
from Alabama, Tennessee, Texas, Louisiana,
Mississippi, South Carolina – other Confederate states.
Their names are here,
not their first name,
only their initials and last.
Seven are marked "unknown;"
the ultimate indignity war can bestow.

Their presence lingers,
whispering of the wastefulness of war:
that they would have rather spent their days
on earth listening to the song of birds
instead of the roar of cannons,

held their sweetheart in their arms
instead of a dying comrade,
walked the fresh green fields of home
instead of far-off fields of blood and pain.

I stand here
wanting to cry for them,
to hold them in my arms,
ease their last breaths.
Wondering how they may have looked,
calling them by Johnny or Jim
or any name that makes them real.
Longing to send a message across time
to a waiting mother who never knew where her boy lay
that I've found him — beneath the red clay of Georgia
but, it's too late.

I turn away
from the tall stone simply inscribed.
"Our Soldiers."
There is nothing I can do now
except visit once in a while, just
to let them know
I feel their pain, their loneliness.

I try not to think of their last moments, dying
for a cause perhaps they never understood,
believing they were wrapped
in the impenetrable armor of youth.
Instead, I see them laughing,
the wind blowing in their hair,
standing strong and straight,
full of challenge and vigor,
the sun in their faces, the moon in their arms.
Life waiting.

J

Jack, Provost Marshal John H. 180
Jackson Guards 200
Jackson, Battle of 159
Jackson, C.S.S. 162, 167, 168
Jackson, Gen. Thomas "Stonewall" 52, 56
Jackson, President Andrew 9, 13, 207
Jemison, Henry 28, 29, 30
Jemison, Pvt. Edwin Francis 24, 28, 29, 30, 31
Jemison, Robert W. 25, 29, 30
Jemison, Sarah 25
Jericho Ford, VA 141
Johnson's Island, OH 64
Johnson, President Andrew 46, 210
Johnston's River Line (see Chattahoochee River Line)
Johnston, Gen. Joseph E. 22, 64, 95, 104, 110, 112, 127, 131, 133
Jones, Gen. David 35

K

Kauffman, Michael 176
Kelly, James Rufus 141, 143, 144, 145
Kennesaw House (Marietta, GA) 84
Kennesaw Mountain 127, 128, 129, 133
Kimmel, Stanley 184
King, Jonas 11
King, Martin 112
Knoxville (TN), Battle of 27, 98

L

LaGrange, GA 61
Lamar Confederates 68
Lanier House (Macon, GA) 201
Lawrenceville Academy 18
Lawrenceville, GA 17, 18, 19
Lee & Gordon's Mills 93
Lee, Gen. Robert E. 21, 32, 35, 39, 52, 74, 76, 93, 162
Leigh, Wilbur 12, 15
Liberty Hall (Crawfordville, GA) 170, 173, 174

Liberty Methodist Church 144, 145
Lincoln, President Abraham 20, 44, 45, 88, 91, 92, 146, 175, 177, 179, 181, 183, 184
Linwood Cemetery (Columbus, GA) 167, 168
Little Round Top 190, 192, 193, 194
Lokey, Capt. William 96, 99, 100, 101, 102
Longstreet, Gen. James 33, 76, 92
Lookout Mountain, Battle of 91, 118
Louisiana Units
    2nd Infantry 24, 25, 26
    12th Infantry 196
    20th Infantry 161
Louisville, KY 140, 186
Lumpkin, John 14, 16
Lytle, Brig. Gen. James 93

M

Macon, GA 27, 56, 142, 147, 161, 163, 167, 173, 195, 199, 201
Madison, GA 18
Magruder, Edward J. 5, 14
Magruder, Gen. John Bankhead 26
Magruder, Miss Eddie 1
Maine Units
    20th Infantry 191, 192
Mallory, Stephen (Sec'y of Confederate Navy) 153, 154
Malvern Hill, Battle of 26, 27, 29, 31, 33, 69
Manassas, First Battle of 5, 109, 158, 159
Manassas, Second Battle of 33, 36, 39,
Marietta, GA 51, 79, 80, 87, 88, 102, 120, 127, 128, 133, 134, 139, 140
Martin, William T. 97
McClellan, Gen. George B. 26, 33, 34, 35, 38
McCook, Col. Dan 111
McDonald, Charles (Governor) 137, 139
McGlasson, Capt. R.B.M. 164
McGuire, George 13
McGuire, Susan 10
McGuire, Terrence 122
McIntosh Volunteers 68
McIntosh, William McPherson 68
McPherson, Maj. Gen. James B. 94

Index